Agile Project Management

AgilePM®

Disclaimer

This handbook, Agile Project Management v2, is based on a subset of the DSDM Agile Project Framework and intended for use as an aid to those undertaking APMG-International's accredited Agile Project Management training or revising for personal certification in Agile Project Management. Readers wishing to know more about or use the DSDM Agile Project Framework are invited to visit the website at www.agilebusiness.org

Note: Agile Project Management training and Agile Project Management personal certification are accredited by APMG-International. Only accredited training providers or their affiliates are allowed to provide courses and examinations in APMG-International's qualification schemes. Readers wishing to know more about APMG-International are invited to visit the website at www.apmg-international.com

Only organisations accredited by the Agile Business Consortium may offer accredited DSDM products and services.

©2010, 2011, 2012, 2013, 2014, 2015, 2017, 2022 Agile Business Consortium Limited

Registered address: Agile Business Consortium, Regus Ashford, The Panorama, Park Street, Ashford, Kent, TN24 8EZ

DSDM®, Atern®, AgilePM® and AgileBA® are registered trademarks of Agile Business Consortium Limited in the United Kingdom and other countries. AgilePgM™ is a trademark of Agile Business Consortium Limited.

PRINCE2® is a Registered Trade Mark of AXELOS Limited in the United Kingdom and other countries

ITIL® is a Registered Trade Mark of AXELOS Limited in the United Kingdom and other countries

All rights reserved. No part of the publication may be reproduced, stored in a retrieval system or transmitted in any form or by any means, electronic, mechanical, photocopying, recording or otherwise, without the prior written permission of the Agile Business Consortium. Applications to reuse, reproduce or republish material in this publication should be sent to the address above, or by email to info@agilebusiness.org

Published by the Agile Business Consortium

First Edition (version 1) first published and printed July 2010 Reprinted November 2011

Version 1.1 published and first printed August 2012. Reprinted March 2013, August 2013

Version 1.2 published and first printed December 2013 Reprinted April 2014

Version 2 published and first printed October 2014. Reprinted April 2015 (with typo amends)
reprinted November 2015 with amends (see page 6), Reprinted May 2017 with amends (see page 6), Reprinted October 2022 with amends (see page 6)

Acknowledgements

Editorial Team: Andrew Craddock, Barbara Roberts, Jennifer Stapleton and Julia Godwin

Production: Kim Whitmore, Emily Ruffle, Mary Henson, Christina Reet, Debbie Cole Creative Marketing, Newble Designs and Cactus

Contents

Section One - Agile Project Foundations

Chapter 1	Introduction	9
Chapter 2	Choosing DSDM as your Agile Approach	11
Chapter 3	Philosophy and Fundamentals	15
Chapter 4	Principles	19
Chapter 5	Preparing for Success	23
Chapter 6.	The DSDM Process	27
Chapter 7	Roles and Responsibilities	31
Chapter 8	DSDM Products	37
Chapter 9	Planning and Control	43
Chapter 10	DSDM Practice - MoSCoW Prioritisation	51
Chapter 11	DSDM Practice - Timeboxing	55
Chapter 12	Other DSDM Practices	61

Section Two - The Agile PM Perspective: Digging Deeper

Chapter 13	Practical Application of the DSDM Principles	69
Chapter 14	Roles and Responsibilities - The Agile PM's View	77
Chapter 15	Project Management Through the Lifecycle	93
Chapter 16	The Effective Use of the DSDM Products	103
Chapter 17	Deliver On Time - Combining MoSCoW and Timeboxing	119
Chapter 18	People, Teams and Interactions	133
Chapter 19	Requirements and User Stories	145
Chapter 20	Estimating	153
Chapter 21	Project Planning Through the Lifecycle	161
Chapter 22	Never Compromise Quality	167
Chapter 23	Risk Management	179
Chapter 24	Tailoring the DSDM Approach	187
Appendix A	Glossary	201
Appendix B	Project Approach Questionnaire (PAQ)	209
Appendix C	Estimating using Planning Poker® and Velocity	211
Appendix D	Index	217

AgilePM®

Foreword

Welcome to the Agile Project Management Handbook, produced by the not-for-profit Agile Business Consortium.

Since its launch in 2010, Agile Business Consortium's Agile Project Management has proved very popular, and has enabled the adoption of Agile Project Management practice worldwide.

This handbook is based on The Agile Project Framework, the latest version of DSDM, and is intended to support the accredited Agile Project Management (AgilePM®) Practitioner training course, as well as providing the definitive source for the AgilePM® Foundation and Practitioner exams. Our aim is to encourage professional development in the field of Agile Project Management.

In today's ever-changing world, organisations and businesses are keen to adopt a more flexible approach to delivering projects, and want to become more agile. However, for organisations delivering projects and programmes, and where existing formal project management processes already exist, the informality of many of the agile approaches is daunting and is sometimes perceived as too risky. These project-focused organisations need a mature agile approach - agility within the concept of project delivery - Agile Project Management. provides:

- an approach that offers agility but retains the concepts of a project, project delivery and project management
- an Agile approach that is stand-alone but also works alongside more formalised project management approaches such as PRINCE2®
- an Agile approach that can be dovetailed into formalised quality processes such as ISO9001 and CMMI enables organisations to gain the benefits of an agile approach without introducing unnecessary risks. This ensures that 'going Agile' becomes a measured and balanced change, keeping what is good in the current organisation and retaining existing good practices around project management and delivery whilst gaining the benefits of a more agile way of working.

DSDM has been for many years the leading, proven, full-project Agile approach, providing governance and rigour along with the agility and flexibility demanded by organisations today. The Agile Business Consortium is pleased to be working with the APM Group to provide Agile Project Management based on DSDM's Agile Project Framework as the 'engine' for driving Agile Project Management. The Agile Project Framework reflects the very latest thinking in corporate-strength agile. The Agile Project Framework has also been designed to link more easily with other Agile approaches, since there is an increasing demand to use a combination of Agile approaches - "blended Agile".

The use of this graphic within the text indicates a potential link to other Agile approaches. The handbook content is based on the DSDM Agile Project Framework with the focus and additional guidance on the Project and Project Management aspects. It does not go into the detail of generic Project Management practices, as this information is readily available elsewhere. It focuses on 'What does agile mean to an Agile Project Manager?' 'What is different?' 'What needs to change?'

Additional information on the DSDM Agile Project Framework can be found at www.agilebusiness.org. DSDM is free to view and free to use. You may also be interested in becoming a member of the Agile Business Consortium. Apart from full access to all Consortium materials, Agile Business Consortium members get significant discounts on products, training and events.

Barbara Roberts

Director for Product Innovation (2010-2019)

Agile Business Consortium

Foreword

APMG is delighted to have collaborated with the Agile Business Consortium in developing this handbook and producing the supporting training courses and qualification.

We are aware of the growing interest in the Agile movement and are particularly pleased to have developed specific guidance for those wishing to run projects in an Agile way.

PRINCE2® is recognised globally as an effective way to manage projects but all project managers have to deal with both the known and the unknown. Unforeseen circumstances and organisational changes can have a dramatic impact on project outcomes. The key to successfully managing projects is to break them into stages, plan the current stage in detail and be flexible regarding the subsequent stages. Agile project management offers flexibility while still recognising the processes that give project managers the confidence to run their projects effectively.

This publication brings Agile to the PRINCE2 community and shows how an Agile approach dovetails very well with the current PRINCE2 philosophy of adopting and tailoring PRINCE2 to meet an organisation's own way of working.

We look forward to hearing of more Agile projects run in a PRINCE2 environment as Practitioners bring together these concepts and deliver even greater value to their clients.

Richard Pharro

CEO

The APM Group

The Structure of this Handbook

The Agile Project Management Handbook is divided into two main sections.

Section One - The Agile Project Foundations - This section provides a simple, but rounded understanding of the core topics associated with Agile Project Management. It forms the basis for the first part of the Agile Project Management accredited training course, and is the source for the Agile Project Management Foundation examination.

Section Two - The Agile Project Manager Perspective - Digging Deeper - This section provides more depth to a number of the topics introduced in Section One. It also introduces some additional topics of particular interest to the Agile Project Manager, either because the Agile Project Manager is responsible for these areas, or because these areas have a direct impact on the Agile Project Manager's ability to deliver successful Agile projects.

Appendices: A Glossary and a full Index are provided, as well as the detail of the Project Approach Questionnaire and guidance on Estimating using Planning Poker and Velocity.

Summary of AgilePM v2 changes from April 2017 to October 2022 reprint

Rebranding
The primary reason for this reprint (October 2022) of the AgilePM v2 Handbook is rebranding in line with Agile Business Consortium

Summary of AgilePM v2 changes from November 2015 to April 2017 reprint

Rebranding
Apart from some minor text changes listed below, the primary reason for this reprint (May 2017) of the AgilePM v2 Handbook is rebranding in line with Agile Business Consortium and APMG International.

Glossary
Exception – term changed to "Management by Exception" and detail revised

Globally
All references to DSDM Consortium, Dynamic Systems Development Method Limited have been updated to Agile Business Consortium and Agile Business Consortium Limited.
All references to info@dsdm.org have been updated to info@agilebusiness.org

Summary of AgilePM v2 changes from April 2014 to November 2015 reprint

Chapter 2 — Choosing DSDM as your Agile Approach
Martin Fowler added to list of Agile Manifesto

Chapter 9 — Planning and Control
"Exception" replaced with "issue"

Chapter 14 — Roles and Responsibilities
Change of paragraph number from 14.15.7 to 14.16.7
In 14.7.1 bullet point "ensuring the non-functional requirements....." moved to 14.6.1 to replace "advising on the achievability....."

Chapter 15 — Project Management through the Lifecycle
First table on page 99 moved to page 98 to be associated with paragraph 15.3.4.
"Outline Plan created......" replaced with "outline created....."
Table on pages 98/99 moved entirely to page 98
Roles associated with products revised to eliminate potential confusion with descriptions in Chapter 16.

Chapter 21 — Project Planning through the Lifecycle
Text added to Foundations in diagram

Glossary
Addition of the term and detail for "Exception"

Globally
Various typos and punctuation amends
Replacing the term final solution, with ultimate solution
Replacing the term Foundation Summary with Foundations Summary

Section One

The Agile Project Foundations

AgilePM

1. Introduction

1.1 DSDM and the Agile Business Consortium

DSDM is a proven framework for Agile project management and delivery, helping to deliver results quickly and effectively. Over the years it has been applied to a wide range of projects - from small software developments all the way up to full-scale business process change. Although DSDM works easily and effectively on small, simple projects, it has always maintained a strong focus on the corporate project-based environment to provide a
"grown-up" approach to Agile in the complex, corporate world.

DSDM was initially created in 1994 through collaboration of a large number of project practitioners across many companies who were seeking to build quality into Rapid Application Development (RAD) processes as they developed, primarily, business-focussed computer solutions.

The contributing companies initially formed the DSDM Consortium (now the Agile Business Consortium) as a not-for-profit organisation to manage the sharing, exploitation and evolution of the intellectual property of DSDM. Initially this was on behalf of, and exclusively for, the Consortium members. However, in 2007, with the full support of its member organisations, the Consortium made DSDM universally available on a free-to-view and free-to-use basis.

1.2 AgilePF - the DSDM Agile Project Framework

AgilePF is an evolution of DSDM Atern®, the previous version of DSDM. It provides the information that is essential to enable any role on a DSDM project to use DSDM effectively and to understand how it is applied in practice.

AgilePF retains DSDM's project-focussed principles, together with its rich set of roles and responsibilities that are ideally suited to a corporate project environment. It also continues to embrace the same robust and fully Agile DSDM practices for establishing and demonstrating control in a project.

At the delivery level, the DSDM process has been simplified to better reflect current trends in evolutionary solution development. The most significant change is in the area of the products, or deliverables, associated with the process. Although the level of formality and indeed inclusion or exclusion of individual products has always been discretionary, the latest product set has been streamlined to align more obviously with the Agile philosophy to keep essential documentation lean, timely and valuable.

2. Choosing DSDM as your Agile Approach

2.1 RAD and Agile - How It All Started

When DSDM was created in 1994, the world of solution delivery through projects was very different from how it is today. For example, the corporate world predominantly used a traditional, sequential, 'Waterfall' approach for their projects. Far too many of these projects were failing, for a variety of reasons, but mainly because projects were just too big and too long, communication and business engagement were poor and progress was measured in percentages complete, rather than delivery of business value. When projects did deliver, they were often late, over budget and delivered the wrong thing. This was due to reliance on specifications which tried, and usually failed, to capture and fix detailed requirements right at the start, coupled with the use of a process in which the identification and management of change was difficult.

To counter these problems, some projects had tried a completely different approach - Rapid Application Development (RAD) - with users of the solution working closely with developers to iteratively and incrementally build software applications, not based on a formalised specification, but on discussions, demonstrations and short feedback loops. This addressed many of the problems of the traditional approach but, in doing so, it introduced a whole new set of problems, particularly around the supportability and scalability of the solutions. RAD provided quick fixes but often its application adversely affected the quality of the solutions because the *disciplines* of analysis and design were thrown out with the up-front phases that used to contain them.

At that time, DSDM was launched to address the problems of the traditional approach (too slow, too big, not transparent enough, not enough ongoing business involvement) as well as the problems introduced by RAD (focus only on speed and quick fixes, no focus on quality, no view of the big picture issues either from the business or the technical perspective). DSDM achieved this by recognising that both approaches had strengths and areas for improvement, and that being effective in all environments requires the ability to deal with wider context issues as well as the here and now. So DSDM brought together the best parts from a traditional approach (control and quality) and from RAD (good communication, business involvement, transparency).

2.2 DSDM, Agile and the Agile Alliance

Ever since its launch, DSDM has been at the forefront of scalable Agile projects and solution delivery. It is equally effective on small straightforward solutions or large complex corporate projects. DSDM has been used effectively on non-IT solutions and is not just about development of software. It is often referred to as "mature Agile", since it grew up with a strong base in the corporate world of projects from 1994 and retains a strong project focus in the 21st century.

As a founder member of the Agile Alliance, DSDM has been at the heart of Agile since 2001. The philosophy and principles of DSDM helped shape the Manifesto for Agile Software Development, although DSDM takes the concept of Agile far wider than just software. The DSDM Agile Project Framework fully adopts the values laid out in the Manifesto.

2.3 How Does DSDM Differ From More Traditional Approaches?

In DSDM, the iterative approach encourages detail to emerge over time; therefore, the current step needs to be completed in only enough detail to allow the project to move to the next step with any shortfall in detailed understanding being dealt with in a subsequent iteration of development. Given the very strong likelihood that business requirements will change over time, and that such change is most likely to happen at the detail level, the effort traditionally spent on detailed up-front work is avoided in DSDM. Solutions built using the DSDM approach address the current and imminent needs of the business rather than, for example, the traditional approach of attacking all the perceived possibilities.

As a result, solutions are more likely to have a better fit with the true business need and are easier to test and easier to integrate into existing and emerging business processes. The development cost of most solutions is only a small part of the total cost of ownership; it therefore makes sense to build simpler solutions that are both fit for purpose on the day of delivery and easier to maintain and modify thereafter. This is preferable to trying to implement a more extensive solution that has been complicated and often compromised by failed attempts to predict future business needs.

Manifesto for Agile Software Development

We are uncovering better ways of developing software by doing it and helping others do it. Through this work we have come to value:

Individuals and interactions over processes and tools

Working software over comprehensive documentation

Customer collaboration over contract negotiation

Responding to change over following a plan

That is, while there is value in the items on the right, we value the items on the left more.

Kent Beck	James Grenning	Robert C. Martin
Mike Beedle	Jim Highsmith	Steve Mellor
Arie van Bennekum	Andrew Hunt	Ken Schwaber
Alistair Cockburn	Ron Jeffries	Jeff Sutherland
Ward Cunningham	Jon Kern	Dave Thomas
Martin Fowler	Brian Marick	

2.4 How Does DSDM Differ From Most Agile Approaches?

DSDM requires basic foundations for the project to be agreed at an early stage. This allows businesses to understand the scope and fundamental characteristics of the proposed solution, and the way it will be created, before development starts. Clarifying and agreeing the foundations for the project from the combined perspectives of business, solution and management reduces the likelihood of nasty surprises on DSDM projects. For larger corporate organisations or organisations with a complex architecture and/or governance standards, agreeing the foundations early in the project is essential.

DSDM also describes a broader set of roles than most Agile approaches giving it a better fit with most corporate environments without compromising agility.

2.5 Why Choose DSDM As Your Agile Approach

DSDM has a broader focus than most other Agile approaches in that it deals with projects rather than just the development and delivery of a product (typically software). The project context requires a focus on the wider business need and on all aspects of the solution that evolves to meet that need.

DSDM may also be used to supplement an existing in-house Agile approach, where this has proved to be lacking. For example, DSDM is often used to provide the full "project" focus to complement Scrum's team-focussed product development process. The Agile Project Management and Scrum pocketbook (available from www.agilebusiness.org) provides guidance on this particular combination.

DSDM also takes a pragmatic approach, recognising that it often needs to work alongside existing standards and approaches. Examples of this are DSDM with PRINCE2, DSDM with ITIL, DSDM with formal quality processes, such as ISO or CMMI and DSDM with a PMO.

DSDM is not only about developing new solutions; projects to enhance existing solutions are also well suited to the DSDM approach.

2.6 Summary of the Benefits of Using DSDM

Using iterative development, DSDM involves the solution's business stakeholders throughout the project lifecycle. This has many benefits, for example:

- The business is better able to direct development of the solution and is more likely to feel ownership of the solution as it evolves and, most importantly, as it transitions into live use
- Prioritisation enables a project to be delivered on time whilst protecting the quality of what is being delivered
- The risk of building the wrong solution is greatly reduced; the ultimate solution is more likely to meet the real business need
- Deployment is more likely to go smoothly, due to the co-operation of all parties concerned throughout development

3. Philosophy and Fundamentals

3.1 Introduction

The DSDM philosophy is that

> *"best business value emerges when projects are aligned to clear business goals, deliver frequently and involve the collaboration of motivated and empowered people."*

This is achieved when all stakeholders:

- Understand and buy into the business vision and objectives
- Are empowered to make decisions within their area of expertise
- Collaborate to deliver a fit-for-purpose business solution
- Collaborate to deliver to agreed timescales in accordance with business priorities
- Accept that change is inevitable as the understanding of the solution grows over time

(Stakeholders encompass everybody inside or outside the project who is involved in or affected by it.)

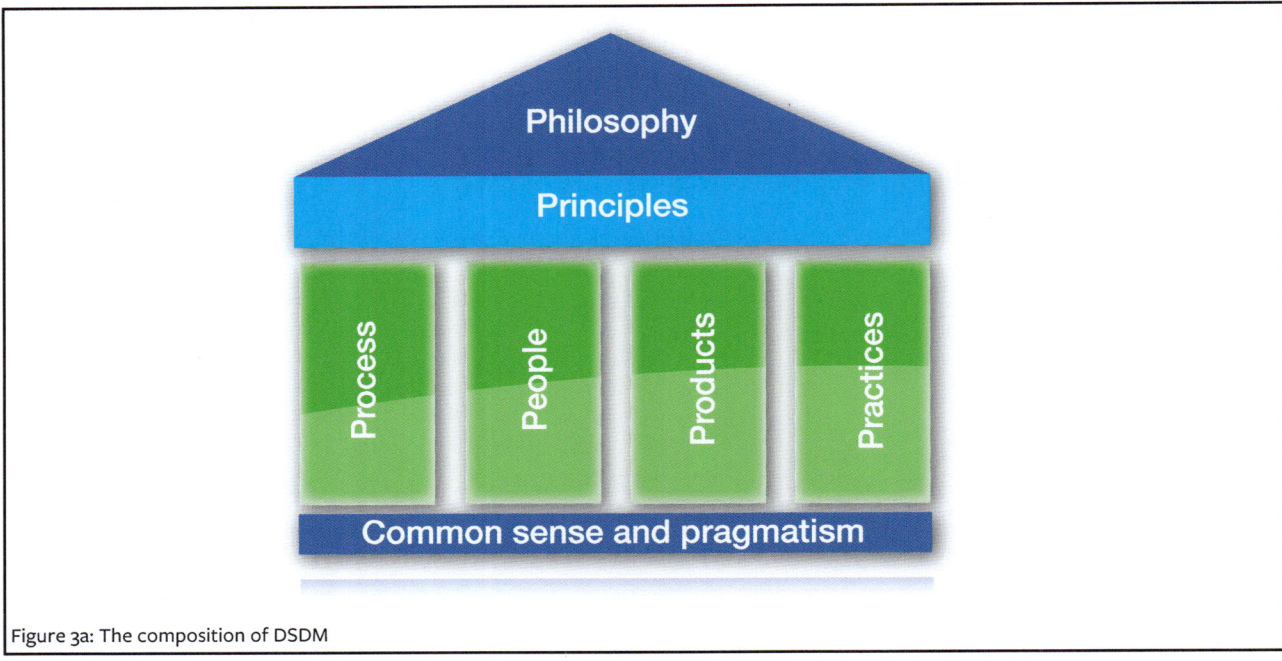

Figure 3a: The composition of DSDM

The DSDM *Philosophy* is supported by a set of eight *Principles* that build the mindset and behaviours necessary to bring the philosophy alive. The principles are themselves supported by *People* (with defined roles and responsibilities), an Agile *Process* (enabling an iterative and incremental lifecycle to shape development and delivery), clearly defined *Products* and recommended *Practices* to help achieve the optimum results.

DSDM's approach and style has always been founded on an underlying ethos of *common sense and pragmatism*. It may be useful to clarify the meaning of these words:

Common sense - "sound practical judgment independent of specialised knowledge or training; normal native intelligence."

Pragmatism - "action or policy dictated by consideration of the immediate practical consequences rather than by theory or dogma."

This is the style of thinking that underpins "the way DSDM works". It is this flexibility of thinking that enables DSDM to avoid the dogma that is sometimes encountered in the world of Agile. The ethos of common sense and pragmatism ensures that "individuals and interactions" continue to take precedence over "processes and tools".

3.2 Understanding Project Variables

Projects have to balance conflicting demands, and the four most common demands are: time, cost, features and quality. Trying to fix all four at the outset of a project is unrealistic, as this would only work in a perfect world where the business need never changes, everything is fully and precisely understood in advance, and problems never happen. This desire to fix everything is the cause of many project failures, as the lack of sufficient contingency results in flawed decisions that are often only noticed towards the end of the project when it is too late to correct them.

For this reason, it is important at the start of a project to ask the question "If we hit a problem, what do we protect (fix) and what can we negotiate (vary) if necessary?"

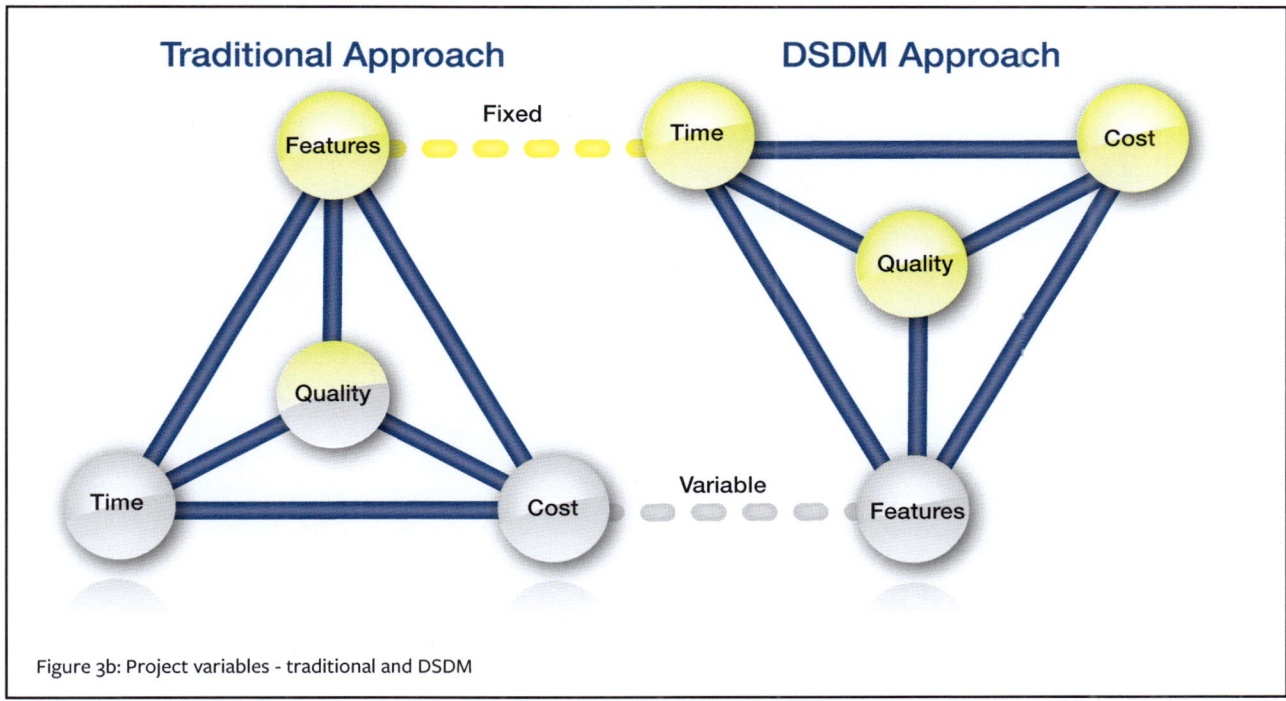

Figure 3b: Project variables - traditional and DSDM

Typically, in the traditional approach to managing a project (left-hand diagram), the feature content of the solution is fixed whilst time and cost are subject to variation. Quality also tends to become an unplanned variable primarily due to the fact that testing is typically left to the end of the project and, as a result of an attempt to make up for previous overruns, is either truncated in terms of testing effort or the time available to fix any defects identified.

By default, DSDM's approach to managing the project (right-hand diagram) fixes time, cost and quality at the end of the Foundations phase while contingency is managed by varying the features (the requirements) to be delivered. As and when contingency is required, the business roles identify the least valuable of the remaining requirements. These are then dropped or deferred in order to keep the project on track.

A DSDM project will always deliver a viable solution, on time and on cost (on budget), as long as the practices of MoSCoW and Timeboxing are followed. Delivery of a Minimum Usable SubseT of requirements is guaranteed as a worst case scenario. However, in all but the most extreme circumstances, the expectation is to deliver far more than the bare minimum.

The iterative and incremental approach to development ensures that the more important requirements are built to the agreed level of quality. Only once this has been achieved does development start on the less important requirements. Incremental delivery of the Evolving Solution ensures that, on the day that the solution is deployed into live use, quality is at the level expected and previously agreed.

3.3 Summary

To enable the philosophy of driving out best business value through projects aligned to clear business goals, frequent delivery and collaboration of motivated and empowered people, DSDM offers eight principles, supported by definition of, and guidance on, people, products, process and practices. All of this guidance needs to be applied with common sense and pragmatism; adapting to the project's environment and context, while preserving the ethos of DSDM presented here.

4. Principles

AgilePM

4.1 Introduction to the DSDM Principles

The eight principles of DSDM support DSDM's philosophy that

> *"best business value emerges when projects are aligned to clear business goals, deliver frequently and involve the collaboration of motivated and empowered people".*

Compromising any of the principles undermines the philosophy of DSDM and introduces risk to the successful outcome of the project. If a team doesn't follow all of these principles then it won't get the full benefit of the approach. The collective application of DSDM's principles brings the philosophy to life.

The eight principles are:

 1. Focus on the business need

 3. Collaborate

 5. Build incrementally from firm foundations

 7. Communicate continuously and clearly

 2. Deliver on time

 4. Never compromise quality

 6. Develop iteratively

 8. Demonstrate control

4.2 Principle 1 - Focus on the Business Need

Every decision taken during a project should be viewed in the light of the overriding project goal - to deliver what the business needs to be delivered, when it needs to be delivered.

4.3 Principle 2 - Deliver on Time

Delivering a solution on time is a very desirable outcome for a project and is quite often the single most important success factor. Late delivery can often undermine the very rationale for a project, especially where market opportunities or legal deadlines are involved. Even for projects without a need for a fixed end date, on-time delivery of intermediate or contributing products is still the best way to demonstrate control over evolution of the solution.

4.4 Principle 3 - Collaborate

Teams that work in a spirit of active cooperation and commitment will always outperform groups of individuals working only in loose association. Collaboration encourages increased understanding, greater speed and shared ownership, which enable teams to perform at a level that exceeds the sum of their parts.

4.5 Principle 4 - Never Compromise Quality

In DSDM, the level of quality to be delivered should be agreed at the start. All work should be aimed at achieving that level of quality - no more and no less. A solution has to be 'good enough'. If the business agrees that the features in the Minimum Usable SubseT meet the agreed acceptance criteria, then the solution should be 'good enough' to use effectively.

4.6 Principle 5 - Build Incrementally from Firm Foundations

One of the key differentiators for DSDM within the Agile space is the concept of establishing firm foundations for the project before committing to significant development. DSDM advocates first understanding the scope of the business problem to be solved and the proposed solution, but not in such detail that the project becomes paralysed by overly detailed analysis of requirements.

Once firm foundations for development have been established, DSDM advocates incremental delivery of the solution in order to deliver real business benefit as early as is practical. Incremental delivery encourages stakeholder confidence, offering a source of feedback for use in subsequent Timeboxes and may lead to the early realisation of business benefit.

4.7 Principle 6 - Develop Iteratively

DSDM uses a combination of Iterative Development, frequent demonstrations and comprehensive review to encourage timely feedback. Embracing change as part of this evolutionary process allows the team to converge on an accurate business solution. The concept of iteration is at the heart of everything developed as part of the DSDM approach. It is very rare that anything is created perfectly first time and it is important to recognise that projects operate within a changing world.

4.8 Principle 7 - Communicate Continuously and Clearly

Poor communication is often cited as the biggest single cause of project failure. DSDM practices are specifically designed to improve communication effectiveness for both teams and individuals.

4.9 Principle 8 - Demonstrate Control

It is essential to be in control of a project, and the solution being created, at all times and to be able to demonstrate that this is the case. High-level plans, designs and standards outline the fundamentals of what needs to be achieved, how, by when, etc. It is also vital to ensure transparency of all work being performed by the team.

4.10 Summary

The eight principles help direct and shape the attitude and mindset of a DSDM team. Compromising any of the principles undermines DSDM's philosophy, as together they deliver a collective value that outweighs their individual benefits.

5. Preparing for Success

5.1 Introduction - Instrumental Success Factors (ISFs)

The following factors are seen as instrumental for positioning DSDM projects for a successful outcome. Where these factors cannot be met, they represent a significant risk to the DSDM approach. Therefore, it is important to identify these risks early and consider how they could be mitigated. Many projects successfully use DSDM whilst still identifying that some of these factors will not be in place.

5.2 Embracing the DSDM Approach

It is important that all project stakeholders and participants understand and accept the DSDM project approach. As well as embracing the DSDM philosophy that *"best business value emerges when projects are aligned to clear business goals, deliver frequently and involve the collaboration of motivated and empowered people"*, this also includes the concept that in order to deliver the right thing at the right time and to handle change dynamically, the project may deliver less than 100% of the possible solution.

5.3 Effective Solution Development Team

People are at the heart of successful DSDM projects and the Solution Development Team is instrumental in ensuring the development of the right solution.

Building an effective team for successful delivery focuses on four elements:

- Empowerment
- Stability
- Skills
- Size

5.3.1 Appropriate empowerment of the Solution Development Team

Each role within the Solution Development Team should be empowered to make decisions based on their expertise, and the team as a whole empowered to make decisions within the boundaries agreed during Foundations. Senior business and technical stakeholders in a project need to ensure that the people they appoint to work as part of the Solution Development Team have the desire, authority, responsibility and knowledge required to make day-to-day decisions.

5.3.2 Solution Development Team stability

The Solution Development Team relies on continuous, informal, and ideally face-to-face communication to build a common understanding of the business problem to be addressed and the solution that is evolving to meet that need. This means that a DSDM project will be put at serious risk if team members are swapped in and out.

5.3.3 Solution Development Team skills

It is important that all the core business knowledge and technical expertise required to build a fit-for-purpose solution is present within the Solution Development Team. DSDM does not require all team members to be multi-skilled experts but they must have good communication skills (listening as well as speaking) and the willingness to work with others, if they are to function as a coherent unit.

5.3.4 Solution Development Team size

DSDM teams rely on informal communication as their first choice. For this to be effective, DSDM suggests that the optimum Solution Development Team size is seven +/- two people. Where more people are needed they should be split into multiple Solution Development Teams.

5.4 Business Engagement - Active and Ongoing

In order for DSDM projects to be successful, it is vital that the business is actively engaged and commits the necessary amount of time at all levels, and that this commitment is maintained throughout the project.

Ensuring active and ongoing business engagement relies on three elements:

- Commitment of business time throughout
- Day-to-day collaboration involving business roles in the Iterative Development of the solution
- A supportive commercial (e.g. contractual) relationship (where appropriate)

5.4.1 Commitment of business time throughout

The business commitment and agreed participation is vital to successful DSDM projects, since these roles provide the business direction to the project. In the early phases, business engagement and business time is needed to properly shape the project. In the later phases, it is needed to guide the detail of solution development.

5.4.2 Active Involvement of the business roles

For successful DSDM projects, contact with the business roles must be ongoing and frequent throughout the project, sufficient to guide the evolution of the solution at the detailed level and to accept that the solution is evolving correctly day to day.

5.4.3 A supportive commercial relationship

The relationship between the sponsoring business and the supplier organisation needs to support collaborative working and the iterative and incremental development of the Evolving Solution without an onerous overhead associated with change at the detail level.

5.5 Iterative Development, Integrated Testing and Incremental Delivery

Each Timebox should ideally deliver a complete, potentially deployable increment of the solution, even though there may not be enough at that point in time to physically deploy it.

Ensuring testing is fully integrated into the iterative and incremental development approach is key both to the reduction of project risk and to the success of the project.

An organisation amenable to incremental delivery of solutions into live use will benefit from early return on investment.

5.6 Transparency

Transparency is about making progress and ongoing work visible to all. Demonstrations of the Evolving Solution at the end of each Timebox provide physical, objective and unquestionable proof of progress. Team Boards and Daily Stand-ups are also very useful for providing clear and up-to-date information on the current state of work. Transparency underpins the demonstration of control (principle 8).

5.7 The Project Approach Questionnaire - Assessing Options and Risks

The Project Approach Questionnaire (PAQ) is a simple checklist used to assess whether the success factors described above are likely to be met or whether action needs to be taken to counter the risk arising from any of them being undermined. The PAQ is first used during during the Feasibility phase of the project to help shape the work of the Foundations phase and again towards the end of Foundations to help finalise the approach to be taken by the project for development and delivery and to drive active management of the project risks.

5.8 Summary

Understanding and assessing the factors that are instrumental for success in the early phases of a DSDM project can help significantly in addressing and mitigating potential risks to the success of the project. Having a common understanding of what needs to be in place is a good starting point for any project and working towards achieving the best starting position for a DSDM project increases the likelihood of a successful project.

6. The DSDM Process

6.1 Overview

In line with the DSDM philosophy that *"best business value emerges when projects are aligned to clear business goals, deliver frequently and involve the collaboration of motivated and empowered people"*, the DSDM approach to development and delivery is both iterative and incremental, with the most important business needs typically being addressed early while less important features are delivered later.

Unlike most Agile approaches, DSDM integrates project management and product development into a single process. For many organisations, DSDM is all that is needed, although some gain value from integrating DSDM with other methods e.g. project management methods, such as PRINCE2 and PMI, or software engineering practices from, say, eXtreme Programming (XP).

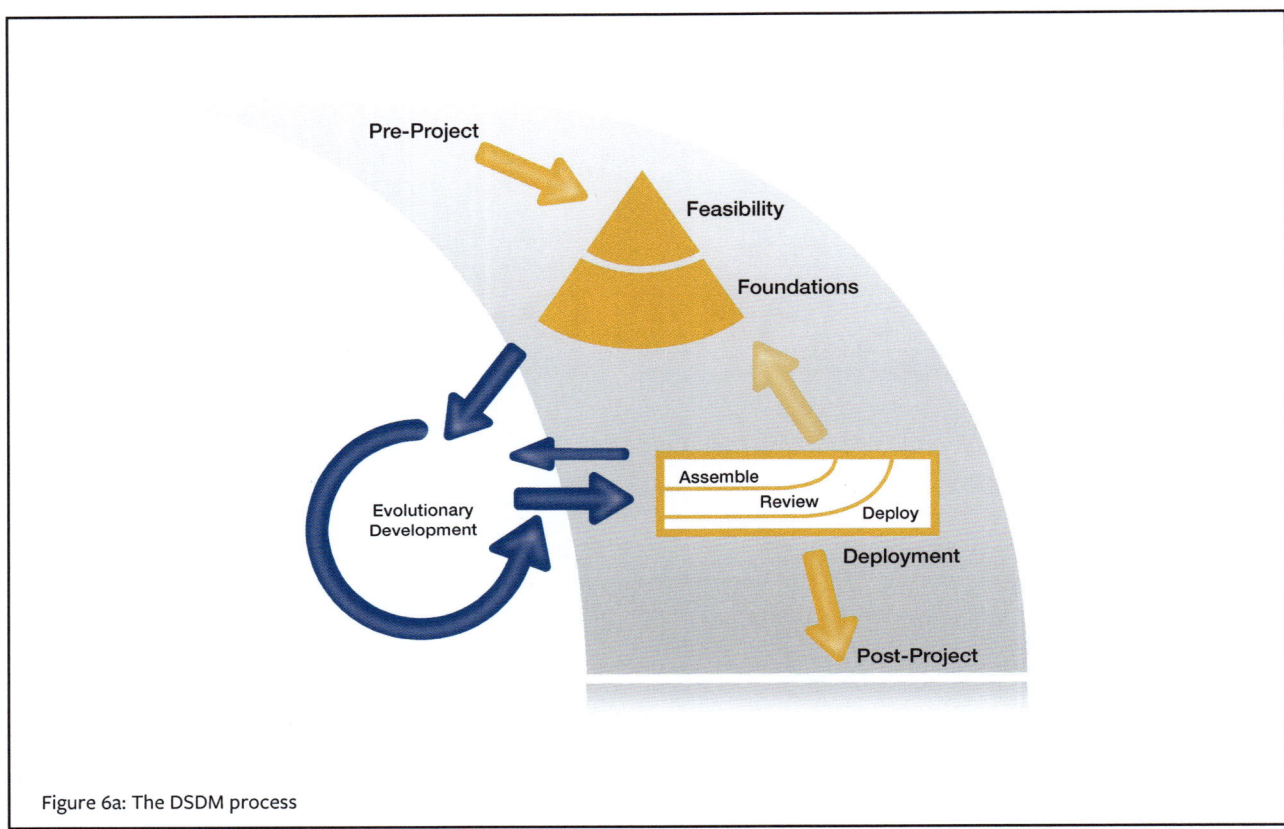

Figure 6a: The DSDM process

The DSDM process model comprises a framework which shows the DSDM phases and how they relate to one another. This process model is then used by each project to derive their lifecycle.

6.2 Pre-Project Phase

The Pre-Project phase ensures that only the right projects are started, and that they are set up correctly, based on a clearly defined objective.

6.3 Feasibility Phase

The Feasibility phase is intended primarily to establish whether the proposed project is likely to be feasible from a technical perspective and whether it appears cost-effective from a business perspective. The effort associated with Feasibility should be just enough to decide whether further investigation is justified or whether the project should be stopped now, as it is unlikely to be viable.

6.4 Foundations Phase

The Foundations phase takes the preliminary investigation from Feasibility to the next level. It is intended to establish a fundamental (but not detailed) understanding of the business rationale for the project, the potential solution that will be created by the project, and how development and delivery of the solution will be managed. By intentionally avoiding low levels of detail, the Foundations phase should last no longer than a few weeks - even for large and complex projects. The detail associated with requirements, and how they should be met as part of the solution, is intentionally left until the Evolutionary Development phase of the project.

The aim of Foundations is to understand the scope of work, and in broad terms, how it will be carried out, by whom, when and where. The Foundations phase also determines the project lifecycle by agreeing how the DSDM process will be applied to the specific needs of this project.

For smaller, simpler projects, the Feasibility and Foundations phases can often be merged into a single phase. For larger, more complex projects, it may sometimes be necessary to revisit Foundations after each Deployment phase.

6.5 Evolutionary Development Phase

Building on the firm foundations that have been established for the project, the purpose of the Evolutionary Development phase is to evolve the solution.

The Evolutionary Development phase requires the Solution Development Team(s) to apply practices such as Iterative Development, Timeboxing, and MoSCoW prioritisation, together with Modelling and Facilitated Workshops, to converge over time on an accurate solution that meets the business need and is also built in the right way from a technical viewpoint.

Working within Timeboxes, the Solution Development Team create Solution Increments, iteratively exploring the low-level detail of the requirements and testing continuously as they move forward.

6.6 Deployment Phase

The objective of the Deployment phase is to bring a baseline of the Evolving Solution into operational use. The release that is deployed may be the ultimate solution, or a subset of the ultimate solution. After the last release, the project is formally closed.

6.7 Post-Project Phase

After the final Deployment for a project, the Post-Project phase checks how well the expected business benefits have been met.

6.8 The Lifecycle in Practice

Whilst there is a clear progression of phases from Pre-Project to Post-Project in the process diagram above, there are also arrows indicating a return path within the process, specifically the arrows from Deployment to Foundations and from Deployment to Evolutionary Development. The process shows the framework and the options available. Each project derives their lifecycle from this process. The lifecycle for the project is defined and agreed as part of the Foundations phase.

6.9 Configuring DSDM for Scalability and Formality

DSDM recognises the real value of Agility in terms of project productivity and solution quality while acknowledging and accepting the necessary constraints that often exist when working in a corporate environment. Such constraints may include financial governance, architecture and/or infrastructure strategies, regulatory governance, vendor agreements and third party support considerations.

The DSDM process can be configured and calibrated to cater for a range of projects from small projects with light governance to larger projects with stronger governance needs. Typically this is achieved by configuring a lifecycle appropriate for a specific project and determining an appropriate level of formality with which the DSDM products are defined, created and approved.

With regards to scaling, the project organisation can easily be refined to support multiple teams, with key roles acting as directors and coordinators across the teams. To support a more complex project structure, products such as the Solution Architecture Definition, Development Approach Definition, Management Approach Definition and the Delivery Plan and Timebox Review Records can be made more elaborate and more formal than would be appropriate for smaller projects.

6.10 Summary

DSDM provides an iterative and incremental process, with a total of six lifecycle phases. Each phase has a specific purpose, together with a number of defined products intended to support the evolution of the solution and the smooth running of the project. The DSDM Agile Project Framework is designed to work effectively with projects of varying size and complexity. Through the tailoring of its various products, DSDM ensures control is demonstrated to a level of formality appropriate to the organisation, thereby running a project so that all the benefits of Agile are achieved without compromising effective project governance.

7. Roles and Responsibilities

7.1 Introduction

People working together effectively are the foundation of any successful project. DSDM recognises this and assigns clear roles and responsibilities to each person in a project, representing the business interests, the solution/technical interests, the management interests and the process interests. Everyone involved in a DSDM project works very closely together in order to break down potential communication barriers.

The best solutions emerge from self-organising, empowered teams. However, these teams, and the people within them, must actively take on the responsibility for their empowerment within the boundaries that have been agreed.

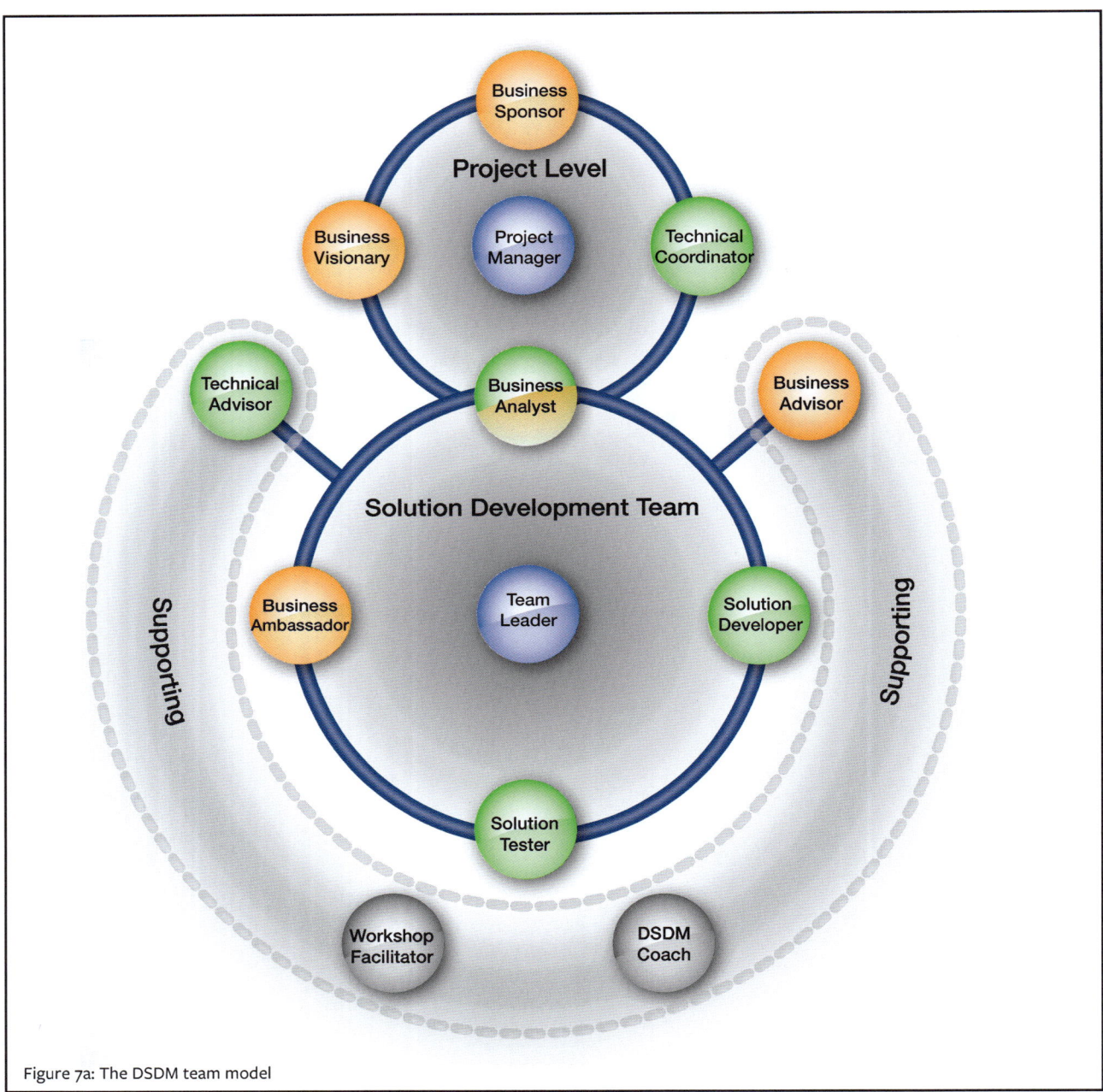

Figure 7a: The DSDM team model

7.2 The DSDM Team Model Explained

7.2.1 Role colour scheme - to represent areas of interest
The colour scheme in the picture of the DSDM Team Model is as follows:

- Orange - Business interests, roles representing the business view
- Green - Solution/technical interests, roles representing the solution/technical view
- Blue - Management interests, roles representing the management/leadership view
- Grey - Process interests, roles representing the process view
- Mix of two colours - A role that covers two separate areas of interest

7.2.2 Role Categories

7.2.2.1 Project-level roles
The project-level roles are Business Sponsor, Business Visionary, Technical Coordinator, Project Manager and Business Analyst. They are the directors, managers and coordinators of the work for the project, where necessary. They may be part of a project board or steering committee for the project and, collectively, have authority to direct the project. They are responsible for the governance of the project, liaising with governance authorities outside the project where necessary.

All roles at the project level need to adopt the facilitative, empowering leadership style that allows Agile teams to learn as they go, getting to an end point by their own means, within an agreed framework of empowerment.

7.2.2.2 Solution Development Team roles
The Solution Development Team roles are Business Ambassador, Solution Developer, Solution Tester, Business Analyst and Team Leader. These roles form the "engine room" of the project. They shape and build the solution and are collectively responsible for its day-to-day development and for assuring its fitness for business purpose. There may be one or more Solution Development Teams within a project. Each team will include all Solution Development Team roles and cover all their responsibilities.

7.2.2.3 Supporting roles
The supporting roles (Business Advisors, Technical Advisors, Workshop Facilitator and DSDM Coach) provide assistance and guidance to the project on an ad hoc basis throughout the lifecycle. The Advisor roles may be filled by one or more subject matter experts, as necessary.

7.2.3 Fulfilling the roles
One DSDM role does not necessarily mean one person. One person may take on one or more roles. One role may be shared by two or more people. Where a role is shared it is vital that the individuals communicate and collaborate closely.

7.3 The Roles

7.3.1 Business Sponsor
This role is the most senior project-level business role. The Business Sponsor is the project champion who is committed to the project, to the proposed solution and the approach to delivering it. The Business Sponsor is specifically responsible for the Business Case and project budget throughout (however formally or informally this may be expressed).

The Business Sponsor must hold a sufficiently high position in the organisation to be able to resolve business issues and make financial decisions.

7.3.2 Business Visionary
This is a senior project-level business role that should be held by a single individual, since a project needs a single clear vision to avoid confusion and misdirection. More actively involved than the Business Sponsor, the Business Visionary is responsible for interpreting the needs of the Business Sponsor, communicating these to the team and, where appropriate, ensuring they are properly represented in the Business Case. The Business Visionary remains involved throughout the project, providing the team with strategic direction and ensuring that the solution delivered will enable the benefits described in the Business Case to be achieved.

7.3.3 Technical Coordinator

As the project's technical authority, the Technical Coordinator ensures that the solution/technical roles work in a consistent way, that the project is technically coherent and meets the desired technical standards. This role provides the glue that holds the technical aspects of the project together while advising on technical decisions and innovation.

The Technical Coordinator performs the same function from a technical perspective as the Business Visionary does from a business perspective.

7.3.4 Project Manager

As well as providing high-level, Agile-style leadership to the Solution Development Team, the role is focussed on managing the working environment in which the solution is evolving. The Project Manager coordinates all aspects of management of the project at a high level but, in line with the DSDM concept of empowerment, the Project Manager is expected to leave the detailed planning of the actual delivery of the product(s) to the members of the Solution Development Team. Managing an empowered team requires a facilitative style rather than a "command and control" style.

It is usual that the Project Manager takes responsibility for the project throughout its duration. This responsibility must include both business and technical delivery aspects of the project, from Foundations (if not Feasibility) through to Deployment.

7.3.5 Business Analyst

The Business Analyst is both active in supporting the project-level roles and fully integrated with the Solution Development Team. The Business Analyst facilitates the relationship between the business and technical roles, ensuring accurate and appropriate decisions are made on the Evolving Solution on a day-to-day basis. The Business Analyst ensures that the business needs are properly analysed and understood by all members of the Solution Development Team.

Active involvement of the business users in the process of evolving the solution is vital to the success of a DSDM project. Therefore it is important to ensure that the Business Analyst does not become an intermediary between Solution Development Team members but, instead, supports and facilitates the communication between them.

7.3.6 Team Leader

The Team Leader ideally acts as the servant-leader for the Solution Development Team and ensures that it functions as a whole and meets its objectives. The Team Leader works with the team to plan and coordinate all aspects of product delivery at the detailed level. This is a leadership role rather than a management role and the person holding it will ideally be elected by his or her peers as the best person to lead them through a particular stage of the project. It is therefore likely that they will also perform another Solution Development Team role (e.g. Business Analyst, Business Ambassador, Solution Developer or Solution Tester) in addition to their team leadership responsibilities.

7.3.7 Business Ambassador

The Business Ambassador is the key representative of the business within the Solution Development Team. During Foundations, the Business Ambassador has significant input into the creation and prioritisation of requirements. Once the requirements have been agreed and baselined (by the end of Foundations), the Business Ambassador then provides the day-to-day detail of the requirements during timeboxed development. This is either based on their own knowledge and experience, or drawing on the experience of Business Advisors.

During the Evolutionary Development phase of the project, the Business Ambassador is the main decision maker on behalf of the business. For this reason, the Business Ambassador needs to be someone who is respected by their business peers and who has sufficient seniority, empowerment and credibility to make decisions on behalf of the business, in terms of ensuring the Evolving Solution is fit for business purpose.

7.3.8 Solution Developer

The Solution Developer collaborates with the other Solution Development Team roles to interpret business requirements and translate them into a Solution Increment that meets functional and non-functional needs of the business as a whole.

7.3.9 Solution Tester

The Solution Tester is an empowered Solution Development Team role, fully integrated with the team and performing testing throughout the project in accordance with the agreed strategy.

7.3.10 Business Advisor

Often a peer of the Business Ambassador, the Business Advisor is called upon to provide specific, and often specialist, input to solution development or solution testing - a business subject matter expert. The Business Advisor may be an intended user or beneficiary of the solution or may, for example, provide legal or regulatory advice with which the solution must comply.

7.3.11 Technical Advisor

The Technical Advisor supports the team by providing specific, and often specialist, technical input to the project, often from the perspective of those responsible for operational change management, operational support, ongoing maintenance of the solution, etc.

7.3.12 Workshop Facilitator

The Workshop Facilitator is responsible for planning, organising and facilitating workshops to ensure that a group of people collaborates to meet a predetermined objective in a compressed timeframe. The Workshop Facilitator should ideally be independent of the outcome to be achieved in the workshop.

7.3.13 DSDM Coach

Where a team has limited experience of using DSDM, the role of the DSDM Coach is key to helping team members to get the most out of the approach, within the context and constraints of the wider organisation in which they work.

7.4 Summary

DSDM identifies roles in two dimensions - categories and interests. Roles are grouped into three categories:

- Project level roles - Business Sponsor, Business Visionary, Technical Coordinator, Project Manager and Business Analyst (also a member of the Solution Development Team)

- Solution Development Team roles - Business Ambassador, Solution Developer, Solution Tester, Team Leader and Business Analyst (also a Project level role)

- Supporting roles - Business Advisor, Technical Advisor, Workshop Facilitator and DSDM Coach

And four interests:

- Business interests - covered by the Business Sponsor, Business Visionary, Business Ambassador and Business Advisor roles

- Solution/technical interests - covered by the Technical Coordinator, Solution Developer, Solution Tester and Technical Advisor roles

- Management interests - covered by the Project Manager and Team Leader roles

- Process interests - covered by the Workshop Facilitator and DSDM Coach roles

The Business Analyst role covers both business and solution/technical interests.

AgilePM

8. DSDM Products

8.1 Introduction to DSDM Products

The DSDM Agile Project Framework describes a set of products to be considered as the project proceeds. These products describe the solution itself (the main deliverable of the project) and anything created to help with the process of evolving it, and anything that is required to help with project governance and control.

Not all products are required for every project and the formality associated with each product will vary from project to project and from organisation to organisation. The formality of the products is influenced by factors such as contractual relationships, corporate standards and governance needs.

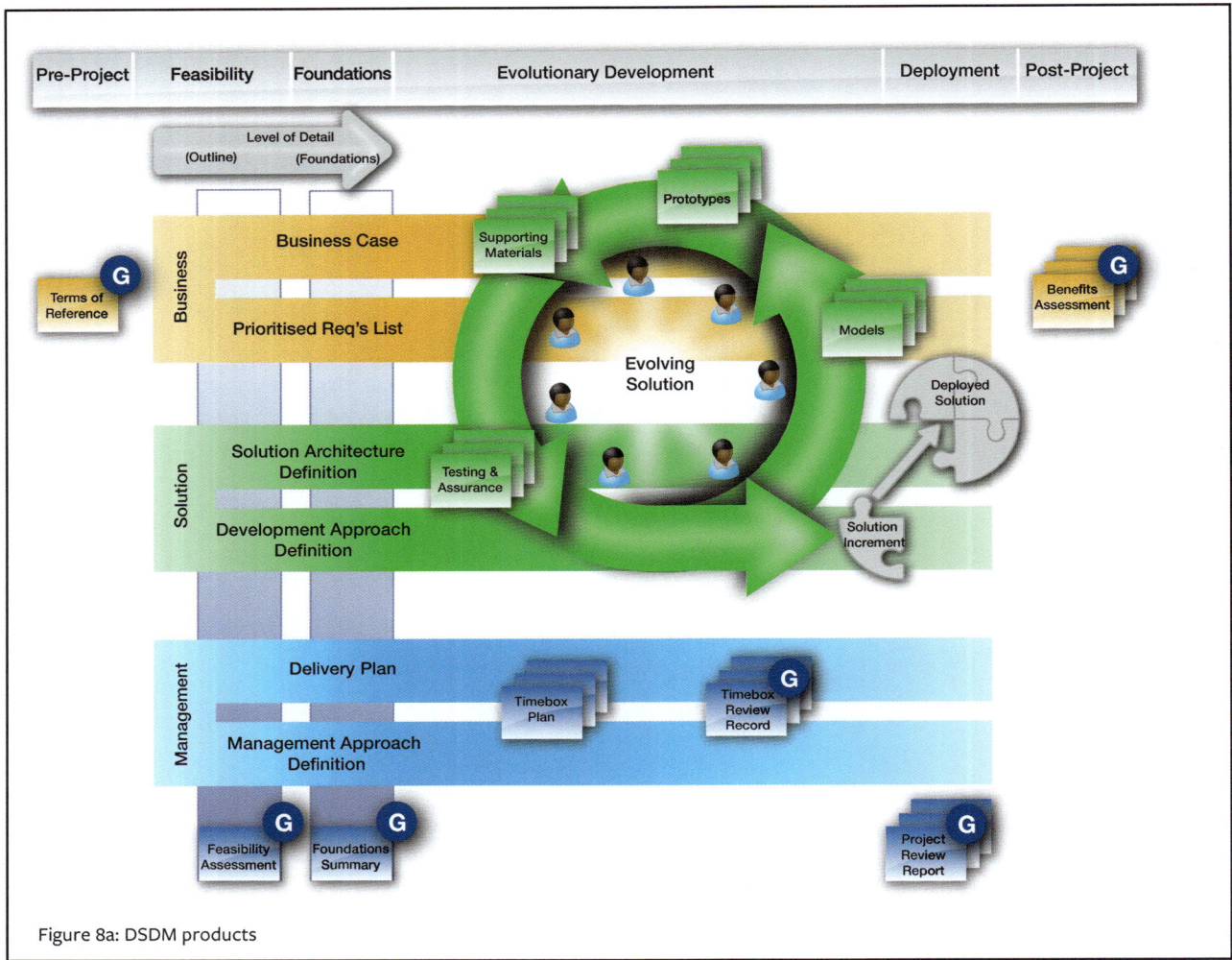

Figure 8a: DSDM products

The products, and where they feature in the project lifecycle, are shown in the diagram above. Orange products are business focussed, green products all contribute to the solution being created by the project and blue products cover project management/control interests.

Several of the products - those marked with G - may also play a part in governance processes such as approval gateways, and may be used to demonstrate compliance of the solution with corporate and regulatory standards where this is required.

8.2 The DSDM Products

8.2.1 Terms of Reference
The Terms of Reference is a high-level definition of the overarching business driver for, and top-level objectives of, the project. The primary aim of the Terms of Reference is to scope and justify the Feasibility phase. It is identified as a governance product because it may be used for purposes such as prioritisation of a project within a portfolio.

8.2.2 Business Case
The Business Case provides a vision and a justification for the project from a business perspective. The business vision describes a changed business as it is expected to be, incrementally and at the end of the project. The justification for the project is typically based on an investment appraisal determining whether the value of the solution to be delivered by the project warrants the cost to produce, support and maintain it into the future, all within an acceptable level of risk.

Baselines of the Business Case are typically created first as an outline by the end of Feasibility, then as a basis for approval of development by the end of Foundations. It is formally reviewed at the end of each Project Increment in order to determine whether further work is justified.

8.2.3 Prioritised Requirements List
The Prioritised Requirement List (PRL) describes, at a high level, the requirements that the project needs to address and indicates their priority with respect to meeting the objectives of the project and the needs of the business. Consideration of requirements begins in Feasibility and a baseline of the PRL describes the scope of the project as at the end of Foundations. After that point, further change will happen naturally in terms of depth, as a result of emergence of detail. Change to the breadth (adding, removing or significantly changing high-level requirements) needs to be formally controlled in order to ensure ongoing alignment with the business vision for the project and to keep control of the scope.

8.2.4 Solution Architecture Definition
The Solution Architecture Definition provides a high-level design framework for the solution. It is intended to cover both business and technical aspects of the solution to a level of detail that makes the scope of the solution clear but does not constrain evolutionary development.

8.2.5 Development Approach Definition
The Development Approach Definition provides a high-level definition of the tools, techniques, customs, practices and standards that will be applied to the evolutionary development of the solution. Importantly, it describes how quality of the solution will be assured. A strategy for testing and review is therefore a key part of the development approach and described in the Development Approach Definition.

8.2.6 Delivery Plan
The Delivery Plan provides a high-level schedule of Project Increments and, at least for the first/imminent Increment, the Timeboxes that make up that Increment. It rarely deals with task-level detail unless there are tasks being carried out by people who are not part of the Solution Development Team or before the Solution Development Team is formed.

8.2.7 Management Approach Definition
The Management Approach Definition reflects the approach to the management of the project as a whole and considers, from a management perspective, how the project will be organised and planned, how stakeholders will be engaged in the project and how progress will be demonstrated and, if necessary, reported. The product is outlined in Feasibility and baselined at the end of Foundations and will only evolve beyond that when circumstances change or if review of the approach identifies areas for improvement.

8.2.8 Feasibility Assessment
The Feasibility Assessment provides a snapshot of the evolving business, solution and management products described above as they exist at the end of the Feasibility phase. Each of the products should be mature enough to make a sensible contribution to the decision as to whether the project is likely to be feasible or not. The Feasibility Assessment may be expressed as a baselined collection of the products or as an executive summary covering the key aspects of each of them.

8.2.9 Foundations Summary

The Foundations Summary provides a snapshot of the evolving business, solution and management products described above as they exist at the end of the Foundations phase. Each of the products should be mature enough to make a sensible contribution to the decision as to whether the project is likely to deliver the required return on investment. Foundations Summary may be expressed as a baselined collection of the products described above or as an executive summary covering the key aspects of each of them.

8.2.10 Evolving Solution

The Evolving Solution is made up of all appropriate components of the ultimate solution together with any intermediate deliverables necessary to explore the detail of requirements and the solution under construction. At any given time, such components may be either complete, a baseline of a partial solution (a Solution Increment), or a work in progress. They include, where valuable: models, prototypes, supporting materials and testing and review artefacts.

At the end of each Project Increment, the Solution Increment is deployed into live use and becomes the Deployed Solution.

8.2.11 Timebox Plan

The Timebox Plan provides depth and detail for each Timebox identified in the Delivery Plan. It elaborates on the objectives provided for that Timebox and details the deliverables of that Timebox, along with the activities to produce those deliverables and the resources to do the work. The Timebox Plan is created by the Solution Development Team and is often represented on a Team Board as work to do, in progress, and done. It is updated at least on a daily basis at the Daily Stand-ups.

8.2.12 Timebox Review Record

The Timebox Review Record captures the feedback from each review that takes place during a Timebox. It describes what has been achieved up to that point together with any feedback that may influence plans moving forwards. Where appropriate, e.g. in a regulated environment, a formal, auditable record of review comments from expert Business Advisors and other roles make this a governance product.

8.2.13 Project Review Report

The Project Review Report is typically a single document that is updated incrementally at the end of each Project Increment by the addition of new sections pertinent to that Increment.

At the end of each Project Increment, the purpose of this product is:

- To capture the feedback from the review of the delivered solution and to confirm what has been delivered and what has not
- To capture learning points from the retrospective for the Increment focussed on the process, practices employed and contributing roles and responsibilities
- Where appropriate, to describe the business benefits that should now accrue through the proper use of the solution delivered by the project up to this point

After the final Project Increment, as part of project closure, a retrospective covering the whole project is carried out that is partially informed by the records for each Project Increment.

8.2.14 Benefits Assessment

The Benefits Assessment describes how the benefits have actually accrued, following a period of use in live operation. For projects where benefits in the Business Case are expected to accrue over a prolonged period, it is possible that a number of Benefits Assessments may be produced on a periodic basis aligned with the timeframe that was used for justifying the investment.

8.3 Summary

The products above are guidelines to the information needed to promote good communication within a project. They are not mandatory, and may not always be presented as documents. However, in circumstances where strong governance and/or proof of compliance with standards is important, there is real benefit to creating formal documents rather than just gaining a shared understanding (which is the normal default for DSDM). Although it may not be obvious, it is important to remember that documentation created as part of the development process and/or tied to the proactive way the project is managed, is likely to provide the most effective and robust audit trail if one is needed.

It is also critically important to remember that DSDM products are only created if and when they add value to the project and/or to the solution it creates. The most important thing is that the stakeholders and participants in the project understand what is needed and what is being delivered and that quality is assured. If documents genuinely help achieve this then create them, if not, don't waste valuable time and effort doing so.

9. Planning and Control

AgilePM

9.1 Introduction

In common with all other Agile methods, DSDM values *responding to change over following a plan* but, unlike some, it places strong emphasis on planning, specifically on *high-level* planning. DSDM's plans shape and structure the project and the work but they do not get into the detail of exactly who does what and when.

Planning in DSDM starts with agreement of strategy - the approach to be taken to evolve the solution - and considers:

- Incremental delivery of the solution - in Project Increments and Timeboxes
- Quality Assurance of the solution - how review and testing activity will be integrated into development

To address these considerations, DSDM defines three Agile Project Planning Concepts, six Testing Concepts and four Tracking and Control concepts

9.2 Project Planning Concepts

9.2.1 Outcome-based planning

A framework of empowerment exists in the hierarchy of a DSDM project. At the highest level, the Business Sponsor has empowered project-level roles to manage the delivery of a valuable business solution that will provide the expected Return on Investment. Below that, the project-level roles have empowered Solution Development Teams who self-organise to deliver the solution envisioned by the Business Visionary and Technical Coordinator to meet the business need.

Within this framework of empowerment:

- The Project Manager is responsible for high-level planning for the project, collaboratively planning for the incremental delivery of the business solution - the outcome required by the Business Sponsor
- The Solution Development Team is responsible for planning the detail of all the work of each Timebox with team members agreeing amongst themselves who will do what work to achieve the objectives agreed at the Kick-Off of that Timebox

9.2.2 Planning to sensible horizons at the right level of detail

The planning horizon defines the period of time to be covered by a plan. The two plans defined by DSDM cover two very different planning horizons with the horizon of the Delivery Plan, being the end of the project or Project Increment and the horizon of the Timebox Plan being the end of a Timebox.

A typical Delivery Plan for a project:

- Will provide a schedule of Timeboxes and any other high-level activities for the imminent Project Increment
- Will have a planning horizon of perhaps 6 weeks to 6 months
- Is likely to include only high objectives and delivery dates for future Project Increments (sensible for a more distant planning horizon)

A typical Timebox Plan:

- Will have a much shorter planning horizon (typically 2-4 weeks)
- Is likely to be much more detailed - maybe describing exactly who intends to do what and when
- Will normally be informally presented on a Team Board and updated at each Daily Stand-up

9.2.3 Plan and re-plan based on best available estimates

Estimates evolve as more is understood about the thing being estimated. Early in a project, estimates will be uncertain and can only be expressed with a low confidence factor typically described by a wide range.

By the end of the Foundations phase, there is a need to be more precise with estimates since the delivery dates and associated costs need to be committed at this point.

As the project proceeds and more becomes known about the requirements and the Evolving Solution, and the accuracy of previous estimates is validated by actual development work, it makes sense to refine predictions of what will be delivered within the fixed timeframe of the current Project Increment and perhaps the project as a whole.

Regardless of the amount of investigation work that has been done, estimate accuracy can be improved by following two essential aspects of estimating best practice, specifically: estimating using more than one technique and estimating in groups.

9.3 Testing Concepts

9.3.1 Testing integrated throughout

Early in a project, it is important to ensure that a strategy for testing is in place and that everybody understands their responsibilities with regards to solution quality and how this is assured by an appropriately rigorous regime of review and testing. Testing should be considered part of the Iterative Development process with testing activity as fully embedded as it can be within the same Timebox as the development activity. This is because the earlier a defect is found, the easier and cheaper it is to fix.

Ideally, the solution will be fully tested and potentially deployable at the end of the Timebox, although it is acknowledged that this may not be achievable in all circumstances.

9.3.2 Collaborative testing

Effective and productive testing involves the collaboration of all stakeholders on the project to increase the productivity of the test-fix-and-retest cycle. This concept is in line with the DSDM principle to Collaborate and should include business and technical, solution development and testing representatives.

9.3.3 Repeatable testing

Since testing needs to support the DSDM principle to Build Incrementally from Firm Foundations, it is important that testing within a Timebox includes not only tests for the new features of the solution being built but, where appropriate, also tests for what has been built previously. It is therefore good practice to ensure tests are readily repeatable. Where appropriate, automation tools can be used to reduce the effort associated with repeating tests.

9.3.4 Prioritised testing

Although test automation tools may help reduce effort associated with repeated tests, there may still be a need to prioritise tests as there is not always time to exhaustively test all aspects of the solution as it evolves. In this circumstance, it may be helpful to prioritise testing on the basis of risk, i.e. on the likelihood of having introduced a defect and/or the impact of such a defect might have. MoSCoW rules could be applied to both the execution of tests and the rectification of defects found.

9.3.5 Independent testing

A product should always be tested by someone other than its creator because it is as critical to test the understanding of a requirement as it is to test that the work done to fulfil that requirement was completed correctly. Even though individuals within a Solution Development Team may hold both Solution Developer and Solution Tester roles it is important that one individual always independently tests the work of another. Active involvement of the Business Ambassador and Business Advisor roles in the project always provides an independent perspective for testing.

9.3.6 Test-Driven Development

The concept of Test-Driven Development (TDD) turns traditional testing practice on its head. Traditionally tests are designed and built in parallel to the design and build of the solution with both being based on individual interpretation of a given requirement. Using a test-driven approach the design and build of the test precedes development of the solution and helps define the requirement. The solution, or feature of it, is then developed until it passes all the specified tests. Research has shown that the practice of Test-Driven Development significantly increases the overall quality of the solution.

9.4 Tracking and Control Concepts

9.4.1 Timeboxing and outcome-based measurement

The use of Timeboxes provides a structure of nested plans to support outcome-based measurement. Outcome-based measurement places the primary focus of measurement on what has been delivered as part of a Solution Increment at the end of a Timebox. The demonstration of the Solution Increment at the end of each Timebox and the formal acceptance by the Business Ambassador, or perhaps the Business Visionary, that what has been delivered is fit for purpose provides the opportunity for outcome-based measurement.

At this level, understanding what has actually been delivered (the actual outcome) compared with what was planned provides the clearest possible indicator as to whether the Project Increment and ultimately the project as a whole is on track. Discipline at the Timebox level is therefore the basis of control not only of the Timebox itself but also for the Project Increment and the project as a whole.

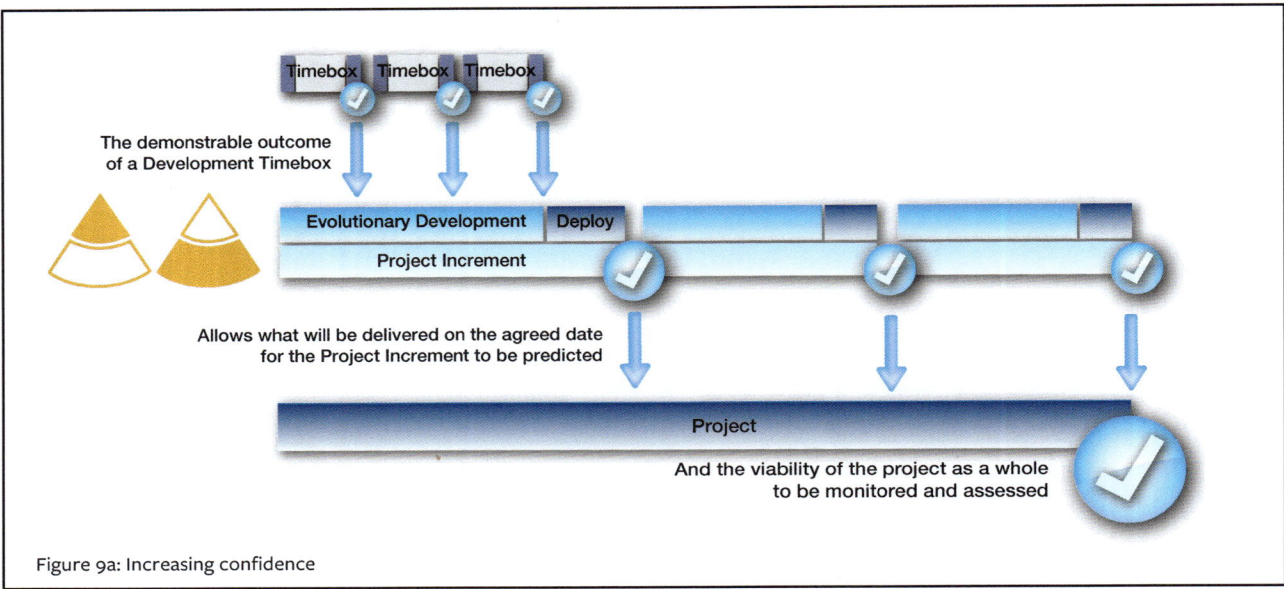

Figure 9a: Increasing confidence

9.4.2 Transparency of process and progress

At the Timebox level, transparency of process and progress comes from the use of a Team Board and the Daily Stand-up that should take place near the Team Board. In combination these make visible the necessary elements of control at the level of the Solution Development Team.

The Team Board makes the detailed plan and the activity against that plan visible to anybody who cares to look. The Team Board clearly shows who is doing what work to meet any particular requirement and, based on estimates of effort required to complete that work, whether the requirement is likely to be fulfilled and demonstrable in the Solution Increment. Issues are also noted on the Team Board along with the ownership of each issue.

The Daily Stand-up, which involves everybody in the Solution Development Team from both the business and technical perspectives, provides an opportunity for each member of the team to describe:

- What they have done since the last Stand-up (describing progress)
- What they intend to do before the next Stand-up (planning in detail to a very close horizon)
- What, if anything, may be blocking their work (making issues visible)

Sharing information in this way provides opportunity for the collaborative, proactive problem solving that characterises an effective Agile team.

9.4.3 Responding to change

In a dynamic business environment following an approach where the detail of understanding of the problem and the detail of what makes up the solution is expected to emerge over time, it is essential that change is not only accepted as inevitable but that it is welcomed as part of the process of getting the solution right. That said, it is equally important: to maintain a *focus on the business need*, to deliver on time, and to *never compromise quality*. This means that change should also be controlled.

Change control in a DSDM project tends to be more formal at the project level than it is at the Solution Development Team level.

At the project level, the Business Visionary is responsible for making sure that the solution meets the business vision and is expected to approve the high-level requirements, described in the Prioritised Requirements List, as a coherent set that reflects the needs and desires of the business. If, as development progresses, there is pressure to make changes to these high-level requirements, then that change should be formally approved by the Business Visionary as being necessary and in line with the business vision. (This is sometimes referred to as a change in breadth.)

At the Solution Development Team level, most of the change will come as a result of a deepening understanding of a requirement or how that requirement will be fulfilled in the Evolving Solution. Change to depth and detail does not represent a formal change of scope and therefore it is primarily at the discretion of the Solution Development Team. The Business Ambassadors and Advisors are empowered to decide what is appropriate and acceptable, within the constraints of time, cost and quality being fixed and requirements being negotiable.

9.4.4 Management by exception

Within the framework of empowerment promoted by DSDM, and using the planning and control concepts described above, day-to-day management of the work required to evolve the solution is left to the Solution Development Team. A degree of tolerance related to the MoSCoW-prioritised scope of what is expected to be achieved is built into the objectives for a Timebox. Typically, the Solution Development Team is empowered to de-scope any Could Have requirement without referring up to the project-level roles. Provided the team is confident that it can deliver a solution within this tolerance, it can make any decisions it needs to around the detail of what will be done and how. If, however, the team believes that the Solution Increment will not meet
all the Must and Should Have requirements agreed or if meeting all the Must and Should Have requirements risks compromising quality, then this is considered to be an issue and should be escalated to the project-level roles for guidance.

Empowerment allows for rapid decision-making at the detailed level and thus rapid progress within a Timebox. Management by exception bridges the boundaries of that empowerment and ensures that, as and when the need arises, project-level roles are involved in making decisions which have a wider impact.

9.5 Planning throughout the Lifecycle

The following diagram describes at a very high level the focus of planning activity in each phase of the project.

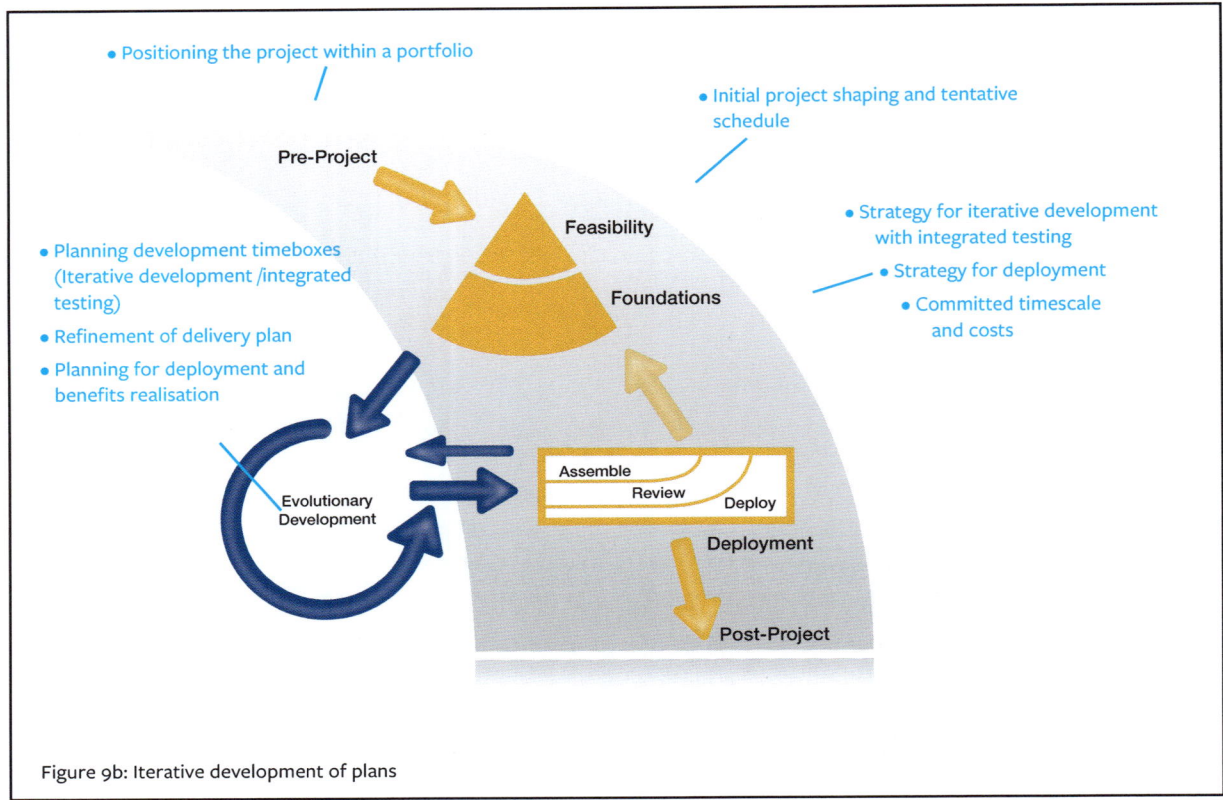

Figure 9b: Iterative development of plans

9.6 Planning and Quality

To ensure successful delivery, quality is considered throughout the DSDM process.

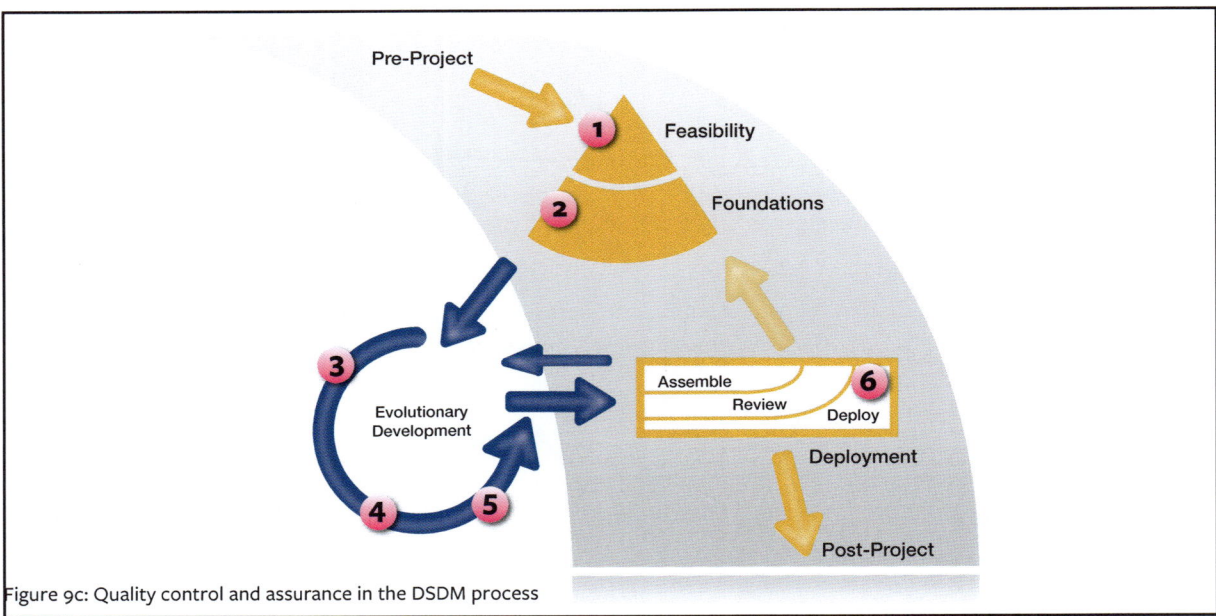

Figure 9c: Quality control and assurance in the DSDM process

9.6.1 High-level risk analysis (Feasibility) ①

High-level risks to achieving the level of quality required are identified alongside any special qualities that the solution needs to have (performance, security, resilience and so on). In light of this, any work required in Foundations to establish how quality will be assured is considered now.

9.6.2 Planning and high-level analysis (Foundations) ②

The quality perspective is included in considering how the solution will be constructed and what business activity is needed to support it in order to:

- Assist in refining good high-level requirements from any requirements which may initially be too vague
- Encourage collaboration between Business roles (focussed on the need), the Solution Developers (focussed on design and build) and Solution Tester (focussed on proving the quality)

This will lead not only to better definition of high-level requirements but also a shared understanding of these and how the solution is likely to evolve to demonstrably meet the business need.

9.6.3 Detailed analysis and planning ③

More detailed analysis is carried out regarding the requirements and acceptance criteria that are being worked on. This is always in the context of what has been built so far. Each of the acceptance criteria is considered from different perspectives before starting to build any given feature. Preparation for the necessary quality assurance activity is started.

9.6.4 Prepare and run ④

- Test preparation:

    - Tests are defined collaboratively for each feature to be constructed. Ideally, this is done in advance of development to form part of the detailed requirement. Where appropriate, testing activity is prioritised

- Running tests:

    - All relevant testing information is captured (the context, what was done and what was seen) in a lightweight and fit-for-purpose way so that tests can be repeated and any actions and the results can be demonstrated to a third party if required. Where possible and appropriate, using tools helps with this

9.6.5 Assess quality and impact ⑤

Defects are identified as early as possible during development, also the actions needed to rectify them. Defect-fixing is prioritised where necessary, treating any defects that are blocking the execution of other agreed tests as a high priority.

At the end of the quality assurance cycle, any residual defects are documented and prioritised so that they can be managed either by scheduling remedial action into a future Timebox or by formally accepting the defect at the end of the Timebox.

9.6.6 Final end-to-end testing and assuring implementation ⑥

Even with testing fully integrated into the development process (as described above), it is still necessary to test both the full package to be delivered and the process by which it will be deployed.

This may be the first opportunity to test the whole solution end-to-end and the only time it is possible to fully test certain non-functional qualities of a solution. A final demonstration that the whole solution is fit for purpose may also be required for governance reasons.

From a technical perspective, every step in the process of deployment also needs to be assured. Walkthroughs of the process and dress-rehearsals of the deployment process should be carried out.

There also needs to be a way of verifying successful deployment once it has happened (which needs to be carefully designed so that it does not impact live operation) and a way to test back-out procedure in case that verification fails as a result of a significant problem occurring during deployment.

9.7 Summary

There have been concerns raised around some of the very informal styles of Agile, citing a perceived lack of planning and control. DSDM addresses these concerns, using as its base the wide experience of DSDM practitioners and DSDM in use within organisations of varying formality. This has allowed the Consortium to evolve a robust but flexible framework to support planning and control within complex project, programme and corporate environments, but which can also work equally effectively on small simple projects. DSDM demonstrates that "Agile and control" and "Agile and planning" are concepts that work very effectively together, provided that planning and control activities are based on an Agile mindset and Agile thinking.

10. DSDM Practice - MoSCoW Prioritisation

10.1 Introduction

In a DSDM project where time has been fixed, it is vital to understand the relative importance of the work to be done in order to make progress and to keep to deadlines. Prioritisation can be applied to requirements/User Stories, tasks, products, acceptance criteria and tests, although it is most commonly applied to requirements/User Stories.

MoSCoW is a prioritisation technique for helping to understand and manage priorities. The letters stand for:

- **M**ust Have
- **S**hould Have
- **C**ould Have
- **W**on't Have *this time*

10.2 The MoSCoW Rules

10.2.1 Must Have

These provide the Minimum Usable SubseT (MUST) of requirements which the project guarantees to deliver. These may be defined using some of the following:

- No point in delivering on target date without this; if it were not delivered, there would be no point deploying the solution on the intended date
- Not legal without it
- Unsafe without it
- Cannot deliver a viable solution without it

DSDM Recommends that the effort associated with delivering the Must Have requirements should not exceed 60% of the total effort available. If the effort to deliver the Must Haves exceeds 60% of the total that is available then the guarantee to deliver this Minimum Usable SubseT is put at risk.

10.2.2 Should Have

Should Have requirements are defined as:

- Important but not vital
- May be painful to leave out, but the solution is still viable
- May need some kind of workaround, e.g. management of expectations, some inefficiency, an existing solution, paperwork etc. The workaround may be just a temporary one

One way of differentiating a Should Have requirement from a Could Have is by reviewing the degree of pain caused by the requirement not being met, measured in terms of business value or numbers of people affected.

10.2.3 Could Have

Could Have requirements are defined as:

- Wanted or desirable but less important
- Less impact if left out (compared with a Should Have)

These are the requirements that provide the main pool of contingency, since they would only be delivered in their entirety in a best-case scenario. When a problem occurs and the deadline is at risk, one or more of the Could Haves provides the first choice of what is to be dropped from this timeframe.

DSDM recommends that the effort associated with delivering the Could Have requirements should be approximately 20% of the total effort available.

10.2.4 Won't Have this time

These are requirements which the project team has agreed will not be delivered (in this timeframe). They are recorded in the Prioritised Requirements List where they help clarify the scope of the project. This avoids them being informally reintroduced at a later date. This also helps to manage expectations that some requirements will simply not make it into the Deployed Solution, at least not this time around.

10.3 MoSCoW Relating to a Specific Timeframe

In a traditional project, all requirements are treated as Must Have, since the expectation is set from the start that everything will be delivered and that typically time (the end date) will slip if problems are encountered. DSDM projects have a very different approach; fixing time, cost and quality and negotiating features. By the end of Foundations, the end-dates for the project and for the first Project Increment are confirmed.

In order to meet this commitment to the deadline, DSDM projects need to create contingency within the prioritised requirements. Therefore the primary focus initially is to create MoSCoW priorities for the project. However, when deciding what to deliver as part of the Project Increment, the next focus will be to agree MoSCoW priorities for that Increment. So at this point, a requirement may have two priorities; MoSCoW for the project and MoSCoW for the Increment. Finally, when planning a specific Timebox (at the start of each Timebox) the Solution Development Team will agree a specific priority for the requirements for this Timebox. At this point, the majority of requirements are Won't Have (for this Timebox). Only requirements that the Solution Development Team plan to work on in the Timebox are allocated a Must Have, Should Have or Could Have priority.

Therefore requirements may have three levels of priority:

- MoSCoW for the project
- MoSCoW for the Project Increment
- MoSCoW for this Timebox

10.4 Summary

MoSCoW Prioritisation (Must Have, Should Have, Could Have, Won't Have *this time*) is primarily used to prioritise requirements although the practice is also useful in many other circumstances.

When prioritising requirements, DSDM recommends that the Must Haves should take no more than 60% of the available effort in a given timeframe and that around 20% of the effort should be associated with Could Haves.

If the effort to deliver the Must Haves exceeds 60% of the total that is available then the guarantee to deliver this Minimum Usable SubseT is put at risk.

MoSCoW Prioritisation is applied at multiple levels - for the project, the Project Increment and the Timebox. In each case, the Could Have requirements provide the primary contingency that makes delivery of the higher priority requirements more likely.

AgilePM

11. DSDM Practice – Timeboxing

11.1 Introduction

DSDM defines a Timebox as a fixed period of time, at the end of which an objective has been met. The Timebox objective is usually completion of one or more deliverables making up a Solution Increment. This ensures the focus for a Timebox is on achieving something complete and meaningful, rather than simply "being busy". At the end of a Timebox, progress and success is measured by completion of products (requirements or other deliverables) rather than completing a series of tasks.

The optimum length for a Timebox is typically between two and four weeks - long enough to achieve something useful, short enough to keep the Solution Development Team focussed. In exceptional circumstances, a Timebox might be as short as a day or as long as six weeks.

Timeboxing is more than just setting short time-periods and partitioning the development work. It is a well-defined process to support the creation of low-level products in an iterative but controlled fashion. Timeboxing incorporates frequent review points to ensure the quality of those products and the efficiency of the Iterative Development process.

By managing on-time/on-target delivery at the lowest level, on-time and on-target delivery at the higher levels can be assured.

The Project Increment and the entire project can also be considered as Timeboxes, as they share the characteristics of delivering a fit-for-purpose solution in a pre-set timeframe. These higher-level Timeboxes are managed through the control applied at the lowest level - the development Timebox. Unless qualified by Project or Increment, the word Timebox always refers to the lowest level Timebox used during the Evolutionary Development of the phase.

11.2 Timebox Options

Every Timebox begins with a Kick-Off and ends with a Close-Out. Beyond this, DSDM recognises two styles of Timebox:

- A DSDM structured Timebox
- A free format Timebox (similar to those in other Agile approaches)

The choice of Timebox style may be driven by factors such as the availability of the Business Ambassador and other business roles or the type of product being developed.

11.2.1 A DSDM Structured Timebox

This is the original DSDM-style Timebox, which provides a standard, repeatable internal structure to a Timebox.

A DSDM structured Timebox comprises three main steps:

- Investigation
- Refinement
- Consolidation

Each of these steps ends with a review.

DSDM Practice - Timeboxing

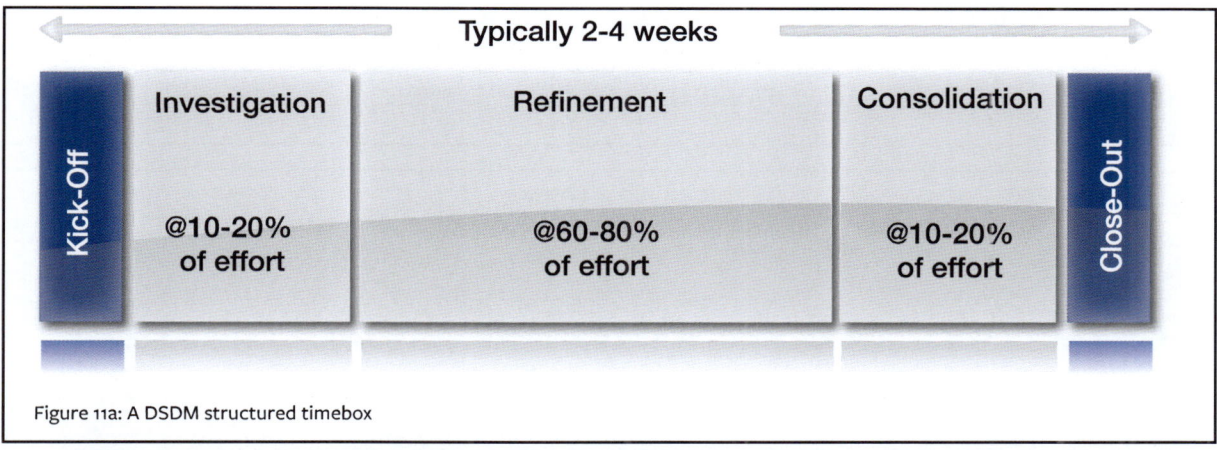

Figure 11a: A DSDM structured timebox

Timebox	Nature of the work done	Suggested timescale
Kick-Off	Short session for the Solution Development Team to understand the timebox objectives and accept them as realistic	Approx 1-3 hours for a 2-3 week Timebox
Investigation	The Investigation includes confirmation of the detail of all the requirements and all the products to be delivered by this timebox. Includes agreement on: • the Timebox deliverables • the acceptance criteria for the deliverables • the measures of success for the Timebox Investigation ends with a review which informs Refinement and may be a valuable governance touch-point	Approx. 10-20% of Timebox
Refinement	Encompasses the bulk of the development, addressing requirements and testing (technical and business testing) the Timebox products, in line with agreed priorities. Refinement ends with a review which informs Consolidation and may be a valuable governance touch-point.	Approx. 60-80% of Timebox
Consolidation	Ties up any loose ends related to Evolutionary Development and ensures all products meet their previously agreed acceptance criteria. Consolidation ends with a review, which informs Close-out and may be a valuable governance touch-point	Approx. 10-20% of Timebox
Close-Out	Formal acceptance of the Timebox deliverables by the Business Visionary and Technical Coordinator. This is followed by a short Timebox retrospective workshop, to learn from the Timebox and to take actions to improve future Timeboxes.	Approx 1-3 hours for a 2-3 week Timebox

11.2.2 A Free Format Timebox

The free format Timebox reflects the style used by other popular Agile approaches, such as a Scrum Sprint. A free format Timebox may be effective where the formality and structure of the DSDM structured Timebox is not possible or helpful.

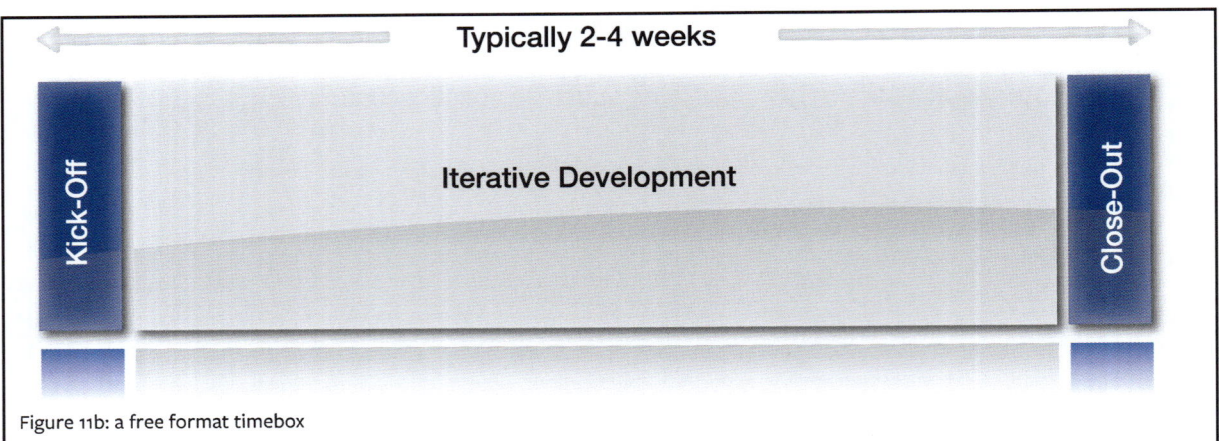

Figure 11b: a free format timebox

Timebox	Nature of the work done
Kick-Off	Short session for the Solution Development Team to understand the timebox objectives, to agree what work (requirements and products) will be taken on in this Timebox and agree their Timebox priorities, and to accept this workload as realistic
Iterative Development	Iterative Development and testing of individual requirements/user stories and other products, as agreed in the Kick-off and in a sequence driven by the agreed priorities for this Timebox. It may still be appropriate to informally adopt the concepts of Investigate, Refine, Consolidate to converge on the accurate solution for each individual requirement/User Story or Product, for example understanding the lower level detail and agreeing the acceptance criteria at the start of the development of a requirement/User Story. This use of Investigate, Refine, Consolidate per requirement/User Story helps to mitigate the risk of too many iterations as the product is elaborated. It is still important that reviews are scheduled during the body of the free format Timebox, to maintain business focus and stakeholder buy-in.
Close-Out	Formal acceptance of the Timebox deliverables by the Business Visionary and Technical Coordinator. This is followed by a short Timebox retrospective workshop, to learn from the Timebox and to take actions to improve future Timeboxes.

11.3 The Daily Stand-up

A key and integral part of all Timeboxes, regardless of the style adopted, is the Daily Stand-up. This is the Solution Development Team's opportunity to share information across the team and to do any day-to-day re-planning and reorganising necessary when issues occur. However, it is important to emphasise that ongoing, informal communication between all team members happens during the day as needed, and not just at the Daily Stand-up.

On a daily basis, the Solution Development Team get together for a Stand-up session. The Stand-up usually takes place at the same time and same place each day (with the Timebox Plan visible), so that others who are not part of the Solution Development Team may listen in. Normally facilitated by the Team Leader, the Stand-up is a daily opportunity for everyone to understand progress against objectives at a detailed level and to expose issues and blockers that may be getting in the way.

The Stand-up:

- Has the following active participants:
    - All members of the Solution Development Team including Business Ambassador(s)
    - Any Business Advisors actively involved in this Timebox
    - Any Technical Advisors actively involved in this Timebox.
- Typically uses a simple format in which each participant in turn describes:
    - What I have been doing since the last stand-up that helps achieve the Timebox objectives
    - What I will be doing between now and the next stand-up to help achieve the Timebox objectives
    - What problems, risks or issues (blockers) I have that will prevent me or the team achieving the Timebox objectives
- Has a short and fixed duration - normally no longer than 15 minutes - 2 minutes per participant + 2 minutes is a good guide
- Is ideally held with all participants standing in a circle by their Team Board, which is sometimes called an Information Radiator

11.4 Timeboxes - The Wider Context

Application of the Timeboxing Practice (described above) in conjunction with the Practice of MoSCoW prioritisation ensures each Development Timebox delivers a fit-for-purpose Solution Increment in the agreed timeframe. On-time delivery at the end of each Timebox keeps the Increment on track and thus the project as a whole on track.

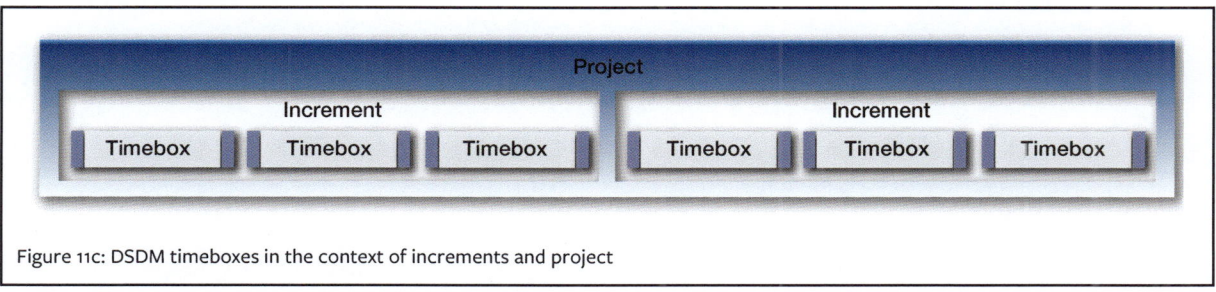

Figure 11c: DSDM timeboxes in the context of increments and project

11.5 Summary

Timeboxing is used in conjunction with MoSCoW Prioritisation to ensure predictable, on-time delivery. Although the term Timebox may be applied to the project as a whole or to a Project Increment, in practical terms the Timeboxing practice is applied only at the lowest level - the typically 2-4 week timeframe in which a Solution Increment is evolved during the Evolutionary Development phases of the project.

DSDM recognises two styles of Timebox:

- The free format Timebox (similar to that used by other Agile approaches)
- The DSDM structured Timebox which segments the Timebox into 3 steps (Investigation, Refinement and Consolidation)
    - Each step ends in a review involving the whole Solution Development Team and may also involve other stakeholders
    - If formalised, these sessions can provide a valuable audit trail of review records for regulatory compliance purposes

12. Other DSDM Practices

12.1 Facilitated Workshops

12.1.1 Introduction

Facilitated Workshops are a specialised type of meeting, with:

- Clear objective deliverables
- A set of people (Participants) specifically chosen and empowered to deliver the required outcome
- An independent person (Workshop Facilitator) to enable the effective achievement of the objective

In Facilitated Workshops, a neutral Workshop Facilitator guides the group through a process which enables them to work together to achieve an agreed goal; whether that be solving a problem, building a plan, gathering requirements or making decisions. The Facilitator has no stake in the outcome of the workshop and no opinion on the content. They are focussed on the group dynamics and enabling the group members to collaborate to achieve their goal(s).

Facilitated Workshops ensure a team-based approach through visual and verbal communication and collaboration, where results can be achieved with speed, commitment and buy-in to the outcome.

Enabling people to communicate and collaborate effectively pays enormous dividends. Facilitated Workshops are an extremely efficient and effective way of achieving this enhanced communication. It is increasingly important for organisations to achieve success through enabling teamwork, interaction and shared understanding.

12.1.2 Workshop benefits

Using Facilitated Workshops brings both direct and indirect benefits to a project. These include:

- Rapid, high-quality decision-making
- Greater buy-in from all stakeholders
- Building team spirit
- Building consensus
- Clarification of issues

12.1.3 Success factors for Facilitated Workshops

The factors which have been found, in practice, to greatly improve the success of Facilitated Workshop are:

- An effective trained, independent Workshop Facilitator
- Flexibility in the format but always with clearly defined objectives
- Thorough preparation before the Workshop, by the Workshop Facilitator and Participants
- A mechanism for ensuring that the outcomes of previous Workshops are built in, where appropriate
- Decisions and agreements that are not forced. If the Participants cannot agree on a point within the Workshop (perhaps due to lack of information or time), the Workshop Facilitator should recognise this outcome and elicit from the group the appropriate action to remedy the shortfall
- Participants receiving a Workshop report, describing decisions, actions and the outcome of the Workshop, very soon after it has been run

12.2 Modelling

12.2.1 Introduction

Modelling is a technique in which visual representations of a problem or a solution are created. A model can be defined as:

- A description or analogy used to help visualise something that cannot be directly observed
- A small but exact copy of something
- A pattern or figure of something to be made

Other DSDM Practices

In IT, the term model has traditionally been used to refer to a set of diagrams.

Modelling techniques are designed to improve communications and prompt the right questions. Many organisations benefit from the use of models, prototypes and mock-ups to establish requirements, to confirm expectations and to test the achievability of objectives. DSDM considers models to be a valuable aid to achieving project success.

Modelling helps to make elements of the solution visible as early as possible. Examples of this could be the use of diagrams, or acting out a new process to be supported by a new IT system. However, the amount of time and effort put into a model should only be just enough to satisfy the purpose of the model and no more.

To enhance clarity, modelling usually incorporates some degree of *abstraction*, which involves omitting certain information from the model to allow clearer focus on another specific aspect.

12.2.2 Modelling perspectives

A coherent picture of a solution area can be gained by considering the perspectives: "what", "where", "when", "how", "who" and "why", and the relationships between them. For example: who performs which processes; what data is needed to support each process. Matrices can be helpful in drawing these relationships.

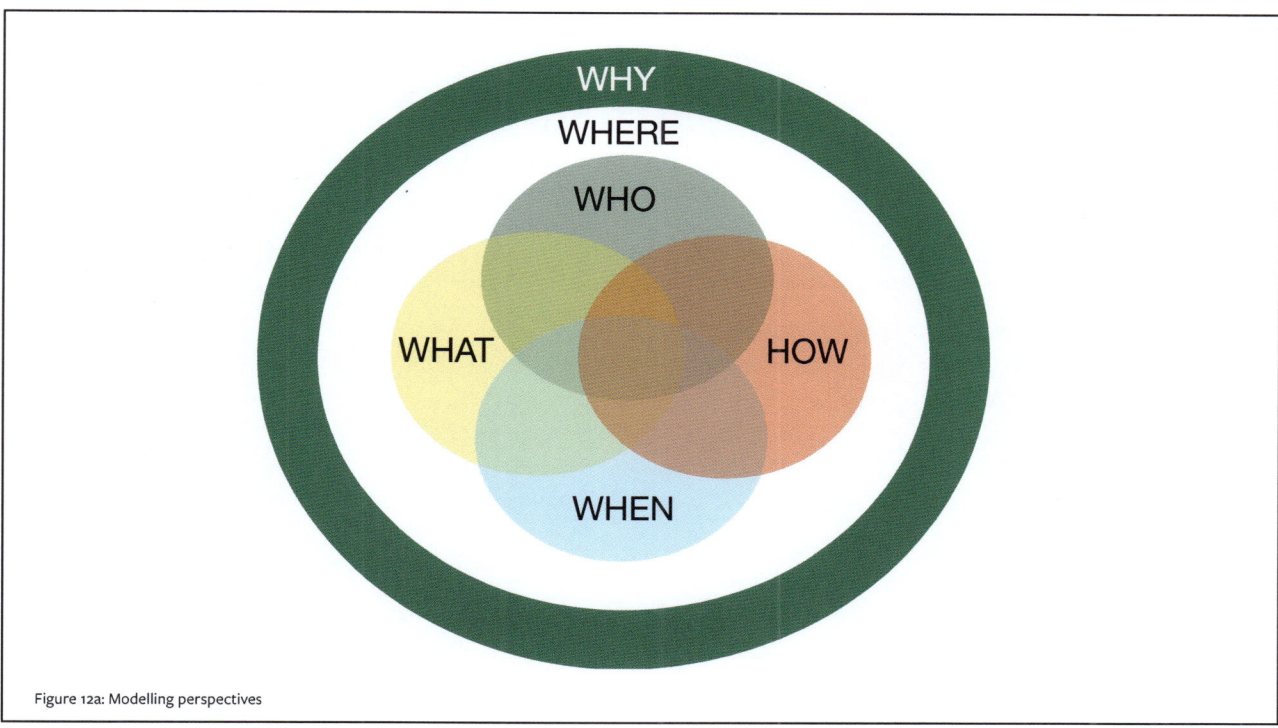

Figure 12a: Modelling perspectives

The table below shows an interpretation of these perspectives from an IT system point of view, but parallels can easily be drawn for other types of project.

WHAT	The information within the solution area, data, relationships and business rules.
HOW	The functions, features and processes within the solution area
WHERE	The locations at which the business operates, in relation to the solution area
WHO	The people: customers, users, stakeholders
WHEN	The events of importance to the business (times and scheduling).
WHY	The business objectives and strategy, as related to the project

12.3 Iterative Development

12.3.1 Introduction

Iterative Development is a process in which the Evolving Solution, or a part of it, evolves from a high-level concept to something with acknowledged business value.

Each cycle of the process is intended to bring the part of the solution being worked on closer to completion and is always a collaborative process, typically involving two or more members of the Solution Development Team.

Each cycle should:

- Be as short as possible, typically taking a day or two, with several cycles happening within a Timebox
- Be only as formal as it needs to be - in most cases limited to an informal cycle of:
    - *Thought* - a consideration of what needs to be done
    - *Action* - to complete the work considered
    - *Conversation* - to review whether the outcome meets the need and to understand what further work is needed if this is not the case

    Note that the cycle actually begins and ends with a conversation
- Involve the appropriate members of the Solution Development Team relevant to the work being done. (At its simplest, this could be, for example, a Solution Developer and a Business Ambassador working together, or it could need involvement from the whole Solution Development Team including several Business Advisors)

12.3.2 Planning Iterative Development

During Foundations, it is very important to decide on a strategy for development that encompasses how the potentially large problem of evolving a solution can be broken down into manageable chunks for delivery in Timeboxes.

12.3.3 Controlling Iterative Development

Each Iterative Development cycle is intended to result in an incremental change to the Evolving Solution that brings it, or more probably a feature of it, progressively closer to being complete or *"done"*. It is quite possible, however, that the review of such an incremental change may reveal that the solution has evolved in a way that is not right. Under such circumstances it is important, wherever possible, to have the option to revert to the previously agreed version and undertake another cycle based on what has been learnt and on any new insight arising from the review. Configuration Management of the solution is therefore an important consideration.

12.3.4 Quality in Iterative Development

One of the defining principles of DSDM is to *never compromise quality*. To achieve this, a required level of quality for the solution should be defined in the early lifecycle phases. During the Evolutionary Development phase continuous verification activity ensures that this level of quality is achieved. Verification may be *static* (a review) or *dynamic* (a test). In DSDM, review and testing activity is at the heart of the Iterative Development practice.

12.3.4.1 Reviews

Reviews can range from informal peer reviews through to highly structured and formal reviews involving experts or perhaps groups of people. The level of formality is often driven by the nature of the product and by corporate or regulatory standards.

12.3.4.2 Testing

There are three broad classes of tests which are useful to consider when dynamically verifying a deliverable:

- Positive tests check that a deliverable does what it should do - e.g. when you add an item to your basket on a web site the item does appear there
- Negative tests check that a deliverable doesn't do what it shouldn't do - e.g. if you put the wrong key into a padlock, you shouldn't be able to open it
- 'Unhappy path' tests check the behaviour of the deliverable when unusual or undefined things happen - e.g. what happens when a car engine overheats? And is that behaviour ok?

Based on these test classes, with some thought it is usually possible to think up multiple positive, negative and unhappy path tests for each acceptance criterion. Every test would typically have the following:

- A defined starting state
- A defined set of actions which we will carry out
- An outcome which we expect to see

12.3.4.3 Roles and responsibilities for review and testing activity

The Technical Coordinator for the project is responsible for the overall quality of the solution from a technical perspective and so is responsible for "ensuring that the non-functional requirements are reasonable at the outset and subsequently met". The Technical Coordinator needs to ensure that appropriate technical reviews are carried out and that testing is sufficiently comprehensive and rigorous to provide confidence that the solution created is fit for purpose.

The Solution Tester is responsible for carrying out all types of testing except for:

- Business acceptance testing: that is the responsibility of Business Ambassador(s) and Business Advisors
- Unit testing of the feature: that is the responsibility of the Solution Developer

As part of a collaborative team, the Solution Tester will be supporting other roles to fulfil their testing responsibilities by providing testing knowledge and expertise.

12.4 Summary

Facilitated Workshops, Modelling and Iterative Development are DSDM practices that help maintain a focus on ensuring the right solution is delivered.

Facilitated Workshops may have a wider application, as they are useful in any circumstance where a group of people need to meet a specific objective in a compressed timeframe. A neutral Workshop Facilitator adds value by managing the group dynamic, leading the workshop participants through a collaborative process to achieve their objective.

Modelling is a practice that uses visual representations of a given problem or solution to enhance communication. A coherent model of a problem or solution can be gained by considering the perspectives: "what", "where", "when", "how", "who" and "why", and the relationships between them.

Iterative Development is the practice used to evolve a solution (or part of it) from a high-level concept to something with acknowledged business value. Iteration is provided through an informal cycle of *thought* (to consider what needs to be achieved), *action* (to evolve the solution) and *conversation* (to discuss whether the solution is right or whether further iteration is required). Review and testing activity is an integral part of the Iterative Development process and ensures that quality is never compromised.

Section Two

The Agile PM Perspective: Digging Deeper

13. Practical Application of the DSDM Principles

13.1 Introduction

In Chapter 4 in this handbook, the DSDM principles were described in outline. In order to run a successful DSDM project, one of the key responsibilities of the Project Manager is to ensure that everybody understands and applies the principles on a day-to-day basis. This chapter takes the description of the principles to the next level and provides practical guidance on what the Project Manager should do to encourage their adoption.

The eight principles support DSDM's philosophy that:

> *"best business value emerges when projects are aligned to clear business goals, deliver frequently and involve the collaboration of motivated and empowered people".*

Compromising any of the principles undermines the philosophy of DSDM and introduces risk to the successful outcome of the project. If a team doesn't follow all of these principles then it won't get the full benefit of the approach. The collective application of DSDM's principles brings the philosophy to life.

The eight principles are:

 1. Focus on the business need

 2. Deliver on time

 3. Collaborate

 4. Never compromise quality

 5. Build incrementally from firm foundations

 6. Develop iteratively

 7. Communicate continuously and clearly

 8. Demonstrate control

13.2 Principle 1 - Focus on the Business Need

 Every decision taken during a project should be viewed in the light of the overriding project goal - to deliver what the business needs to be delivered, when it needs to be delivered.

In practical terms the Project Manager needs to ensure that members of the project team:

- Understand and respect the true business priorities by ensuring MoSCoW prioritisation is correctly applied to requirements and deliverables at all times
    - During the Foundations phase, the primary focus of the Project Manager is to ensure MoSCoW is properly applied as the requirements in the Prioritised Requirements List are prioritised
    - Beyond the Foundations phase, as requirements change and as the solution evolves the Project Manager must ensure that the continual reprioritisation necessary to converge on an accurate business solution is effective and continues to follow MoSCoW rules
    - At the Kick-Off for each Timebox, the Project Manager needs to ensure agreement to the MoSCoW priorities for requirements to be addressed, products to be delivered and acceptance criteria to be met by the end

of the timebox. These priorities must be business-driven although other scheduling considerations such as dependency management may influence these priorities

- Establish a valid business case
    - A well thought through business case will add momentum to a project by providing an urgency for delivery and a sound business focus for team members
    - It is not the responsibility of the Project Manager to define or document the business case - that lies primarily with the Business Visionary, assisted by the Business Analyst. The Project Manager simply needs to ensure that the relevant work to generate the business case is given the attention it needs
- Ensure continuous business sponsorship and commitment
    - The Project Manager must always remember that the ultimate owner of the project is the Business Sponsor. It is therefore vitally important to keep the Sponsor properly and accurately informed about progress and actively engaged in the high-level decision-making and issue resolution as required
    - On a Timebox-by-Timebox basis, the Project Manager needs to ensure that the Business Visionary is engaged in necessary review activity to ensure the solution is evolving in line with the business vision stated in the Business Case
    - On a day-to-day basis, the Project Manager needs to ensure that Business Ambassadors and Business Advisors are actively engaged in guiding the evolution of the solution to meet the business need
- Guarantee delivery of the Minimum Usable SubseT
    - In practical terms, this is primarily about proper application of the MoSCoW rules - ensuring sufficient contingency (in Should Have and Could Have requirements) is available to guarantee that the Must Have requirements will be met
    - Another key responsibility the Project Manager has is to ensure that the resources needed to work on evolving the solution are available and properly applying themselves to solution development work

13.3 Principle 2 - Deliver on Time

Delivering a solution on time is a very desirable outcome for a project and is quite often the single most important success factor. Late delivery can often undermine the very rationale for a project, especially where market opportunities or legal deadlines are involved. Even for projects without a need for a fixed end date, on-time delivery of intermediate or contributing products is still the best way to demonstrate control over evolution of the solution.

In practical terms, the Project Manager needs to ensure that members of the project team:

- Timebox the work
    - One of the key responsibilities of the Project Manager is to create a realistic Delivery Plan by the end of the Foundations phase. The plan should clearly describe a schedule of Project Increments and, for the first/imminent Increment a schedule of properly resourced and appropriately focused Timeboxes
    - At the Kick-Off for each Timebox, the Project Manager needs to ensure that everybody in the Solution Development Team understands and is fully committed to delivering, on time, a Solution Increment that properly reflects business priorities
- Focus on business priorities
    - Again, at the Kick-Off for each Timebox, the Project Manager needs to ensure that the work to be done and the solution to be delivered are properly business-focussed. The Project Manager does not provide the focus or set the priorities - that comes from the Business roles - he/she just needs to ensure that they are properly set and agreed by the end of the Kick-Off

- Always hit deadlines
    - The Project Manager needs to constantly emphasise the importance of on-time delivery as this is the one control that must not be allowed to slip at the Timebox level. Progress is measured by what is delivered in the time allowed and not by how long it takes to deliver what is agreed. This is a fundamental of control in a DSDM project so every Timebox must finish on time - Always - Without exception
- Build confidence through predictable delivery
    - Over time, everybody will get used to the fact that Timeboxes always end on time and that what varies is what is actually delivered by the end of the Timebox
    - Demonstrating steady progress by delivering a demonstrable Solution Increment at the end of each Timebox (even if it does not include every feature that was requested) helps build confidence in what the team can do. The Project Manager should keep reinforcing this message with the Solution Development Team until it becomes embedded as their default way of working
    - A combination of sustainable working hours and true respect for MoSCoW priorities at the Timebox level will allow for estimates to be validated and a velocity to be established that can be used to predict what is likely to be included in the Solution Increment delivered for Deployment. It is absolutely vital that the Project Manager enforces a sustainable pace. Pushing a team, or allowing them to be pushed, into working longer than an 8-hour day will lead to lower productivity and significant unpredictability as fatigue and even burn-out takes its toll on the team. For the same reasons, the Project Manager must also ensure that the team do not push themselves too hard for too long

13.4 Principle 3 - Collaborate

Teams that work in a spirit of active cooperation and commitment will always outperform groups of individuals working only in loose association. Collaboration encourages increased understanding, greater speed and shared ownership, which enable teams to perform at a level that exceeds the sum of their parts.

In practical terms, the Project Manager needs to ensure that members of the project team:

- Involve the right stakeholders at the right time throughout the project
    - During the Feasibility and Foundations phases, the Project Manager needs to ensure that the project-level roles (Business Sponsor, Business Visionary, Technical Coordinator) and, where appropriate, the Business Analyst and any required Business and Technical Advisors, are actively engaged in shaping the project
    - During the Evolutionary Development phase, the Project Manager needs to ensure that all resources that have been agreed to be involved in the project continue to be sufficiently engaged to properly fulfil their role
    - At all times, the Project Manager needs to ensure all stakeholders are kept informed of the status of the project, and any specialist resources required to assist in the project are engaged as required
- Encourage proactive involvement from the business representatives
    - Proactive business engagement in a DSDM project is critical to its success. The Project Manager needs to ensure that the right people are engaged at the right time and to the right extent by constantly monitoring and, where required, intervening to make it happen
    - Where appropriate the Project Manager should coach the team to behave in the collaborative way required by DSDM
- Ensure that all members of the team are empowered to take decisions on behalf of those they represent
    - The Project Manager must ensure that an appropriate framework of empowerment exists - with the Business Visionary properly empowering Business Ambassadors and Advisors to shape the detail of the solution and the Technical Coordinator properly empowering the Solution Developers and Testers to build the solution to the agreed levels of quality

- Where the concept of empowerment is not right, the Project Manager should expect to intervene either to ensure that the right people are engaged at the right level and where necessary to consider coaching to ensure the right patterns of behaviour are exhibited at both the project and Solution Development Team level
- Build a one-team culture
  - It is important that the Project Manager promotes an environment where more emphasis is placed on success, or failure, of the team as a whole, rather than focusing on individual performance
  - However, where the team dynamic is disrupted by the persistent poor performance or behaviour of an individual, the Project Manager will need to intervene, perhaps even to the extent of removing that individual from the team, if that is what is required to maintain team morale

13.5 Principle 4 - Never Compromise Quality

In DSDM, the level of quality to be delivered should be agreed at the start. All work should be aimed at achieving that level of quality - no more and no less. A solution has to be 'good enough'. If the business agrees that the features in the Minimum Usable SubseT meet the agreed acceptance criteria, then the solution should be 'good enough' to use effectively.

In practical terms, the Project Manager needs to ensure that members of the project team:

- Agree the level of quality from the outset, before development starts
  - This is best achieved by ensuring that:
    - maintainability is considered early in the project lifecycle
    - the development approach is properly considered during the Foundations Phase. (This is the responsibility of the Technical Coordinator but the Project Manager should ensure it happens)
    - acceptance criteria are properly defined for all requirements in the Prioritised Requirements List. (This is the responsibility of the Business Analyst but the Project Manager should ensure it happens)
- Ensure that quality does not become a variable
  - On a Timebox-by-Timebox basis the Project Manager needs to:
    - ensure that the team prioritise quality of higher priority requirements (ensuring they are developed to the agreed standard and meet required acceptance criteria) over starting development on lower priority requirements
    - ensure that the Technical Coordinator is involved in appropriate Timebox reviews as development progresses
- Test early, test continuously and test to the appropriate level
  - This is primarily the responsibility of the Technical Coordinator and Solution Tester but the Project Manager needs to ensure that:
    - the development approach integrates testing with development as far as is practical; where appropriate a strategy for testing should be included in the Development Approach Definition by the end of Foundations
    - products delivered at the end of each Timebox are reviewed and tested to the extent defined by the development approach and any specific acceptance criteria defined at the Timebox Kick-Off
- Design and document appropriately
  - There is a common misconception in the Agile world that everything the team needs to do should be encapsulated in User Stories. This is definitely not the case in a DSDM project where high-level analysis and design activity conducted during the Foundations phase is intended to shape the solution and the approach to its development

- Where appropriate, this high-level solution design (from both a business and a technical perspective) should be documented in the Solution Architecture Definition (SAD). The Project Manager is not responsible for producing the SAD but must ensure that, as far as possible, the solution design:
  - Remains at a high level during Foundations
  - Is intended to guide development and, as such, is understood and accepted by the Solution Development Team
  - Does not unnecessarily constrain Iterative Development and the emergence of detail

13.6 Principle 5 - Build Incrementally from Firm Foundations

One of the key differentiators for DSDM within the Agile space is the concept of establishing firm foundations for the project before committing to significant development. DSDM advocates first understanding the scope of the business problem to be solved and the proposed solution, but not in such detail that the project becomes paralysed by overly detailed analysis of requirements.

Once firm foundations for development have been established, DSDM advocates incremental delivery of the solution in order to deliver real business benefit as early as is practical. Incremental delivery encourages stakeholder confidence, offering a source of feedback for use in subsequent Timeboxes and may lead to the early realisation of business benefit.

In practical terms, the Project Manager needs to ensure that members of the project team:

- Carry out appropriate analysis and enough design up front to create strong foundations for all subsequent work
- Formally reassess priorities and informally reassess ongoing project viability with each delivered Increment

Guidance for this is covered in the advice provided for the principles above

13.7 Principle 6 - Develop Iteratively

DSDM uses a combination of Iterative Development, frequent demonstrations and comprehensive review to encourage timely feedback. Embracing change as part of this evolutionary process allows the team to converge on an accurate business solution. The concept of iteration is at the heart of everything developed as part of the DSDM approach. It is very rare that anything is created perfectly first time and it is important to recognise that projects operate within a changing world.

In practical terms, the Project Manager needs to ensure that members of the project team:

- Build business feedback into each iteration
  - The Project Manager needs to ensure that the level of business involvement from Business Ambassadors and Advisors at the Timebox level is sufficient to support this
- Recognise that most detail should emerge later rather than sooner
  - The Project Manager needs to ensure that the Foundations phase of the project does not turn into a detailed analysis and design phase
  - The work of Foundations should shape the project and act as a framework of guidance and necessary constraints rather than be detailed and prescriptive
  - Where necessary, the Project Manager will need to reassure the team and the project stakeholders that the emergence of detail is both expected and is intended to reduce the risk of developing the wrong solution
- Embrace change - the right solution will not evolve without it
  - Again, where necessary, the Project Manager will need to reassure the team and the project stakeholders that change is both inevitable and, in a DSDM project, seen as positive. By embracing change, the risk of developing the wrong solution is reduced

- The Project Manager also needs to ensure that the team continues to make progress throughout the project. It is important that requested changes are therefore properly considered and that any additional work associated with change is properly traded off against less important work. For major change (identified by a change to the high-level requirements baselined in the Prioritised Requirements List at the end of Foundations), formal change control may be required, with the Business Visionary approving any changes and formally acknowledging the trade-offs needed to enable the change

13.8 Principle 7 - Communicate Continuously and Clearly

Poor communication is often cited as the biggest single cause of project failure. DSDM practices are specifically designed to improve communication effectiveness for both teams and individuals.

In practical terms, the Project Manager needs to ensure that members of the project team:

- Make full and proper use of the DSDM practices such as Workshops, Modelling and features of the process such as Timeboxing and the associated daily stand-ups to communicate amongst themselves
- Provide opportunity for anybody who is interested to keep themselves informed of what is happening on a project by making the activity and outputs of the DSDM practices visible
- Keep documentation lean and timely and ensure that it is only created where it adds genuine value to the development or support of the solution
- Manage the expectations of the stakeholders at all levels throughout the project - ideally by involving them in the DSDM process (e.g. inviting them to end of Timebox demonstrations) rather than by creating a parallel stream of written progress reports
- Always aim for honesty and transparency in all communication within and external to the project team

13.9 Principle 8 - Demonstrate Control

It is essential to be in control of a project, and the solution being created, at all times and to be able to demonstrate that this is the case. High-level plans, designs and standards outline the fundamentals of what needs to be achieved, how, by when etc. Being open and honest about how closely the reality of solution development is adhering to those fundamentals and being clear about how the project team is adapting their activities (and, where necessary, the plans, designs and standards themselves) to best meet the business need, is the basis of demonstration of control.

In practical terms, the Project Manager needs to ensure that members of the project team:

- Make plans and progress visible to all
    - The Delivery Plan should be presented in a form that everybody understands and should be kept current and realistic based on the understanding of what has been achieved on a Timebox-by-Timebox basis
    - Timebox Plans, ideally in the form of a Team Board (or tool-based equivalent, where necessary), should be visible to everybody with an interest in the project. The Solution Development Team should be updating the Board at least daily (at the Daily Stand-up) as it is their plan for their work
- Measure progress through focus on delivery of products rather than completed activities
    - Business value can only be achieved through use of the solution the project creates. Something 'almost done' actually has less business value than something not started (because it exists in some form and adds complexity to the solution and so increases maintenance costs). The only meaningful measure of progress is therefore the delivery Solution Increments that demonstrate that this value can be achieved

- The Project Manager needs to actively encourage the Solution Development Team to focus on completing higher priority features before starting work on lower priority ones in order to minimise wasted development time on partially completed features that may never be completed - especially if the lower priority ones promise to be more interesting to work on
- Use an appropriate level of formality for tracking and reporting, allowing project-level roles to continually assess the viability of the project
  - As described above, the best way to track progress is through delivery of products and the best way to keep stakeholders informed of progress is to involve them in the development process. The PM should encourage the engagement of stakeholders in end of Timebox demonstrations rather than spend time writing progress reports that are often left unread and tend to lack detail for those who are interested enough to read them

Principles - Agile Project Manager Top Tips

- Make the principles visible to all, so that everyone understands their importance
- Encourage all team members to flag up if they believe any of the principles are being broken
- Breaking one or more principles means the behaviours being adopted pose a risk to the project that needs to be addressed
- Ensure that *Demonstrate control* is not viewed as "just a Project Manager issue"
- Consider organising a short workshop at the start of the project for the team to agree how each of the principles will be achieved
- Consider including a review of how well the principles have been applied during each increment review and deciding how to change behaviours, if necessary, in the next increment

14. Roles and Responsibilities
The Agile PM's View

The DSDM Roles were introduced in chapter 7. More detailed guidance on each of the roles is provided in this chapter including a description of specific responsibilities associated with each of them. For completeness the summary information from chapter 7 is repeated in this chapter.

14.1 Introduction

People working together effectively are the foundation of any successful project. DSDM recognises this and assigns clear roles and responsibilities to each person in a project, representing the business interests, the solution/technical interests, the management interests and the process interests. Everyone involved in a DSDM project works very closely together in order to break down potential communication barriers.

The best solutions emerge from self-organising, empowered teams. However, these teams, and the people within them, must actively take on the responsibility for their empowerment within the boundaries that have been agreed. At the same time, it is important they:

- Respect each other's knowledge, experience, skills and opinions
- Take personal responsibility for their work and the dependence of the other team members on them
- Have the courage to challenge ways of working, to improve their team collaboration and working processes

14.2 The DSDM Team Model Explained

14.2.1 Role colour scheme - to represent areas of interest

The colour scheme in the DSDM Team Model diagram is as follows:

- Orange - Business interests, roles representing the business view
  - Typically taken by business personnel, e.g. Business Ambassador providing day-to-day business direction, Business Visionary providing high-level direction and a view of the future
- Green - Solution/technical interests, roles representing the solution/technical view
  - Contributing to the technical development of the solution, e.g. Solution Developers creating the solution, Technical Coordinator providing technical leadership and direction
- Blue - Management interests, roles representing the management/leadership view
  - Facilitating the management/leadership aspects of the project, e.g. Project Manager and Team Leader following the DSDM process and managing/leading a DSDM project (using Agile leadership competencies)
- Grey - Process interests, roles representing the process view
  - Facilitating the process aspects of the project, e.g. Workshop Facilitator managing the workshop process, DSDM Coach embedding the DSDM framework
- Mix of two colours - A role that straddles two separate areas of interest, e.g. Business Analyst, has both a business and a solution/technical focus

Roles and Responsibilities The Agile Project Manager's View

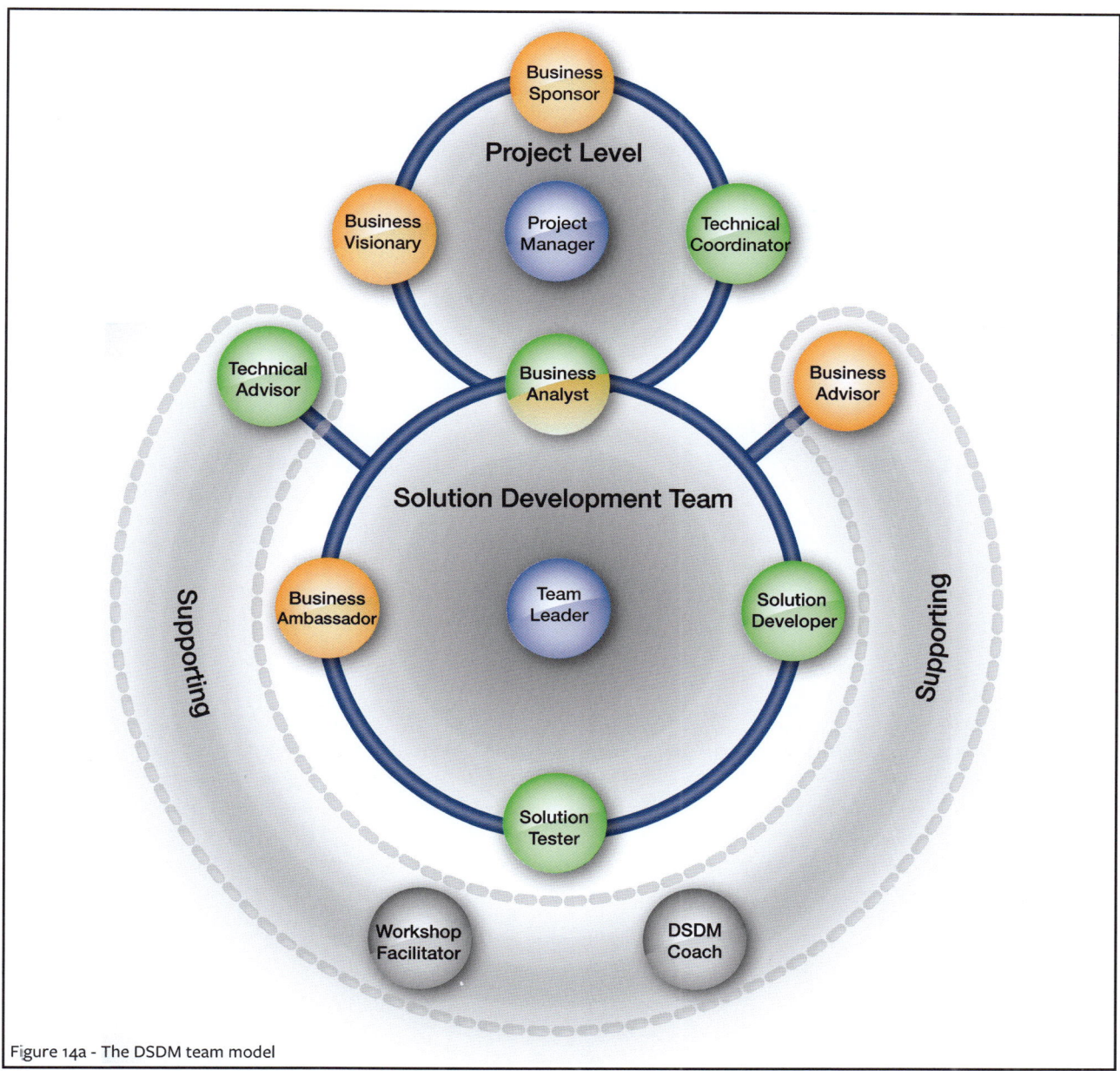

Figure 14a - The DSDM team model

14.2.2 Role categories

14.2.2.1 Project-level roles

The project-level roles (Business Sponsor, Business Visionary, Technical Coordinator, Project Manager and Business Analyst) are the directors, managers and coordinators of the work for the project, where necessary. They may be part of a project board or steering committee for the project and, collectively, have authority to direct the project. They are responsible for the governance of the project, liaising with governance authorities outside of the project. The Business Sponsor provides the overall strategic direction and controls the funding/budget for the project. The Business Visionary and the Technical Coordinator hold the business and technical visions, respectively, for the project. The Project Manager ensures that project funds are used effectively to create the envisaged solution within the agreed timescale.

The Business Analyst is intentionally positioned as part of the project level as well as part of the Solution Development Team. This allows the Business Analyst to, for example, help the business to formulate the Business Case and also to be involved in assisting the business in defining their requirements during Feasibility and Foundations, sometimes before the full Solution Development Team is assigned. The role then continues in supporting the Solution Development Team alongside the project-level roles, as the more detailed requirements emerge.

All roles at the project level need to adopt the facilitative, empowering leadership style which allows Agile teams to learn as they go and reflect, adapt and enhance process. They need to ensure the freedom of the Solution Development Team to do the job, getting to an endpoint by its own means, within an empowerment framework for the team.

The project-level roles:

- Build projects around motivated individuals
- Trust the teams, confident that everyone will work to the best of their ability
- Give the teams the environment and support they need

14.2.2.2 Solution Development Team roles

The Solution Development Team roles are Business Ambassador, Solution Developer, Solution Tester, Business Analyst and Team Leader. These roles form the "engine room" of the project. They shape and build the solution and are collectively responsible for its day-to-day development and for assuring its fitness for business purpose. There may be one or more Solution Development Teams within a project. Each team will include all Solution Development Team roles and cover all their responsibilities.

The membership of each Solution Development Team should be stable throughout a project, however, in the worst case, each Solution Development Team should remain stable for a Project Increment. Each member of the Solution Development Team is an empowered individual who takes personal ownership for their area of responsibility and represents the interests of their peers.

14.2.2.3 Supporting roles

The supporting roles (Business Advisors, Technical Advisors, Workshop Facilitator and DSDM Coach) provide assistance and guidance to the project on an ad hoc basis throughout the lifecycle. The Advisor roles may be filled by one or more subject matter experts, as necessary. The Advisor roles are not the empowered decision-makers - that is the responsibility of the roles within the Solution Development Team - but they advise the Solution Development Team in areas where specialist expertise is needed (e.g. legal and compliance matters, technical knowledge, business-specific rules and regulations).The supporting roles engage with the project as and when necessary. For example, a Business or Technical Advisor will be actively involved during Foundations and then for the particular Timeboxes where their expertise is needed to properly shape the Evolving Solution.

14.2.3 Levels of engagement

All DSDM roles need to be appropriately engaged in the project to fulfil the responsibilities of their role sufficiently. Project-level roles need to be engaged sufficiently to ensure that the ongoing work of the project remains aligned to the business need, is generating a solution to the agreed quality and continues to be viable in terms of the Business Case. Project-level roles therefore need to be engaged in high-level reviews and planning sessions and perhaps in more detailed sessions where key issues and strategic decisions need their input. Their involvement is not normally needed or expected day to day but is more likely to be focussed around the beginning and end of Timeboxes and perhaps at key review points within them. Solution Development Team roles need to be actively engaged in the project on a day-to-day basis working at the detailed level; shaping, building, reviewing and testing the Solution Increment delivered at the end of each Timebox. All Solution Development Team roles must attend the Daily Stand-up in order to maintain a common understanding of progress and any issues and, as a self-organising team, agree detailed plans and actions needed to meet their delivery commitments. Continuous, open, honest communication and day-to-day collaboration are the key to making good progress with transparency of progress, and work being done, being important in demonstrating control. Where project-level roles do engage at a lower level of detail, it is important that they do so as observers and leaders and as the owners of issues rather than as managers of the team or the work being undertaken.

14.2.4 Fulfilling the roles

One DSDM role does not necessarily mean one person. One person may take on one role, or one person may cover two or more roles. Conversely, one role may be split between two or more people. However, where a role is split between individuals, it is vital that these individuals communicate and collaborate closely.

> *For example:*
>
> *On a large IT project, the Technical Coordinator's responsibilities may be allocated to more than one person, e.g. the System Designer/Architect, the Networks Manager, the Infrastructure Manager, etc.*
>
> *On a branding project, Solution Developer responsibilities may be split, with one Solution Developer focusing on logo design, another on key marketing messages*

Conversely, in smaller projects, one person often performs more than one role.

> *For example:*
>
> *One person may carry out the responsibilities both of the Project Manager and the Team Leader. However, some roles are typically only fulfilled by one person, whatever the size of the project, e.g. there should only be one Business Visionary (rather than a group of visionaries) and one Business Sponsor. It is also often true, however, that one person fulfils both the Business Sponsor and the Business Visionary roles.*

Issues such as geographical constraints or staff availability can affect the creation of the ideal project team, but it is strongly recommended that all the roles are considered and that their individual responsibilities are all understood and accepted as appropriate. The role definitions can be used as the basis for personal terms of reference for a project.

14.3 The Project Manager Role

As well as providing high-level, Agile-style leadership to the Solution Development Team, the role is focused on managing the working environment in which the solution is evolving. The Project Manager also coordinates all aspects of management of the project at a high level but, in line with the DSDM concept of empowerment, the Project Manager is expected to leave the detailed planning of the actual delivery of the product(s) to the members of the Solution Development Team. Managing an empowered team requires a facilitative style rather than a "command and control" style.

Although the Project Manager role is focused on getting the project delivered, appropriate sourcing of the role will depend on the skills and knowledge required and on the project itself; the Project Manager may come from the business, or may come from the solution/technical side. For some projects, especially formal contractual projects being delivered by external suppliers, there may be two Project Managers, one from the business (the customer) and one from the solution/technical side (the supplier).

It is usual that the Project Manager takes responsibility throughout the duration of the project. This must include both business and technical delivery aspects of the project, from Foundations (if not Feasibility) through to Deployment.

14.3.1 Responsibilities

- Ensuring effective and timely communication and provision of information to project governance authorities (Business Sponsor, project board, steering committee, etc.) and stakeholders not actively engaged in the project with the agreed and appropriate level of frequency and formality
- Performing high-level project planning and scheduling, but not detailed Timebox planning or task planning
- Collaborating with the Solution Development Team and other appropriate stakeholders to create and agree the Delivery Plan (the schedule of Project Increments and the Timeboxes within them)
- Monitoring progress against the baselined Delivery Plan
- Managing risk and any issues as they arise, collaborating with senior business or technical roles as required to resolve them
- Motivating and ensuring empowerment of the teams to meet their objectives

- Monitoring and ensuring appropriate involvement and communication between required members of the multi-disciplinary Solution Development Team
- Handling problems escalated from the Solution Development Team
- Providing help and guidance to the Solution Development Team where difficult situations arise
- Attending Daily Stand-up meetings, as appropriate, to keep a current understanding of the team's progress and issues, and to flag up to the team, where necessary, any important external issues that they need to be aware of

14.4 Business Sponsor

This role is the most senior project-level business role. The Business Sponsor is the project champion who is committed to the project, to the proposed solution and the approach to delivering it. The Business Sponsor is specifically responsible for the Business Case and project budget throughout (however formally or informally this may be expressed).

The Business Sponsor must hold a sufficiently high position in the organisation to be able to resolve business issues and make financial decisions. This role has a crucial responsibility to ensure and enable fast progress throughout the project.

The Business Sponsor should be committed, supportive and available for the duration of the project, providing a clear escalation route. On smaller projects, the Business Sponsor role will always be fulfilled by a single person. However, on larger projects or in complex organisations, the Business Sponsor's financial responsibilities may be fulfilled by a higher authority such as an investment board or an executive committee. In this circumstance, DSDM expects the business to agree a specific person to "front" the role. This ensures the project deals with a single ultimate decision maker and a single ultimate escalation point, and is protected from a lack of clarity through differing views about the project.

14.4.1 Responsibilities
- Owning the Business Case for the project
- Ensuring ongoing viability of the project in line with the Business Case
- Holding the budget for the project
- Ensuring that funds and other resources are made available as needed
- Ensuring the decision-making process for escalated project issues is effective and rapid
- Responding rapidly to escalated issues and being the ultimate point for resolution of conflict within the project
- Empowering the business roles within the project, to appropriate levels, within their responsibilities
- Keeping themselves informed of progress and issues, e.g. by attending demonstrations at the end of Timeboxes and asking questions of other roles who are more actively engaged

14.5 Business Visionary

This is a senior project-level business role that should be held by a single individual, since a project needs a single clear vision to avoid confusion and misdirection. More actively involved than the Business Sponsor, the Business Visionary is responsible for interpreting the needs of the Business Sponsor, communicating these to the team and, where appropriate, ensuring they are properly represented in the Business Case. The Business Visionary remains involved throughout the project, providing the team with strategic direction and ensuring that the solution delivered will enable the benefits described in the Business Case to be achieved. At the end of the project, the Business Visionary will own the Deployed Solution and will be responsible for the realisation of any benefits associated with it.

14.5.1 Responsibilities
- Defining the business vision for the project
- Communicating and promoting the business vision to all interested and/or impacted parties
- Monitoring progress of the project in line with the business vision
- Owning the wider implications of any business change from an organisational perspective

- Contributing to key requirements, design and review sessions, particularly where aspects of the solution being considered address key elements of the business vision
- Identifying and owning business-based risk
- Defining, and approving changes to, the high-level requirements in the Prioritised Requirements List, i.e. any changes that affect the baselined scope or significantly alter the balance of priorities
- Ensuring collaboration across stakeholder business areas within the scope of the project
- Ensuring business resources are available to the project as needed
- Promoting the translation of the business vision into working practice, i.e. ensuring full business adoption of the solution created by the project
- Empowering the business roles within the Solution Development Team, to appropriate levels, within their responsibilities
- Where the Solution Development Team cannot agree, acting as an arbiter of business differences related to the business need and the way this is addressed in the Evolving Solution

14.6 Technical Coordinator

As the project's technical authority, the Technical Coordinator ensures that the solution/technical roles work in a consistent way, that the project is technically coherent and meets the desired technical standards. This role provides the glue that holds the technical aspects of the project together while advising on technical decisions and innovation.

The Technical Coordinator performs the same function from a technical perspective as the Business Visionary does from a business perspective.

14.6.1 Responsibilities

- Agreeing and controlling the technical architecture
- Determining the technical environments
- Advising on and coordinating each team's technical activities
- Identifying and owning architectural and other technically based risks
- Ensuring the non-functional requirements are achievable and subsequently met
- Working with the Business Analyst to evaluate the technical options and decide the best way to turn the high-level business requirements into a technical solution
- Advising on and coordinating each team's approach to estimating, to reflect technical best practice and current technical understanding
- Promoting appropriate standards of technical best practice
- Controlling the technical configuration of the solution
- Approving the solution as technically fit for purpose prior to deployment
- Managing technical aspects of the transition of the solution into live use
- Empowering the technical roles within the Solution Development Team to appropriate levels within their responsibilities
- Acting as the final arbiter of technical differences between Solution Development Team members

14.7 Business Analyst

The Business Analyst is both active in supporting the project-level roles and fully integrated with the Solution Development Team. The Business Analyst facilitates the relationship between the business and technical roles, ensuring accurate and appropriate decisions are made on the Evolving Solution on a day-to-day basis. The Business Analyst ensures that the business needs are properly analysed and understood by all members of the Solution Development Team.

Active involvement of the business users in the process of evolving the solution is vital to the success of a DSDM project.

Therefore it is important to ensure that the Business Analyst does not become an intermediary between Solution Development Team members but, instead, supports and facilitates the communication between them.

14.7.1 Responsibilities
- Assisting the Business Visionary in the formulation and promotion of the business vision, as appropriate
- Modelling the organisation's current and future state in the area of the solution and identifying opportunities, risks and impacts
- Working with the Business Visionary and the Solution Development Team to formulate and communicate solution options
- Working with the project-level roles in formulating the Business Case and organising Benefits Assessments
- Supporting and facilitating unambiguous and timely communication between business and technical participants in the project
- Ensuring the requirements defined are of good quality and are analysed and managed appropriately
- Managing development, distribution and baseline approval of all communication related to business requirements and their interpretation, with particular focus on ensuring the prioritised requirements list is kept up to date, as the detail expands and evolves
- Ensuring that the business and organisational implications of day-to-day evolution of the solution are properly modelled and thought through
- Ensuring the impact of business decisions is reviewed in the context of the project
- Ensuring the business and technical components of the solution collectively provide a cohesive whole for the business
- Taking responsibility for tracking business requirements through to business acceptance
- Liaising with the Business Visionary in organising support for the solution through implementation into live use

14.8 Team Leader

The Team Leader ideally acts as the servant-leader for the Solution Development Team and ensures that it functions as a whole and meets its objectives. The Team Leader works with the team to plan and coordinate all aspects of product delivery at the detailed level. This is a leadership role rather than a management role and the person holding it will ideally be elected by his or her peers as the best person to lead them through a particular stage of the project. It is therefore likely that they will also perform another Solution Development Team role (e.g. Business Analyst, Business Ambassador, Solution Developer or Solution Tester) in addition to their team leadership responsibilities. It is also feasible that the person carrying out the Team Leader role could be different from one Timebox to another, for example where they have a different focus.

14.8.1 Responsibilities
- Facilitating the team focus on the on-time delivery of agreed products
- Encouraging full participation of team members within their defined roles, responsibilities and empowerment
- Ensuring that the Iterative Development process is properly focused and controlled
- Ensuring that all testing and review activity is properly scheduled and carried out
- Managing risks and issues at the Timebox level, escalating to the Project Manager, Business Visionary or Technical Coordinator as required
- Monitoring progress on a day-to-day basis for all team activities
- Facilitating communication of team progress with the Project Manager
- Facilitating the Daily Stand-ups, ensuring they are timely, focused and brief
- Facilitating reviews and retrospectives with the team

14.9 Business Ambassador

The Business Ambassador is the key representative of the business needs within the Solution Development Team and, as such, needs to have the desire, authority, responsibility and knowledge to fulfil the role.

During Foundations, the Business Ambassador has significant input into the creation and prioritisation of requirements. Once the requirements have been agreed and baselined (by the end of Foundations), the Business Ambassador then provides the day-to-day detail of the requirements during timeboxed development. This is either based on their own knowledge and experience, or drawing on the experience of the Business Advisors.

During the Evolutionary Development phase of the project, the Business Ambassador is the main decision-maker on behalf of the business. For this reason the Business Ambassador needs to be someone who is respected by their business peers and who has sufficient seniority, empowerment and credibility to make decisions on behalf of the business, in terms of ensuring the Evolving Solution is fit for business purpose. It is also important that the person fulfilling this role has the confidence to recognise where their own knowledge is insufficient and to bring in Business Advisors to support them.

Typically the Business Ambassador role is someone who is already busy. For this reason they must be able to commit the appropriate (and agreed) amount of time throughout Timebox development to help guide the Evolving Solution in the right direction to meet the business needs. For some projects, this may require a full-time commitment as the only way to meet the deadline. However, this is unusual and actually introduces a risk that the Business Ambassador may become unaware of events occurring in the business. For most projects, the Business Ambassador commitment is a part-time one, at a level agreed during Foundations. But it is also important that where an Ambassador is committing time to the project, some of their normal workload can be delegated, so that all their work (day-to-day business and DSDM project) can be achieved in a normal working week. It is important that the amount of commitment expected is openly discussed and agreed at a workable level.

14.9.1 Responsibilities

- Contributing to all requirements, design and review sessions
- Providing the business perspective for all day-to-day solution development decisions
- Providing the detail of business scenarios to help define and test the solution
- Communicating with other users, involving them as needed and getting their agreement
- Providing day-to-day assurance that the solution is evolving correctly
- Organising and controlling business acceptance testing of the solution
- Taking responsibility for the creation of the business user and support documentation for the ultimate solution (this responsibility may be delegated, for example to a specialist such as a Technical Author, but the ultimate responsibility remains with the Business Ambassador)
- Ensuring business participants in the Deployed Solution are properly trained and supported

14.10 Solution Developer

The Solution Developer collaborates with the other Solution Development Team roles to interpret business requirements and translate them into a Solution Increment that meets functional and non-functional needs. A person assuming a Solution Developer role needs to be appropriately empowered by the Technical Coordinator to make day-to-day decisions in their area of expertise. They should ideally be allocated full-time to the project they are working on. Where they are not full-time, the project ought to be their first priority. If this cannot be achieved, significant risk is introduced with regard to timeboxing. This risk needs to be managed proactively by the Project Manager.

14.10.1 Responsibilities

- Working with all other Solution Development Team roles to iteratively develop:
    - The Solution Increment

- Models required for the properly controlled development of the solution
- Models and documents as required for the purpose of supporting the Deployed Solution in live use
- Testing the output of their own work prior to independent testing
- Agreeing and adhering to technical constraints
- Adhering to the organisation's technical implementation standards and best practice
- Participating in any quality assurance work required to ensure the delivered products are truly fit for purpose
- Recording (and later interpreting) the detail of any
  - Changes to the detailed requirements
  - Changes to the interpretation of requirements which result in re-work within the solution
  - Information likely to impact on the ongoing evolution of the solution

14.11 Solution Tester

The Solution Tester is an empowered Solution Development Team role, fully integrated with the team and performing testing throughout the project in accordance with the agreed strategy.

14.11.1 Responsibilities

- Working with business roles to define test scenarios and test cases for the Evolving Solution
- Carrying out all types of technical testing of the solution as a whole
- Liaising with the Business Analyst and Business Ambassador to help clarify acceptance criteria for requirements
- Creating test products as appropriate, e.g. test cases, test plans and test logs
- Reporting the results of testing activities to the Technical Coordinator for quality assurance purposes
- Keeping the Team Leader informed of the results of testing activities
- Assisting the Business Ambassador(s) and Business Advisor(s) so that they can plan and carry out their tests well enough to ensure that the important areas are covered

14.12 Business Advisor

Often a peer of the Business Ambassador, the Business Advisor is called upon to provide specific, and often specialist, input to solution development or solution testing - a business subject matter expert. The Business Advisor will normally be an intended user or beneficiary of the solution or may be a representative of a focus group. However they may, for example, simply provide legal or regulatory advice with which the solution must comply.

14.12.1 Responsibilities

Based on the specialism for which the Business Advisor has been engaged:

- Providing specialist input into relevant:
  - Requirements, design and review activities
  - Day-to-day project decisions
  - Business scenarios to help define and test the solution
- Providing specialist advice on, or help with:
  - Developing business user and support documentation for the ultimate solution
  - Deployment of the solution releases into the business, as appropriate

14.13 Technical Advisor

The Technical Advisor supports the team by providing specific, and often specialist, technical input to the project, often from the perspective of those responsible for operational change management, operational support, ongoing maintenance of the solution, etc.

14.13.1 Responsibilities

The Technical Advisor supports the Solution Development Team through the provision of detailed, and often specialist, technical input and advice with regards to:

- Requirements, design and review sessions
- The operational perspective for day-to-day decisions
- Operational or support scenarios to help define and test the solution
- Assurance that the solution is evolving correctly
- Operational acceptance testing
- Development of technical support documentation
- Training of technical operations and support staff
- Incremental Deployment of the solution releases, as appropriate

14.14 Workshop Facilitator

The Workshop Facilitator is responsible for managing the workshop process and is the catalyst for preparation and communication. The Workshop Facilitator is responsible for organising and facilitating a session that allows the participants to achieve the workshop objective.

The Workshop Facilitator should be independent of the outcome to be achieved in the workshop.

14.14.1 Responsibilities

Before each workshop:

- Agreeing the scope of the workshop with the workshop owner (the person who wants the workshop to take place)
- Planning the workshop, including agreement of empowerment and the decision-making process
- Familiarisation with the subject area of the workshop, if necessary
- Engaging with participants prior to the workshop to:
    - Confirm their suitability as a participant (in terms of knowledge, state of empowerment and their need to be at the workshop)
    - Ensure their full understanding of the workshop objectives
    - Understand any major areas of interest and concern in the subject area
    - Encourage completion of any required preparation work

During each workshop:

- Facilitating the workshop to meet its objectives

At the conclusion of each workshop

- Reviewing the workshop outcome against its objectives

After each workshop

- Ensuring the workshop results are distributed to participants and other agreed stakeholders, as necessary

14.15 DSDM Coach

Where a team has limited experience of using DSDM, the role of the DSDM Coach is key to helping team members to get the most out of the approach, within the context and constraints of the wider organisation in which they work. The DSDM Coach should ideally be certified as a DSDM Coach to ensure that their competence to fulfil this role has been independently validated. As with any method of working in any context, the approach cannot be followed blindly. If there is something in the project environment that will inhibit the effectiveness of a particular DSDM technique, then it is vital that the potential problem is addressed. Typically, there are two ways of addressing such a problem: the first is to influence the environment to allow the technique to be effective; the second is to adapt or substitute the technique. Either way, an expert in DSDM - the DSDM Coach - will have the knowledge and experience to help.

14.15.1 Responsibilities

- Providing detailed knowledge and experience of DSDM
- Tailoring the DSDM process to suit the individual needs of the project and the environment in which the project is operating
- Helping the team use DSDM practices and helping those outside the team appreciate the DSDM philosophy and values
- Helping the team work in the collaborative and cooperative way typical of DSDM and all Agile approaches
- Building DSDM capability within the teams at all levels

14.16 Key Project Manager Relationships

14.16.1 The Project Manager and the Business Sponsor

Although it is important that the Project Manager takes responsibility for project delivery it is vital that the ownership of the project remains with the Business Sponsor. The Project Manager needs to ensure that the Business Sponsor understands and accepts the importance of the responsibilities associated with their role - particularly those related to issue resolution. The Project Manager should make it clear that escalation of issues to the Business Sponsor will probably be infrequent but that, if it does occur, it will require swift and decisive action.

Wherever possible, the Project Manager should try and establish a relationship with the Business Sponsor where both parties are comfortable just talking about the project and then make a point of doing so on a regular basis. A 5-minute conversation is likely to be the most effective way of ensuring the Business Sponsor remains aware of, and hopefully comfortable with, what is going on in the project. Where the Business Sponsor may not be comfortable, potential issues can often be avoided through quiet conversation and agreement on a way forward. Even where formal bodies such as Steering Committees exist, the Project Manager should talk to the Business Sponsor outside of that forum ensuring that there are no surprises for the Business Sponsor at the meeting and, ideally, agreeing a common position on any issues in advance.

14.16.2 The Project Manager and the Business Visionary

Along with the Technical Coordinator, the Business Visionary is an equal in authority to the Project Manager:

- Each of the three roles has authority for their interest group
    - the Business Visionary for all business-related decisions
    - the Technical Coordinator for all technical quality decisions
    - the Project Manager for decisions related to how the project should be managed
- All three are collectively empowered by the Business Sponsor to ensure that the right solution is created for the business as a whole and delivered as efficiently as possible

The Project Manager needs to ensure that the Business Visionary fully understands the responsibilities associated with the role and remains close enough to the project throughout the lifecycle in order to fulfil them. During Feasibility and Foundations phases, the Business Visionary must be actively engaged in, and ideally driving, activities to:

- Create and promote the business vision

- Shape the business case
- Define and prioritise high-level requirements

As with the Business Sponsor, the Project Manager should establish a relationship with the Business Visionary in which simple, informal conversation about project progress and issues is the norm.

During Evolutionary Development, as a minimum of engagement, the Project Manager should encourage the Business Visionary to attend and actively participate in the End of Timebox reviews and subsequent project-level re-prioritisation and re-planning activities.

14.16.3 The Project Manager and the Technical Coordinator

Along with the Business Visionary, the Technical Coordinator is an equal in authority to the Project Manager:

- Each of the three roles have authority for their interest group
    - the Business Visionary for all business-related decisions
    - the Technical Coordinator for all technical quality decisions
    - the Project Manager for decisions related to how the project should be managed
- All three are collectively empowered by the Business Sponsor to ensure that the right solution is created for the business as a whole and delivered as efficiently as possible

The Project Manager needs to ensure that the Technical Coordinator fully understands the responsibilities associated with the role and remains close enough to the project, throughout the lifecycle, as is needed to fulfil them. During Feasibility and Foundations phases the Technical Coordinator must be actively engaged in, and ideally driving, activities to ensure:

- A firm architectural foundation for the solution is established
- Non-functional requirements are sensible and achievable
- A sensible Agile development approach (standards and practices to be applied) is agreed with all members of the Solution Development Team

As with the Business Sponsor, the Project Manager should establish a relationship with the Technical Coordinator in which simple conversation about project progress and issues is the norm.

During Evolutionary Development, as a minimum of engagement, the Project Manager should encourage the Technical Coordinator to attend and actively participate in the End of Timebox reviews and subsequent project-level re-prioritisation and re-planning activities.

14.16.4 The Project Manager and the Business Analyst

The Business Analyst participates in the project in association with both the project-level roles and the Solution Development Team. In both cases, the Business Analyst is there to assist the roles in ensuring the solution that evolves is genuinely fit for purpose.

At the project level, the Project Manager needs to establish a close relationship with the Business Analyst, working together to ensure that the right solution evolves in the most effective way and that any issues inhibiting that effectiveness are dealt with swiftly and appropriately. This requires a clear mutual understanding of responsibilities and a genuine respect for each other's role.

An experienced Business Analyst who lacks experience with DSDM may be tempted into two ways of working that are typical of the role in more traditional project approaches but this must be avoided in an Agile project:

1. Working at a detailed level early in the lifecycle - this is typical in approaches where detailed analysis and design activity precedes development. This early detail is highly inappropriate in an Agile environment where detail is expected to emerge over time during Evolutionary Development
2. Writing everything down in detailed documents - perhaps with a focus on getting formal up-front agreement to this prior to development work commencing. Again, this is typical in more traditional approaches but inappropriate when using an

Agile approach. Iterative Development relies on a much less formal mechanism for agreeing what is needed and checking that is delivered

In both cases, the Project Manager should encourage the Business Analyst to work in an Agile way.

14.16.5 The Project Manager and the Team Leader

The Project Manager and the Team Leader roles are focussed on different levels of detail and based on day-to-day interactions with different roles.

- The Project Manager interacts primarily with the project-level roles and other stakeholders collectively providing high-level direction and dealing with equally high-level planning and issue management
- The Team Leader works at the detail level, working in a facilitative style with the Solution Development Team and associated Business and Technical Advisors dealing with day-to-day planning and management of the work needed to evolve the solution.

The relationship between the two roles is critical to the success of the project. From the Project Manager's perspective, there is a need to balance empowerment of the Solution Development Team (including the Team Leader) to get the job done, with a need to understand whether things are progressing smoothly in line with the commitment made to deliver what has been agreed at the end of each Timebox.

This is best achieved by the Project Manager participating actively in agreed Timebox review points and acting as an observer at the Daily Stand-up.

In a relationship where conversation, rather than more formal mechanisms of communication is the norm, a quiet, supportive conversation about any issues the Project Manager has observed at the Stand-up is the best way to maintain the required balance of empowerment and control.

Where the same individual holds both the Project Manager and Team Leader role, great care must be taken to ensure that the style of management and leadership is properly aligned with the situation - e.g. retaining a peer-to-peer relationship at the Solution Development Team-level rather than a manager-to-worker relationship.

14.16.6 The Project Manager and the Solution Development Team

The relationship between the Project Manager and the Solution Development Team tends to be informal and hands off where the Project Manager behaves more as an 'observer' than 'manager'. The Project Manager should adopt a facilitative style of management whenever there is a need to engage directly with the Solution Development Team - for example, at least in the first instance, helping the team resolve its own issues rather than immediately starting to manage them.

Balancing empowerment with control is critical and the Project Manager should use a combination of 'management by objective' and 'management by exception'.

Management by objective requires the Project Manager to ensure that the Solution Development Team understands the objectives they have agreed for themselves at the beginning of each Timebox and the importance of meeting the delivery commitments they have made to meet that objective.

Management by exception is one of the tracking and control concepts (see chapter 9.4.4) that requires the Project Manager to exert control if, for whatever reason, the team believe that they are unable to meet the commitments they have made.

One key exception to the hands-off approach is where issues between team members are not being resolved. In this circumstance, it may be necessary for the Project Manager to be proactive in resolving any issues likely to disrupt the morale and productivity of the team as a whole.

14.16.7 The Project Manager and other stakeholders

The first of the responsibilities described for the Project Manager is:

> *Ensuring effective and timely communication and provision of information to project governance authorities and stakeholders not actively engaged in the project with the agreed and appropriate level of frequency and formality.*

It is important that the Project Manager keeps other stakeholders informed about progress, future plans and any major risks and issues associated with the project. Communication in this regard should always be open and honest.

In communicating with stakeholders, it is best to adopt the philosophy that there is no 'good news' or 'bad news' there is only 'news'. It is important that the stakeholders understand this and the Project Manager should avoid being drawn into the world of politics and the 'management of the message'. The Project Manager should focus instead on managing the issue itself.

Where required, the Project Manager may play a part in facilitating communication between other project-level roles and their stakeholder peers - effectively helping them meet their responsibilities - but must not fall into the trap of accepting those responsibilities or inappropriately owning the relationship between the project and individual stakeholders.

14.17 Summary

DSDM identifies roles in two dimensions - categories and interests. Roles are grouped into three categories:

- Project roles
- Solution Development Team roles
- Supporting roles

Within a DSDM project, the different interests are represented using colours:

- Orange represents the business interests
- Green represents the solution/technical interests
- Blue represents management interests
- Grey represents process interests

The Business Analyst role is coloured a mix of orange and green since this role often straddles the boundary between business and solution/technical interests.

On a DSDM project, one role may be fulfilled by several people, or one person may fulfil several roles.

DSDM values individuals and interactions over processes and tools. The roles and responsibilities defined by DSDM are both comprehensive and carefully considered. The Project Manager should ensure that everybody who participates in a DSDM project understands their role, their responsibilities and the importance of respecting these in the context of a collaborative, productive, whole-project team.

AgilePM

Roles and Responsibilities - Agile Project Manager Top Tips

- Getting a good Business Ambassador is often challenging, as these are knowledgeable and skilled people, usually key to the business. That is the reason why the project needs them, as their input drives the quality of the ultimate solution

- Check that the business has confidence in the person taking the Business Ambassador role. This person will be making the majority of the day-to-day decisions on behalf of the business during Evolutionary Development

- It is possible (although unusual) that the Visionary and the Ambassador are the same person fulfilling two roles. It is also possible that the Visionary and Sponsor are the same person fulfilling two roles. However there is no point in one person fulfilling the Business Ambassador and Business Advisor roles, since the Ambassador only calls on the Business Advisors to provide detailed subject matter expertise that they don't possess themselves

- There should ideally be a single Business Sponsor, and a single Business Visionary for a DSDM project

    - Having multiple Sponsors is not too much of an issue provided you as a PM have an agreed escalation mechanism and direct contact with an empowered decision-maker at this level

    - Having multiple Business Visionaries is a very big problem, however, as a business vision created by committee rarely has the clarity, power and applied passion that a vision created by a single mind has

    - Often the demand for multiple Business Visionaries has its origin in the politics of the organisation. Where this is the case, try to identify a single Business Visionary (typically the person most passionate about the change that is needed) and use a body such as a Steering Group to ensure that all views are properly represented and the solution retains the organisation-wide balance that is needed

- It is good practice to use the DSDM Team Model diagram (in section 14.2) to fill in the names for each role and to make this visible to the whole team and relevant stakeholders from the start of the project

- Consider discussing the responsibilities for each role with the role owners, to ensure they are happy with what is expected from them

- Where you are fulfilling both the Project Manager role and the Team Leader role (a common combination), always be aware of which role you are in at any point in time, as the behaviours are different. For example, at a Stand-up, wearing your Team Leader "hat", you are an active participant, but you are not acting as the Project Manager at this point

- Make every effort to have Solution Testers working inside the team rather than as part of a separate QA function, which always builds in delay and can create divisions across the project

- On a large multi-team project, it can be very useful to have a Technical Coordination Team. Each team member covers all teams but only in one or more of the role's responsibilities.

- If resources are tight, consider combining the roles of Business Analyst and Team Leader. Both roles have a keen interest in the feasibility, cohesion and acceptability of what is being built

15. Project Management Through the Lifecycle

15.1 Introduction

In Chapter 6, the DSDM process was introduced. This section focuses on the practicalities of what the DSDM Project Manager needs to consider in each phase as the project progresses through the various phases.

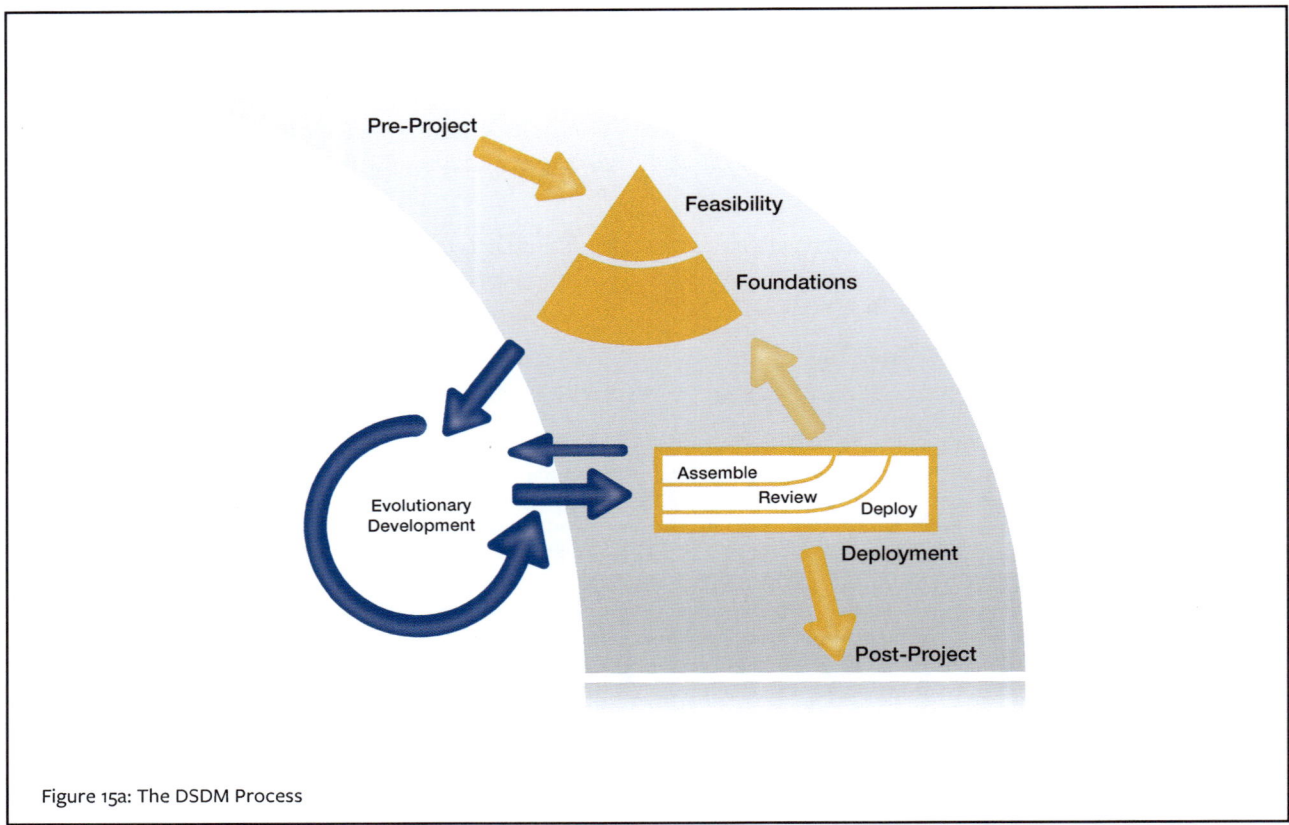

Figure 15a: The DSDM Process

15.2 The DSDM Process and the Project Lifecycle

The diagram above describes a process with a start and an endpoint defined by the Pre- and Post-Project phases respectively.

Each phase has a purpose and should be addressed in any project, but the amount of effort and the formality associated with each one will vary from organisation to organisation and from project to project.

The Pre-Project phase at its simplest and most informal may take the form of a conversation between a person with an idea for a project and a person prepared to sponsor it. In larger more formal organisations, the Pre-Project phase might involve the creation of a formal proposal for a project (the DSDM Terms of Reference) that can be considered by an investment committee to decide whether the project is aligned with the current strategic goals for the business and whether it warrants any further investigation at this time.

The objective of the Foundations phase is to establish firm and enduring foundations for the project from the Business, Solution Development and Management perspectives, including agreement of a realistic Business Case for the project (describing timescales, budget, scope of the development and expected business value). For projects where any of this is unclear at the outset and where significant effort is required to establish a good understanding of what is needed or expected, a formal Feasibility phase should precede Foundations.

The Feasibility phase takes the form of an initial, very high-level consideration of the Business, Solution Development and

Project Management through the Lifecycle

Management aspects of the project. It is aimed at determining whether the project is likely to be feasible:

- From a technical perspective - is it likely that a solution can be created to meet the business need?
- From a business perspective - is it likely to be cost effective to create that solution?

If the project is unlikely to be feasible in either regard, it makes sense to establish this as early as possible, with limited effort and cost.

So for larger, more complex projects, a sequence of Pre-Project, Feasibility and Foundations phases makes sense, whereas for smaller, simpler projects, where there are no concerns about feasibility, a project may sensibly move straight from Pre-Project to Foundations.

The DSDM philosophy is that:

> *"best business value emerges when projects are aligned to clear business goals, deliver frequently and involve the collaboration of motivated and empowered people".*

One of the key decisions made during Foundations relates to whether the solution can be delivered and deployed into live use incrementally, thus delivering value early. By the end of Foundations, the Delivery Plan is expanded from the outline created in Feasibility to provide more detail. It describes the project lifecycle moving on from the Foundations phase by defining the number of planned Project Increments, each comprising an Evolutionary Development phase and a Deployment phase. The project is closed as part of the Deployment phase of the final Project Increment. Where a business considers it valuable, the Post-Project phase focuses on measuring the actual benefit realised by the delivered solution.

Three **examples** of project lifecycles that can be created from the DSDM process are shown below

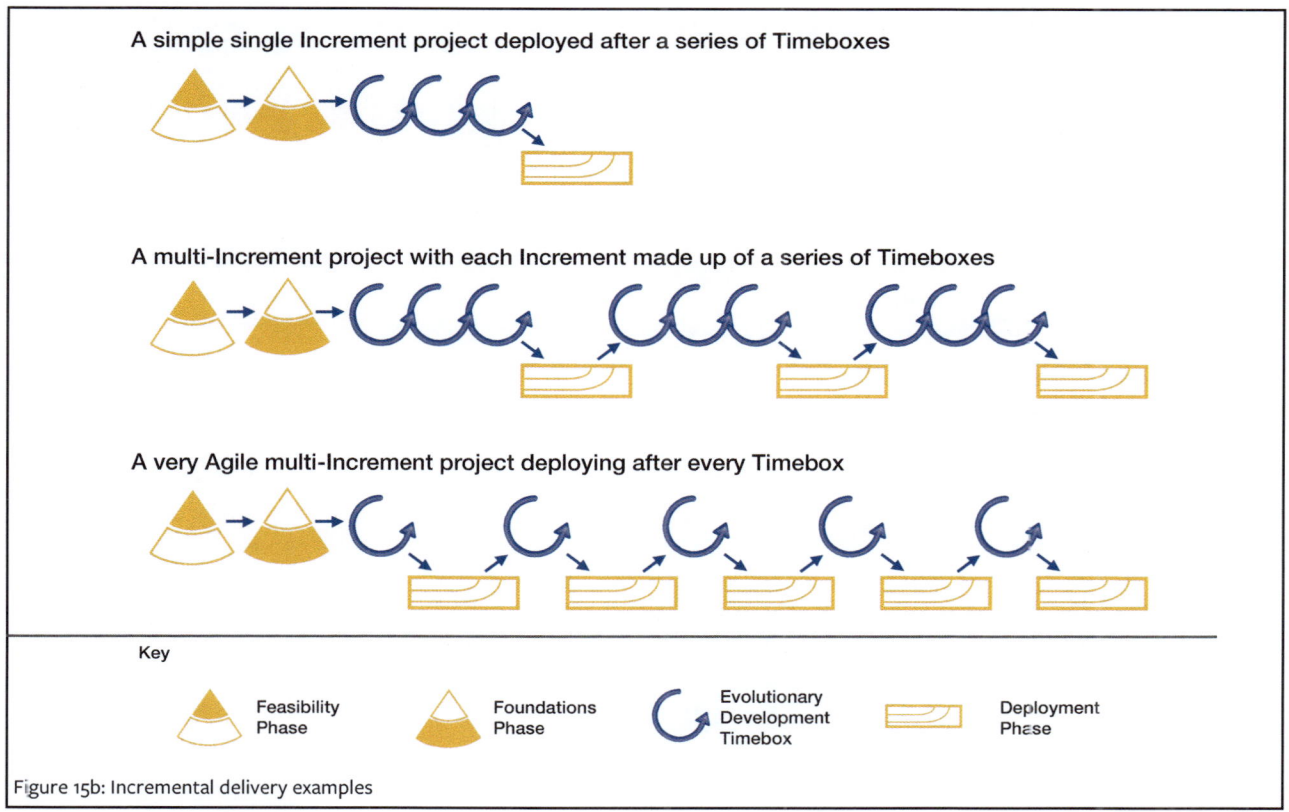

Figure 15b: Incremental delivery examples

15.3 Project Management Focus Phase by Phase

15.3.1 Pre-Project

There is no involvement from the Project Manager Pre-Project.

15.3.2 Feasibility

Working primarily with the project-level roles including the Business Analyst, the Project Manager organises the work of the Feasibility phase to establish whether the project is likely to be feasible.

Early in the phase, the Project Manager needs to establish what work needs to be done and which of the six key foundation products need to be created in outline. It may be decided not to create any of the DSDM products at this point, or to create a subset of products. What is required will be dictated by organisational standards and the specific needs of the project. It is, however, very important that the products are all considered and that the thinking behind them occurs.

Product	Key roles involved	Purpose and detail required at Feasibility (see chapter 16 - Products - for more detail)
Business Case	Business Analyst, Business Sponsor	The Business Case is an important product as it provides justification for starting the project and beyond that the drive required to maintain momentum on a project as it moves through the lifecycle. By the end of Feasibility, the Business Case will contain limited detail but it should be sufficient to enable a decision on whether further work and expenditure is justified. The Business Case may be created in a specific template form or, especially at this point in the project, may be expressed as high-level concepts and justifications in a less formal presentation
Prioritised Requirements List (PRL)	Business Analyst, Business Visionary	The PRL describes the requirements for the project as a whole and defines its scope. By the end of the Feasibility phase, it is likely to be made up of a small number of very high-level requirements, typically less than 10. This very high-level list will be broken into more detail during the Foundations phase
Solution Architecture Definition (SAD)	Business Analyst, Technical Coordinator, Business Visionary, Project Manager	The Project Manager should be confident that the business and technical aspects of the solution are coherent and will be instrumental in ensuring the right people are involved at the right time primarily during the Foundations phase of the project. At Feasibility, this product will probably be little more than a 'sketch' of the potential overall solution to a business problem
Development Approach Definition (DAD)	Technical Coordinator, Project Manager	The Development Approach Definition describes how the development team will work, the standards they will follow, etc. At this point, a DAD is likely only to exist in the form of a pre-existing standard or as a very high-level outline of the overall DSDM approach to be followed

Project Management through the Lifecycle

Product	Key roles involved	Purpose and detail required at Feasibility (see chapter 16 - Products - for more detail)
Delivery Plan	Project Manager, Business Visionary, Technical Coordinator	At this point the Delivery Plan can only exist in outline as very little is known about the business problem, the proposed solution and the way the project will be structured to deliver that solution. Any pre-existing constraints such as delivery dates driven by, for example, regulatory or marketing imperatives should be stated and any preliminary thoughts on timescales, resources and costs will be useful to support the outline of the Business Case
Management Approach Definition (MAD)	Project Manager, Business Sponsor	At this point, the focus of the Management Approach should be dealing with fundamental issues such as solution sourcing (e.g. will it be an in-house development or an out-sourced one? Is it a new 'green field' development or an enhancement of an existing solution?). The Project Approach Questionnaire should be used at this point to identify any potential issues with the use of the DSDM approach so that these can be considered during the Foundations phase
Feasibility Assessment	Project Manager, Business Sponsor	The Feasibility Assessment may be a physical document in its own right or it may take the form of a presentation of some kind. It may be also be a collection of the products above or an executive summary of what they contain. Regardless of its form or format, it is intended to propose a very high-level solution (or a limited set of solution options) to meet the business problem that has been posed and, at an equally high level, a justification for moving into the Foundations phase. At the end of Feasibility, there are no certainties, because none are possible at this point, but there should be enough to *indicate* to a Business Sponsor whether a successful project is *likely* to meet the business need in a cost effective way

Note: The Feasibility Assessment may be a useful Governance product that can be presented to an investment committee or similar authority responsible for determining whether the project should proceed to the Foundations phase.

15.3.3 Foundations

Working primarily with the project-level roles including the Business Analyst, and involving Business and Technical Advisors and as many of the Solution Development Team as possible, the Project Manager organises the work of the Foundations phase to establish firm and enduring foundations for the rest of the project. Note that ideally members of the Solution Development Team should be involved throughout Foundations in order to build a deep understanding of requirements, their origin and their rationale. However, as a minimum, the Project Manager must ensure that they are properly engaged before the end of the phase in order to understand the requirements well enough to provide sensible estimates of the work needed to fulfil them.

Early in the phase, the Project Manager needs to establish what work needs to be done and which of the six key foundation products need to be created or evolved from an outline created in the Feasibility phase. There may be no need to create some of the products or evolve them beyond their Feasibility outline. Organisational standards and the specific needs of the project will dictate whether they are required but every effort should be made to ensure that they are lightweight and guiding rather than detailed and prescriptive. Regardless of whether or not products are worked on, it is very important that they are all considered and the thinking behind them occurs.

In the table below, two products are identified as 'mandatory' and must be created in some form. One is identified as 'recommended' and it is vital that the purpose of this product is fulfilled in some way even if a physical document is not actually produced. The rest of the products should be created where they add value. The intended users of each of the products should be involved in their creation at least as reviewers, wherever possible.

Product	Key roles involved	Purpose and detail required at Foundations (see chapter 16 - Products - for more detail)
Business Case (Recommended)	Business Analyst, Business Sponsor	The Project Manager needs to ensure that by the end of the Foundation phase the Business Case (whether formally documented or not) clearly communicates: • A vision for the business as it will be on successful completion of the project • Estimated costs for development and predicted benefits for the solution in live use • Any analysis that may be required to justify the project The Project Manager should be confident that the Business Case is strong enough to ensure the appropriate focus and resources for the project. As the project progresses, the strength of the Business Case can be used in negotiations with senior management to maintain appropriate organisation-wide focus on, and support for, the project
Prioritised Requirements List (PRL) (Mandatory)	Business Analyst, Business Visionary, Business Ambassador	The Project Manager needs to ensure that by the end of the Foundations phase all high-level requirements are captured in the PRL and, at least for the first/imminent Project Increment: • Are granular enough to fit comfortably into a Timebox with a number of others • Have acceptance criteria associated with them to help understand when they are complete • Have been estimated with a confidence level sufficient to agree a fixed timescale and budget for the project • Have been properly prioritised in accordance with the MoSCoW guidelines • Have been approved by the Business Visionary as representing the full breadth of scope of the project sufficient to achieve the business vision

Product	Key roles involved	Purpose and detail required at Foundations (see chapter 16 - Products - for more detail)
Solution Architecture Definition (SAD)	Business Analyst, Technical Coordinator, Business Visionary, Project Manager	The Project Manager needs to ensure that by the end of the Foundations phase, both the business and technical aspects of the solution architecture are understood by all project participants, in particular the Solution Development Team, sufficiently to frame the development of the solution but without unnecessarily constraining Iterative Development of the Solution. Note that the content of the SAD will vary considerably from project to project and standard templates for this document should be used with extreme caution
Development Approach Definition (DAD)	Technical Coordinator, Solution Dev. Team, Project Manager	The Project Manager needs to ensure that by the end of the Foundations phase the Solution Development Team fully understand and accept the way of working it describes. Note: that the DAD is often not created as a physical document unless required as part of a Quality Management System - in which case it may be a component of a Quality Plan or similar
Delivery Plan (Mandatory)	Project Manager, Business Visionary, Technical Coordinator, Solution Dev. Team	The Project Manager needs to ensure that by the end of the Foundations phase a viable plan exists, at least for the first Project Increment, that clearly demonstrates that all the Must, Should and Could Have requirements can be delivered in a series of Timeboxes assuming agreed resource levels and timescales. This plan will, of course, be subject to continual change as the project progresses but will be tracked against its baseline at the end of Foundations
Management Approach Definition (MAD)	Project Manager Business Sponsor	The Project Manager needs to ensure that by the end of the Foundations phase the approach to managing the project is understood and agreed. In particular, any potential issues arising from completion of the Project Approach Questionnaire must have been considered and dealt with, possibly by appropriate tailoring of the DSDM approach
Foundations Summary	Project Manager, Business Sponsor	As with the Feasibility Assessment, this may be a physical document in its own right or it may be a collection of the products above or an executive summary of what they contain. Regardless of its form or format, it is intended to provide a summary of the foundations that have been established for the project. Supported by appropriate presentation and debate, this should give the Business Sponsor and all senior stakeholders sufficient confidence that the project should proceed into Evolutionary Development or, where appropriate, not proceed any further

Note: The Foundations Summary may be a useful Governance product that can be presented to an investment committee or similar authority responsible for determining whether the project should proceed beyond the Foundations phase.

15.3.4 Evolutionary Development

During the Evolutionary Development phase, the Project Manager passes the day-to-day management of the Timeboxes to the Solution Development Team(s) and focuses mainly on ensuring the project environment is optimised for Agile development of the solution in Timeboxes.

On a Timebox-by-Timebox basis, the Project Manager needs to participate in (and perhaps even facilitate) the Timebox Kick-Off. The objective of the Timebox Kick-Off is to ensure that the Solution Development Team understands and accepts what needs to be done and is able to commit to delivering a Solution Increment at the end of the Timebox that meets agreed (MoSCoWed) requirements and acceptance criteria. At this point, the Project Manager should take responsibility for ensuring all people and resources are committed to the project for the duration of the Timebox, sufficient to allow the team to meet the commitment it makes. Beyond the Kick-Off, the Solution Development Team self-organise to meet their commitment, taking responsibility for the planning and execution of all detailed analysis of requirements, solution design, build and testing tasks. The tracking and control concept of 'management by exception' guides the Project Manager to remain 'hands off' during a Timebox, responding only to exceptions escalated by the Solution Development Team.

The Project Manager should also participate in the Timebox Close-Out, primarily to measure progress (in line with the tracking and control concept of 'outcome based measurement') and to feed learning and an understanding of what was not completed in the Timebox (typically lower priority requirements and acceptance criteria) back into the wider Delivery Plan.

On a day-to-day basis, the Project Manager should monitor (but not try to control) what is going on at the team level and where appropriate participate in the reviews at agreed points in the Timebox (typically the end of Investigation and end of Refinement reviews for a structured Timebox).

Product	Key roles involved	Purpose and detail required (see chapter 16 - Products - for more detail)
Timebox Review Records	Team Leader, Any Advisor roles with responsibility for regulatory compliance	These may be created during the Timebox at key review points, formally capturing feedback and required actions or just at the end of the Timebox where they act as a formal summary and business acceptance of what has been delivered. They may be as formal as a document using an agreed template or as informal as notes from a Timebox Close-Out review appropriately shared with participating stakeholders. The Project Manager must ensure that Timebox Reviews are as thorough and formal as they need to be and that Timebox Review Records (where it is agreed they should be produced) are created at the time - not days or weeks after the event - and are genuinely fit for their intended purpose
Delivery Plan	Project Manager, Business Visionary, Technical Coordinator, Solution Dev. Team	It is unusual that everything planned for a Timebox is delivered and that no issues arise that have an impact on future plans. To remain current, relevant and useful, the Project Manager needs to update the Delivery Plan at least at the end of each Timebox.

Note: Timebox Review Records may be a useful Governance product if they are updated at key review points in the Timebox and capture feedback from Business and Technical Advisors expert in the regulatory requirements and at subsequent reviews (or the end of the Timebox) to capture acknowledgement that the feedback has been actioned.

In terms of ensuring that the project environment is optimised for Agile development, the Project Manager should do everything possible to protect the Solution Development Team from being distracted by demands to do unplanned work and to ensure that tools and facilities to support Agile working remain available as planned. Managing the engagement of Business Ambassadors and Advisors, Technical Advisors and any part-time resources is a key focus of the Project Manager - ensuring everybody is engaged during a Timebox to the extent that was agreed at the Kick-Off.

During the Evolutionary Development phase, the Project Manager works primarily with the Business Visionary and Technical Coordinator to plan the imminent Deployment phase.

Key products for consideration by the Project Manager during Evolutionary Development are described in the top table on the opposite page.

15.3.5 Deployment

During the Deployment phase, the Project Manager coordinates the day-to-day activities associated with bringing the Solution Increment into live operational use. The tasks to be completed are owned by the Business Visionary (responsible for business change activities) and the Technical Coordinator (responsible for the technical transition into live use) in collaboration with key members of the Solution Development Team and stakeholders outside the project organisation. The Project Manager is responsible for ensuring everything is coherent and that the right people are involved at the right time to complete the work required.

Also during the Deployment phase, an Increment Retrospective is held to allow the whole project team to reflect on what was delivered, what was not delivered that might have been and the implications of that reality on future plans. A second, but equally important, aspect of the Increment Retrospective reflects on the way of working as it was in reality, including the extent to which responsibilities associated with each of the roles were fulfilled, the way the DSDM process and practices were applied, the effectiveness of the tools used, etc.

The findings of the retrospective are captured in the Project Review Report described in the bottom table below.

Product	Key roles involved	Purpose and detail required (see chapter 16 - Products - for more detail)
Project Review Report	Project Manager, Business Visionary, Technical Coordinator, Team Leader	The Project Review Report contains 2 key elements associated with each completed Project Increment. The first is a record of what has been delivered (and what has not) and any learning associated with the way the Project Increment was run. The second is an assessment of the business value of what has been delivered - specifically which of the benefits outlined in the Business Case should now accrue through live use of the Solution Increment

The Review step in the Deployment phase is a useful, and for many organisations, an essential, Governance checkpoint. It is the point at which it is formally agreed that the Solution Increment created in preceding Timeboxes will be deployed into live use. It is also the point at which it is formally agreed to either proceed to the next Project Increment, to revisit the Foundations phase (to assess the viability of, and plan the next Project Increment) or to close the project.

On completion of the final Project Increment, following a final retrospective (captured in the Project Review Report) the project is formally closed.

15.3.6 Post-Project

There is no involvement from the Project Manager Post-Project, since the project has now closed down.

15.4 Summary

DSDM describes a process containing a series of phases each with an individual purpose contributing to the lifecycle of a project and the delivery of a valuable business solution. Early in the project, during the Feasibility and Foundations phases, the Project Manager needs to work with other project-level roles to shape the project - determining how the project will be structured to best meet the business objectives and how the process, people, practices and products will interoperate to keep the project on track and demonstrably under control.

During Feasibility and Foundations phases, the Project Manager takes an active part in ensuring that the necessary work required to justify the project and to establish firm project foundations - from the business, technical and management perspectives - is properly scheduled and that the right people are involved to set the project up for success.

As the project progresses through the Evolutionary Development phase, the Project Manager ensures that the Solution Development Team are as fully empowered as possible to organise themselves to deliver increments of the Evolving Solution. With the detailed planning and scheduling of solution development work being handled with the Solution Development Team, the Project Manager is free to manage the wider project environment including proactive high-level project planning and risk management and ongoing engagement of business and specialist/advisory roles. Through attending Daily Stand-ups (as an observer) and pre-agreed Timebox Review sessions the Project Manager is able to keep up to date with project progress at the detail level and to keep stakeholders informed and their expectations managed.

Note: *Since this chapter provides an overview of the PM role through the lifecycle, the Agile Project Manager Top Tips that will apply throughout the lifecycle are included elsewhere, within the chapters on particular topics, rather than being repeated here.*

16. The Effective Use of the DSDM Products

16.1 Introduction to the Products

The products form part of the DSDM Agile Project Framework, as summarised in the diagram below, and are introduced in Chapter 8. For ease of reference, that content is duplicated in this chapter with more detail provided for the Project Manager about the roles **R**esponsible for their production, **A**ccountable for their content, **C**ontributing to and **I**nformed by their content (RACI).

Not all products are required for every project and the formality associated with each product will vary from project to project and from organisation to organisation. The formality of the products is influenced by factors such as contractual relationships, corporate standards and governance needs.

DSDM identifies two distinct types of product:

- *Evolutionary products* evolve over time. They typically, but not always, span a number of project phases and may be baselined more than once during that time
- *Milestone products* are created in a phase and typically fulfill a specific purpose within that phase as a checkpoint or to facilitate governance processes

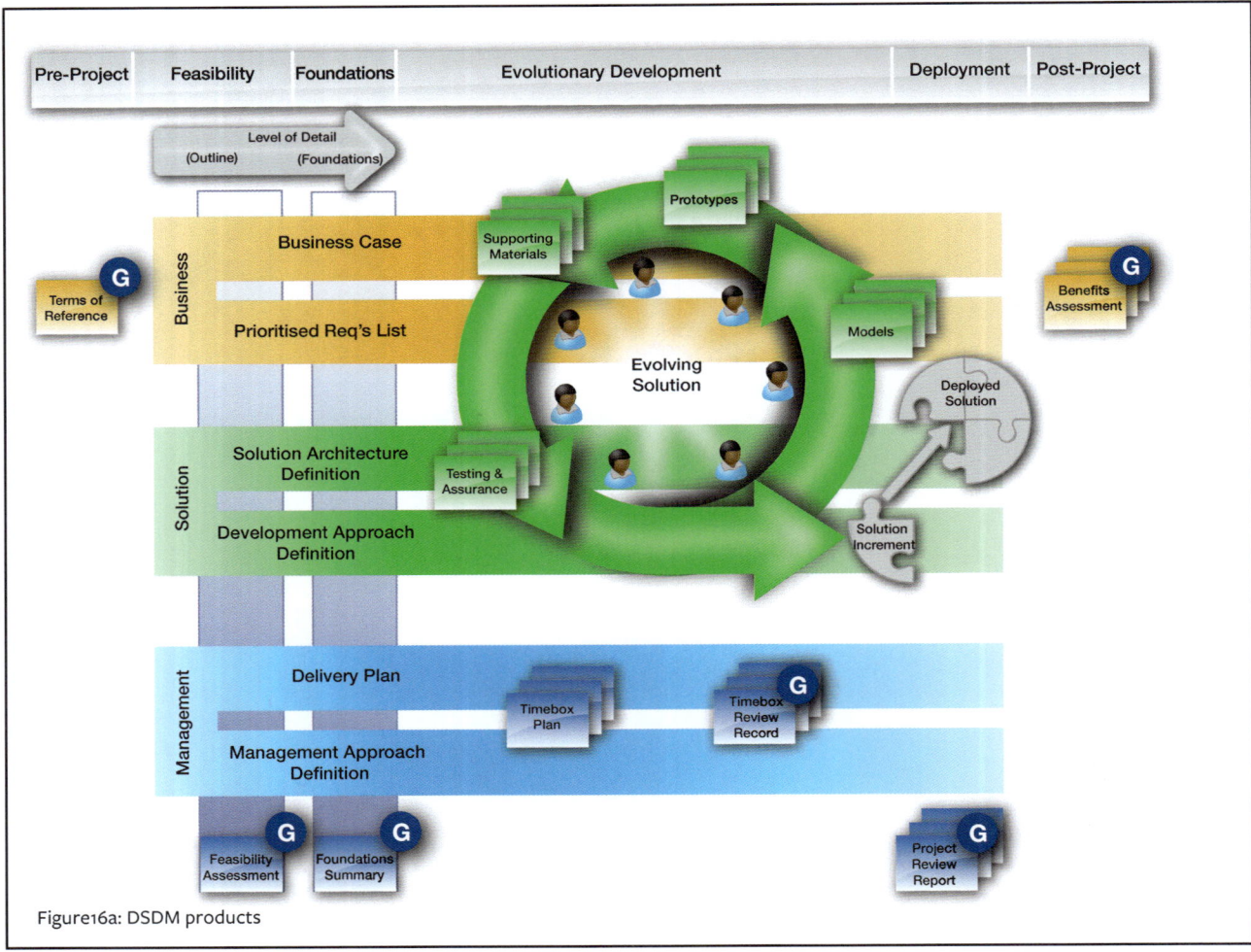

Figure 16a: DSDM products

The products, and where they feature in the project lifecycle, are shown in the diagram above. Orange products are business-focused, green products all contribute to the solution being created by the project and blue products cover project management/control interests. Several of the products - those marked with **G** - may also play a part in governance processes such as approval gateways, and may be used to demonstrate compliance of the solution with corporate and regulatory standards where this is required.

16.2 Terms of Reference

16.2.1 Description

The Terms of Reference is a Milestone Product. It is a high-level definition of the overarching business driver for, and top-level objectives of, the project. The primary aim of the Terms of Reference is to scope and justify the Feasibility investigation. It is identified as a Governance product because it may be used for purposes such as prioritisation of a project within a portfolio.

16.2.2 Roles and responsibilities

RACI	Role	Rationale
Responsible (Produced by)	Anybody	Anybody can have an idea for a project
Accountable (Approved by)	Business Sponsor	Person with budget for the Feasibility Investigation
Contributors	Anybody	Anybody can help shape the idea
Informed (Produced for)	Project Governance Authority	To check alignment with strategic goals and help prioritise within a portfolio
	Business Analyst Technical Coordinator	To ensure, by reference, objectives and proposed solutions emerging during Foundations phase are appropriately aligned

Agile Project Manager Top Tips

- On receipt of an approved Terms of Reference (in whatever form that may take) arrange a meeting with the Business Sponsor, the Business Visionary, the Business Analyst and the Technical Coordinator to gain a shared view of the business need and to start managing expectations of the Feasibility phase

16.3 Business Case

16.3.1 Description

The Business Case is an Evolutionary Product. It provides a vision and a justification for the project from a business perspective. The business vision describes a changed business as it is expected to be, incrementally and at the end of the project. The justification for the project is typically based on an investment appraisal determining whether the value of the solution to be delivered by the project warrants the cost to produce, support and maintain it into the future, all within an acceptable level of risk.

Baselines of the Business Case are typically created first as an outline by the end of Feasibility, then as a basis for approval of development by the end of Foundations. It is formally reviewed at the end of each Project Increment in order to determine whether further work is justified. It should be kept in mind informally throughout the project to inform decisions in line with benefit delivery and become aware of any potential threats to the viability of project at the earliest point.

AgilePM

16.3.2 Roles and responsibilities

RACI	Role	Rationale
Responsible (Produced by)	Business Analyst	Skills and experience with business case production and working collaboratively with the senior business and technical roles
Accountable (Approved by)	Business Sponsor	Responsible and accountable for return on investment
Contributors	All project-level roles, Business and Technical Advisors (as appropriate)	Business, Solution and Management considerations will all impact on the Business Case
Informed (Produced for)	Project Governance Authority	Approval for project to proceed and to help prioritise the project within a portfolio
	The entire project team	Everybody involved needs to understand what is needed and why

Agile Project Manager Top Tips

- As a Project Manager, the Business Case should be your friend
    - A strong business case will strengthen many discussions you may have with regards to securing necessary resources and prioritising the involvement of part-time resources
    - The business case enables focus to be kept on what is important throughout the project. If there is an indication that the project is losing focus or becoming unviable (whether through formal or informal assessment of the project against the Business Case) then early action can be taken

16.4 Prioritised Requirements List

16.4.1 Description

The Prioritised Requirement List (PRL) is an Evolutionary Product. It describes, at a high level, the requirements that the project needs to address, and indicates their priority with respect to meeting the objectives of the project and the needs of the business. Consideration of requirements begins in Feasibility and a baseline of the PRL demarcates the scope of the project as at the end of Foundations. After that point, further change will happen naturally in terms of depth, as a result of emergence of detail. Change to the breadth (adding, removing or significantly changing high-level requirements) still needs to be formally controlled in order to ensure ongoing alignment with the vision for the project and to keep control of the scope.

16.4.2 Roles and responsibilities

RACI	Role	Rationale
Responsible (Produced by)	Business Analyst	Skills and experience with eliciting and defining requirements
Accountable (Approved by)	Business Visionary	Responsible for ensuring that requirements align with business vision
Contributors	Business Ambassador and Business Advisor	Provide the detailed knowledge and experience to shape the requirements
Informed (Produced for)	The entire project team	Everybody involved needs to understand the requirements needed and why

The Effective Use of the DSDM Products

Agile Project Manager Top Tips

- The Prioritised Requirements List is the single most important product from a practical perspective. The priority of the requirements will drive the Delivery Plan and the lower priority (Could Have and, if necessary, Should Have) requirements will provide essential contingency for the project
- Ensure that the MoSCoW rules are properly applied when prioritising requirements. It is not the Project Manager's responsibility to set the priority - just to ensure that they are prioritised correctly and effectively
- Ensure that the Business Analyst and Business Visionary are involved throughout the project at key decision points to ensure that the priorities remain true and shape future plans accordingly
- The Prioritised Requirements List can be used as the basis for a simple traceability tool in order to track in one place the many charts, post-its, etc. used by Solution Development Teams

16.5 Solution Architecture Definition

16.5.1 Description

The Solution Architecture Definition is an Evolutionary Product. It provides a high-level design framework for the solution. It is intended to cover both business and technical aspects of the solution to a level of detail that makes the scope of the solution clear but without going into a level of detail that constrains evolutionary development.

16.5.2 Roles and responsibilities

RACI	Role	Rationale
Responsible (Produced by)	Business Analyst	Responsible for overall design of business process and organisation change
	Technical Coordinator	Responsible for overall design and integrity of technical aspects of solution
Accountable (Approved by)	Business Visionary	Responsible for delivering the required business change
	Project Manager	Responsible for ensuring the products of the project are delivered
Contributors	All Business and Solution Roles (including Advisors)	Provide detailed knowledge and experience to help shape the business and technical architectures
Informed (Produced for)	Solution Development Team	Building a solution within the framework described needed and why

Agile Project Manager Top Tips

- Remember that the Solution Architecture Definition addresses both business and technical aspects of the solution. For many projects, a tool such as a piece of software is pointless without the necessary business change to exploit it
- Ensure that all those responsible for shaping the architecture take ownership of this and collaborate to define a high-level design framework that fully integrates both business and technical aspects of the solution

16.6 Development Approach Definition

16.6.1 Description

The Development Approach Definition is an Evolutionary Product. It provides a high-level definition of the tools, techniques, customs, practices and standards that will be applied to the evolutionary development of the solution. Importantly it describes how quality of the solution will be assured. A strategy for Testing and Review would therefore be a key part of the development approach and described in the Development Approach Definition.

16.6.2 Roles and responsibilities

RACI	Role	Rationale
Responsible (Produced by)	Technical Coordinator	Responsible for defining technical quality standards and ensuring development best practices are applied
Accountable (Approved by)	Project Manager	Responsible for ensuring the products of the project are delivered
Contributors	Business and Technical Advisors	Understand the business and technical constraints that the development approach needs to accommodate
	DSDM Coach	Understands the way Agile Teams should ideally work and has the knowledge and experience to tailor the approach around business, technical constraints
Informed (Produced for)	Solution Development Team	Responsible for building the solution in a professional way and to the required level of technical quality
	Quality Managers / Auditors / Assessors	Need to understand whether the approach that was agreed is being followed as described (may be particularly relevant in regulated environments)

Agile Project Manager Top Tips

- A team works best when team members understand and accept the rules that bind and unite them and the part each one of them will play in the development of the solution
- Regardless of whether the Development Approach Definition is created in physical form, the Project Manager should ensure that all members of the Solution Development Team understand and accept the approach to development and have ideally helped to shape it
- Remember that the Business Ambassador is part of the Solution Development Team and that Business Advisors may need to be deeply involved in development so ensure that they understand the approach and are ready, willing and able to participate in the project on that basis
- Where appropriate, especially when the team is new to the Agile way of working, consider engaging a DSDM Coach to help shape the approach - this will help achieve greater buy-in to the approach among the team, optimise productivity and increase the likelihood of success for the project

16.7 Delivery Plan

16.7.1 Description

The Delivery Plan is an Evolutionary Product. It provides a high-level schedule of Increments for the project and, at least for the first/imminent Increment, the Timeboxes that make up that Increment. It rarely deals with task level detail unless there are tasks being carried out by people who are not part of the Solution Development Team or before the Solution Development Team is formed.

16.7.2 Roles and responsibilities

RACI	Role	Rationale
Responsible (Produced by)	Project Manager	Responsible for ensuring increments of the solution are delivered, predictably within agreed budget and time constraints
Accountable (Approved by)	Business Visionary Technical Coordinator	Responsible for ensuring the incremental delivery of business value is optimal for the business as a whole
Contributors	Solution Development Team and other roles as appropriate	Help shape the plan based on business need and capability to deliver the solution
Informed (Produced for)	All project participants and stakeholders	Everybody needs to understand at a high level what is happening when and who is participating

Agile Project Manager Top Tips

- By the end of Foundations, the Delivery Plan must describe a scenario in which all the requirements (Must, Should and Could Haves) can be delivered within the constraints of the agreed timescale and costs. It is important to start from a point where achieving everything, however unlikely that may be in the end, is at least theoretically possible
- Do whatever is possible to resist being drawn into an agreement at the end of the Foundations phase where time and cost are fixed without contingency and all requirements are Must Have. A project must have contingency if it is to be successful, otherwise by default quality will be compromised.
- Do not be drawn in to committing to dates, costs and resource levels before the end of the Foundations phase. By the end of Feasibility, indicative timescales and costs may be available but these are estimates and must only be presented with a confidence range e.g. 1000-2000 days of effort or £500,000 +/- 50%

16.8 Management Approach Definition

16.8.1 Description

The Management Approach Definition is an Evolutionary Product. It reflects the approach to the management of the project as a whole and considers, from a management perspective how the project will be organised and planned, how stakeholders will be engaged in the project, how progress will be demonstrated and, if necessary, reported. The product is baselined at the end of Foundations and will only evolve beyond that when circumstances change or if review of the approach identifies areas for improvement.

16.8.2 Roles and responsibilities

RACI	Role	Rationale
Responsible (Produced by)	Project Manager	Responsible for ensuring the project is properly set up for the predictable delivery of project products
Accountable (Approved by)	Business Sponsor	Needs to be confident that the project is set up right to deliver what is needed at the right time for the right price
Contributors	Business Visionary and Technical Coordinator	Understand the capabilities and constraints associated with the project environment and contributors to the project
	DSDM Coach	Understands the way an Agile project should operate and has the knowledge and experience to tailor the approach around project and environmental constraints
Informed (Produced for)	All project participants and stakeholders	Everybody needs to understand at a high level how the project will be managed

Agile Project Manager Top Tips

- Use the Project Approach Questionnaire (PAQ) to help identify risks and issues associated with using the DSDM approach. Ensure that the PAQ is completed collaboratively, involving as many project participants, or likely participants, as possible
- During Feasibility, focus primarily on major issues that will impact the fundamental nature of the project such as:
    - Solution sourcing (e.g. in-house or out-sourced, bespoke development or package purchase)
    - Regulatory and other governance needs and constraints
    - Pre-existing constraints and major dependencies (e.g. externally fixed end date)
- During Foundations, focus primarily on setting up the project for success including ensuring:
    - The right people are in the right roles at all levels (where possible, including Advisors) and that all participants understand and accept their responsibilities
    - The approach is appropriately tailored to deal with issues and risks identified through use of the PAQ
    - The Business Visionary and Technical Coordinator have helped shape and fully accept the chosen approach
    - Where Agile experience is limited, the option of engaging a DSDM coach to help define the approach has been considered
- Where applicable, ensure that aspects of the management approach such as organisation, governance and reporting align with any programme-level expectations

16.9 Feasibility Assessment

16.9.1 Description

The Feasibility Assessment is a Milestone Product. It provides a snapshot of the evolving Business, Solution and Management products described above as they exist at the end of the Feasibility phase. Each of the products should be mature enough to make a sensible contribution to the decision as to whether the project is likely to be feasible or not. The Feasibility Assessment may be expressed as a baselined collection of the products or as an executive summary covering the key aspects of each of them.

16.9.2 Roles and responsibilities

RACI	Role	Rationale
Responsible (Produced by)	Project Manager	Responsible for project status reporting
Accountable (Approved by)	Business Sponsor	The champion of the project, responsible for the Return on Investment
Contributors	All roles involved with producing the constituent / contributing products	Ensure that the overall assessment accurately reflects the conclusions in the constituent / contributing products
Informed (Produced for)	Project Governance Authority	Who need to decide whether or not the project should proceed and as proposed

Agile Project Manager Top Tips

- Bear in mind

    - The purpose of this product is to allow the right decision to be made as to whether the project should proceed or not at this point in time

    The approval needed at this point is sufficient only to establish firm and enduring foundations for the project (i.e. to complete the work of the Foundations phase) - full approval of the project is not being asked for at this point

- When creating this product as an executive summary for governance reasons, think carefully about its purpose and the target audience. Remember:

    - The longer the document and the greater the detail the less likely it will be read or reac properly so keep it as short and focused as possible

    - Include only information relevant to the decisions needed

        - The decision required is to either to proceed into a Foundations phase if the project is likely to be viable or to stop the project now if it is not likely to be viable. Approval for the whole project is not being requested at this time.

        - If any of the decision makers need more information they can ask for it - encourage them to do so rather than try to guess their needs

        - Much useful information will have been discovered that may be useful later. If necessary, this should be recorded elsewhere - and properly considered at the appropriate time

        - Don't fall into the trap of stating everything in the document just to 'prove' it has been considered

    - Ensure that any assessments and recommendations genuinely and accurately reflect those in the contributing products - involve the people *Responsible* and *Accountable* for those products in the creation of this one or, at the very least, in its review

AgilePM

16.10 Foundations Summary

16.10.1 Description

The Foundations Summary is a Milestone Product. It provides a snapshot of the evolving Business, Solution and Management products described above as they exist at the end of the Foundations phase. Each of the products should be mature enough to make a sensible contribution to the decision as to whether the project is likely to deliver the required return on investment. The Foundations Summary may be expressed as a baselined collection of the products described above or as an executive summary covering the key aspects of each of them.

16.10.2 Roles and responsibilities

RACI	Role	Rationale
Responsible (Produced by)	Project Manager	Responsible for project status reporting
Accountable (Approved by)	Business Sponsor	The champion of the project, responsible for the Return on Investment
Contributors	All roles involved with producing the constituent /contributing products	Ensure that the overall assessment accurately reflects the conclusions in the constituent /contributing products
Informed (Produced for)	Project Governance Authority	Who need to decide whether or not the project should proceed and as proposed

Agile Project Manager Top Tips

- Bear in mind
    - The purpose of this product is allow the right decision to be made as to whether the project should proceed or not
    - The approval needed is to complete at least the first Project Increment and may be approval for the whole project
- When creating this product as an executive summary for governance reasons, think carefully about its purpose and the target audience. Remember:
    - The longer the document and the greater the detail the less likely it will be read or read properly so keep it as short and focused as possible
    - Include only information relevant to the decisions needed
        - Approval for the whole project is not necessarily required at this time - only the first Project Increment may be approved if there is any doubt about longer term commitments
        - If any of the decision makers need more information they can ask for it - encourage them to do so rather than try to guess their needs
        - Much useful information will have been discovered that may be useful later. If necessary this should be recorded elsewhere - and properly considered at the appropriate time
        - Don't fall into the trap of stating everything in the document just to 'prove' it has been considered
    - Ensure that any assessments and recommendations genuinely and accurately reflect those in the contributing products - involve the people *Responsible* and *Accountable* for those products in the creation of this one or, at the very least, in its review

16.11 Evolving Solution

16.11.1 Description

The Evolving Solution is an Evolutionary Product. It is made up of all appropriate components of the ultimate solution together with any intermediate deliverables necessary to explore the detail of requirements and define the solution under construction. At any given time, such components may be either complete, a baseline of a partial solution, or a work in progress. They include, where valuable, models, prototypes, supporting materials and testing and review artefacts.

At the end of each Project Increment, a baseline of the Evolving Solution is deployed into live use and becomes the *Deployed Solution*.

16.11.2 Roles and responsibilities

RACI	Role	Rationale
Responsible (Produced by)	Solution Development Team	Responsible for building all aspects of the solution
Accountable (Approved by)	Business Visionary	Responsible for ensuring the solution that is delivered is fit for business purpose
	Technical Coordinator	Responsible for ensuring the solution that is delivered is technically fit for purpose
Contributors	All roles and invited stakeholders	Anybody can help ensure the optimum solution is developed over time
Informed (Produced for)	Business Sponsor	Responsible for the Return on Investment
	Solution Participants	Users of the end-products of the project and part of the wider solution in live business use

Agile Project Manager Top Tips

- Ensure the right people are involved to the right extent at the right time in the iterative development and incremental delivery of the Evolving Solution

16.12 Timebox Plan

16.12.1 Description

The Timebox Plan is an Evolutionary Product that provides depth and detail for each Development Timebox identified in the Delivery Plan. It elaborates on the objectives provided for that Development Timebox and details the deliverables of that Timebox, along with the activities to produce those deliverables and the resources to do the work. The Timebox Plan is created by the Solution Development Team and is often represented on a Team Board as work to do, in progress, and done. It's updated at least on a daily basis at the Daily Stand-ups.

AgilePM

16.12.2 Roles and responsibilities

RACI	Role	Rationale
Responsible (Produced by)	Solution Development Team	Responsible for self-organising to 'say what they will do'
Accountable (Approved by)	Project Manager, Technical Coordinator, Business Visionary	Jointly responsible for acknowledging that the team are properly focussed on the timely delivery of a fit for purpose solution increment
Contributors	Business and Technical Advisors	Help define the detail of what needs to be done
Informed (Produced for)	Solution Development Team	Responsible for self-organising and doing what they said they would do

Agile Project Manager Top Tips

- It is not the responsibility of the Project Manager to be involved in the creation of the Timebox Plan. This should be left to the Solution Development Team
- In your role as agile Project Manager:
    - Ensure that the Solution Development Team fully understand and appropriately commit to delivering a solution that meets a given set of requirements appropriately prioritised for the Timebox
    - Be comfortable that the Timebox plan produced by the Solution Development Team is realistic and properly aligned to their actual availability and the delivery commitment they have made
    - Take ownership of the provision of any additional resources the team may need
    - Take ownership of those risks and issues associated with the work of the Timebox that the Solution Development Team believe are outside of their control or influence

16.13 Timebox Review Record

16.13.1 Description

The Timebox Review Record is an Evolutionary Product, capturing the feedback from each review that takes place during a Development Timebox. It describes what has been achieved up to that point together with any feedback that may influence plans moving forwards. Where appropriate, e.g. in a regulated environment, a formal, auditable record of review comments from expert Business Advisors and other roles make this product a Governance product.

16.13.2 Roles and responsibilities

RACI	Role	Rationale
Responsible (Produced by)	Team Leader	Responsible for ensuring that the Iterative Development process is properly focused and controlled and that all testing and review activity is properly carried out
Accountable (Approved by)	Business Visionary	Acknowledging whether the Solution Increment (comprising deliverables of the Timebox) is fit for business purpose
	Technical Coordinator	Acknowledging whether the solution increment is technically fit for purpose
	Business and Technical Advisors	Where appropriate, confirming regulatory and other standards have been met
Contributors	Solution Development Team	Describing what they have done, how and to what extent
Informed (Produced for)	Project Governance Authority	Being assured that development is properly controlled and that all testing and review activity is properly carried out
	Project Manager	To formally track progress towards delivery of the ultimate solution

Agile Project Manager Top Tips

- The Project Manager is not responsible for the subject or the outcome of Timebox reviews, just that they are properly planned and scheduled, and are sufficiently rigorous to allow the accountabilities of the Business Visionary and the Technical Coordinator to be met

16.14 Project Review Report

16.14.1 Description

The Project Review Report is a Milestone Product. It is typically a single document that is updated, incrementally, at the end of each Project Increment by the addition of new sections pertinent to that Increment.

At the end of each Project Increment, the purpose of this product is:

- To capture the feedback from the review of the delivered solution to confirm what has been delivered and what has not
- To capture learning points from the retrospective for the Increment focused on the process, practices employed and contributing roles and responsibilities
- Where appropriate to describe the business benefits that should now accrue through the proper use of the solution delivered by the project up to this point

After the final Project Increment, a Project Retrospective, in part informed by these Increment reviews, is prepared as part of the closure of the project.

AgilePM

16.14.2 Roles and responsibilities

RACI	Role	Rationale
Responsible (Produced by)	Project Manager	Responsible overall for the delivery of the product
Accountable (Approved by)	Business Visionary	Responsible for ensuring the solution is fit for business purpose
	Technical Coordinator	Responsible for ensuring the solution is technically fit for purpose
	Team Leader	Responsible for ensuring that the iterative development process is properly focused and controlled and that all testing and review activity is properly carried out
Contributors	All project roles and stakeholders	Anybody may contribute to the effectiveness of the way of working identifying potential weaknesses and flaws and suggesting improvements
Informed (Produced for)	All project participants and stakeholder and those responsible for supporting future projects (e.g. PMO)	Interested in knowing what has been achieved, the value of what has been delivered and any learning for the future.
	Project Governance Authority	Require assurance that development is properly controlled and that all testing and review activity is properly carried out

Agile Project Manager Top Tips
- This product is complex and has multiple objectives. The Project Manager needs to think carefully about which, if any, of these objectives are relevant to one or more of:
    - The ongoing project or the life of the delivered Solution (in terms of future plans for development, etc.)
    - The governance needs of the project
    - The learning needs of the project team or the wider organisation and create a review record tailored to that specific need
- For multi-Increment projects, the Project Manager will also need to agree with the Project Governance Authority whether a review record is required:
    - For each Project Increment (created at the end of each Increment)
    - For the project as a whole (to mark the close of the project)
    - Both of the above
- Finally, the Project Manager needs to agree an appropriate format for this record (e.g. formal document, a presentation, a brief email, an informal conversation with stakeholders, etc.)

16.15 Benefits Assessment
16.15.1 Description
The Benefits Assessment is a Milestone Product. It describes how the benefits have actually accrued, following a period of use in live operation. Note: It may be meaningful to review the benefits accrued per Increment and collate those into the assessment for the whole project. For projects where benefits in the Business Case are expected to accrue over a prolonged period, it is possible that a number of Benefits Assessments may be produced on a periodic basis aligned with the timeframe used for justifying the investment.

The Effective Use of the DSDM Products

16.15.2 Roles and responsibilities

RACI	Role	Rationale
Responsible (Produced by)	Business Visionary	Responsible for translation of the Business Vision into working practice
	Business Analyst	Responsible, for ensuring that benefits are assessed against business case and business need
Accountable (Approved by)	Business Sponsor	Responsible for the Return on Investment
Contributors	Solution Participants	Users of the end-products of the project and part of the wider solution in live business use can share their experience of the effectiveness and impact of any business changes resulting from the project
Informed (Produced for)	Project Governance Authority	Need to understand whether the investment in the project was justified and understand differences between predicted and accrued value

Agile Project Manager Top Tips

- The Project Manager role is not involved Post-Project, since by this point the project has been closed

16.16 Products RACI (Summary Table)

	Terms of Reference	Business Case	Prioritised Requirements List	Solution Architecture Definition	Development Approach Definition	Delivery Plan	Management Approach Definition	Feasibility Assessment	Foundations Summary	Evolving Solution	Timebox Plan	Timebox Review Record	Project Review Report	Benefits Assessment
Business Sponsor	A	A				I	A	A	A	I		I	I	A
Business Visionary		C	A	A		AC	C	C	C	A	A	A	A	R
Business Advisor		(C)	C	C	C	C	I	C	C	C	C	AC	C	
Technical Coordinator	I	C		R	R	AC	C	C	C	A	A	A	A	
Technical Advisor		(C)		C	C	I	C	C	C	C	C	AC	C	
Project Manager		C		A	A	R	R	R	R	I	A	I	R	
Business Analyst	I	R	R	R		C	I	C	C	C	I	C	C	R
Business Ambassador*			C											
Solution Development Team		I	I	C	I	C	I	C	C	R	RI	C	C	
Team Leader*												R	A	
DSDM Coach					C		C	C	C	C			C	
Project Governance Authority	I	I			I	I	I	I	I			I	I	I
Anybody	RC									I				C

*Where different to collective responsibility of the Solution Development Team

16.17 Summary

The products above are guidelines to the information needed to promote good communication within a project. The majority are not mandatory, and may not always be presented as documents. However, in circumstances where strong governance and/or proof of compliance with standards is important, there is real benefit in creating formal documents rather than just gaining a shared understanding (which is the normal default for DSDM). Although it may not be obvious, it is important to remember that documentation created *as part of* the development process and/or tied to the proactive way the project is managed, is likely to provide the most effective and robust audit trail if one is needed.

It is also critically important to remember that DSDM products are only created if and when they add value to the project and/or to the solution it creates. The most important thing is that the stakeholders and participants in the project understand what is needed, what is being delivered and that quality is assured. If documents genuinely help achieve this then create them, if not, don't waste valuable time and effort doing so.

DSDM Products - Agile Project Manager Top Tips

- Think carefully about the intended value of every product listed above
- Where it has value, determine what is required to deliver that value
    - Do not blindly revert to formal documents - think about the best way to share the value identified
        - If formal documents are required, like the solution itself, they can evolve through Evolutionary Development as the detail emerges, rather than attempt to create them at the outset or at the end.
        - Any documents that are created should be as brief and focused as possible:
            - Think… "If the reader has 5 minutes (and only 5 minutes) to read and understand this document then what is the best way to present the key information in that time?"
            - Do not waste time creating large complex documents that people do not have the time or enthusiasm to read and which quickly become obsolete
            - Do not create a document solely for the purpose of "ticking a box"
    - Consider not only writing a brief document but also presenting it to key stakeholders in a short meeting (either individually or collectively). This is the best way to get useful feedback
- Other tips - associated with each of the products described - are embedded above.

17. Deliver On Time - Combining MoSCoW and Timeboxing

17.1 Introduction

DSDM brings together the practices of MoSCoW prioritisation and Timeboxing (as described in chapters 10 and 11) to enable on-time delivery of projects consistently and predictably, time after time. Individually, the practices of MoSCoW prioritisation and Timeboxing are very effective. However, it is the combination of these practices that provides the core strength of DSDM.

This combination allows DSDM teams to build a reputation for on-time delivery and, combined with some level of flexibility around requirements, this timely consistency is often a key factor underpinning many successful businesses.

The starting point for delivering projects to meet the business need is to understand what the business actually needs and when they need it.

17.2 Why use MoSCoW?

The use of MoSCoW works particularly well on projects that have a fixed deadline. It also overcomes the problems associated with simpler prioritisation approaches which are based on relative priorities:

- The use of a simple high, medium or low classification is weaker because definitions of these priorities tend to rely on individual opinion and fail to set an expectation of what will be delivered. In particular, a categorisation with a single weakly defined middle option, such as medium priority, allows for indecision "Will I get this or won't I?"
- The use of a simple sequential 1,2,3,4... priority is weaker because it deals less effectively with items of similar importance. There may be prolonged and heated discussions over whether an item should be one place higher or lower

By comparison, the specific use of Must Have, Should Have, Could Have or Won't Have *this time* provides a clear indication of that requirement and sets realistic expectations for its completion. At a project or increment level:

- Must Have requirements - will deliver the guaranteed Minimum Usable SubseT and will remain the primary focus for all team members. These Must Haves alone will provide significant business benefit and a viable solution
- Should Have requirements - are likely to be delivered in normal circumstances, and it is reasonable for the business to expect delivery of most of the Should Haves
- Could Have requirements - may be delivered, but since they are the least important / least valuable to the business, they will always be used to provide the first level of contingency if problems occur, in order to protect delivery of higher priority requirements within the agreed time and cost constraints for the project or for the Project Increment
- Won't Have this time - these requirements may be important for the future, and need to be considered as part of the bigger picture, but will not be delivered in the current timeframe. Prioritising a requirement as a Won't Have can be very powerful in keeping the focus at this point in time on the more important Could Haves, Should Haves and particularly the Must Haves

17.3 Ensuring Effective Prioritisation

17.3.1 Balancing the priorities

When deciding the effort to be allocated to Must Have requirements, it is important to remember that anything other than a Must Have is, to some degree, contingency, since the Must Haves define the Minimum Usable SubseT which is guaranteed to be delivered.

DSDM recommends:

- Getting the percentage of project/Project Increment Must Haves (in terms of effort to deliver) to a level where the team's confidence to deliver them is high - typically no more than 60% Must Have effort
- Agreeing a pool of Could Haves for the project/Project Increment that reflects a realistic level of contingency - typically around 20% Could Have effort. Creating a sensible pool of Could Haves sets the correct expectations for the business from the start - that these requirements/User Stories may be delivered in their entirety in a best case scenario, but the primary project/Project Increment focus will always be on protecting the Must Haves and Should Haves

This spread of priorities provides enough contingency to ensure confidence in a successful project outcome. Note, when calculating effort for a timeframe, i.e. the 100% figure, Won't Haves (for this timeframe) are excluded.

DSDM's recommendations for the balance of priorities reflect a typical project scenario. Projects with a higher level of risk, for example the risk of unknown technology or an unproven team, may decide to use a lower percentage of Must Haves. The important thing for effective MoSCoW prioritisation is to match the balance of priorities to the individual risk profile of the project, rather than simply applying a mathematical ratio without thinking.

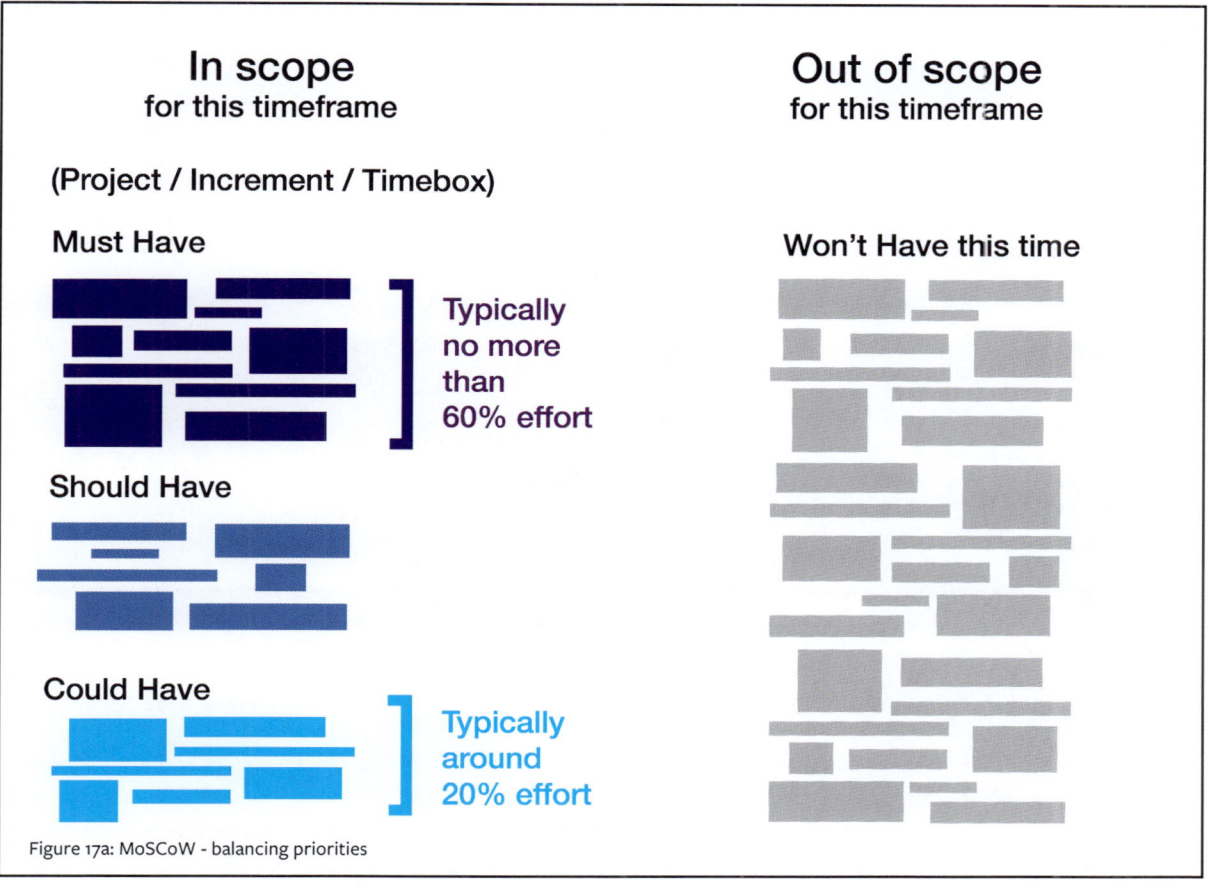

Figure 17a: MoSCoW - balancing priorities

Levels of Must Have effort above 60% introduce a risk of failure, unless the team is working in a project where all of these criteria are true:

- Estimates are known to be accurate
- The approach is very well understood
- The team is well established, the team members have a proven record with effective collaborative working and their productivity is known
- The environment is understood and low risk in terms of the potential for external factors to introduce delays

In some circumstances, the percentage of Must Have effort may be significantly less than 60%. However, this can be used to the benefit of the business by providing the greatest possible flexibility to optimise value delivered across a larger proportion of Should Haves.

When the use of DSDM is new, there is sometimes initial concern by the business that the team will stop or ease off once the Must Haves have been delivered. However, in reality the team always remain focused on delivering as much as can be fitted in during the time available. Additionally, the transparency of Agile projects ensures that the amount of effort and the work planned is always visible.

17.4 MoSCoW - An Integral Part of DSDM's Planning Process

Achieving a sensible balance of effort for priorities is an integral part of the planning process, whether this is planning the project, planning an Increment or planning an individual Timebox.

At the project and Project Increment levels, getting a sensible balance is the responsibility of the whole team. This is usually a collaborative effort, with:

- the business roles working to ensure the priorities reflect their true business needs and grouping the requirements to provide an effective and valuable solution to meet business deadlines
- the solution/technical roles working to ensure plans to deliver these priorities are realistic, achievable, reflect technical constraints and are being planned in the most efficient way possible within the business' priorities
- the Business Analyst considering the links between requirements, the availability of information and helping to identify viable groups of requirements
- the Project Manager weighing up the various risks to ensure that the balance of priorities being agreed reflects the level of known risk on this particular project

When using MoSCoW priorities to plan at the Development Timebox level - to create the Timebox Plan - the same logic on the balance of priorities applies, but here the planning activity is owned and driven by the Solution Development Team roles (Team Leader, Business Ambassador, Business Analyst, Solution Developer and Solution Tester). At this point the Project Manager is an interested bystander only, while ensuring that:

- the balance of effort across the priorities is being applied sensibly
- the team is aware of any significant risks for this Timebox and reflect this in the balance of priorities
- the whole team takes ownership of their estimates and their plan

17.4.1 Agreeing up front how priorities will work

DSDM defines what the different priorities mean - the MoSCoW Rules. But whereas the definition of a Must Have is not negotiable, the difference between a Should Have and a Could Have can be quite subjective. It is very helpful if the team agree, at the start of their project, how these lower level priorities will be applied. This agreement is often facilitated by the Project Manager or the Business Analyst. Understanding in advance some objective criteria that separate a Should Have from a Could Have and ensuring that all roles on the project buy into what has been agreed can avoid much heated discussion later. Look for defined boundaries that decide whether a requirement is a Should Have or a Could Have.

> *Examples:*
>
> *At what point does the number of people impacted raise a Could Have to a Should Have?*
>
> *What balance of effort expended to benefit predicted would differentiate a Should have from a Could Have?*

Ideally this agreement is reached before the requirements are captured.

17.4.2 When to prioritise

Every item of work has a priority. Priorities are set before work commences and the majority of this prioritisation activity happens during Foundations. However, priorities should be kept under continual review as work is completed. As new work arises, either through introduction of a new requirement or through the exposure of unexpected work associated with existing requirements, the decision must be made as to how critical it is to the success of the current work using the MoSCoW rules. When introducing new requirements, care needs to be taken not to increase the percentage of Must Have requirement effort beyond the agreed project level. The priorities of uncompleted requirements should be reviewed throughout the project to ensure that they are still valid. As a minimum, they should be reviewed at the end of each Timebox and each Project Increment.

17.4.3 Discussing and reviewing priorities

Any requirement defined as a Must Have will, by definition, have a critical impact on the success of the project. The Project Manager, Business Analyst and any other member of the Solution Development Team should openly discuss requirements prioritised as Must Have where they are not obviously Must Haves ("Without this would we cancel the project/increment?"). It is up to the Business Visionary or their empowered Business Ambassador or Advisor to explain why a requirement is a Must Have.

Escalation in the decision-making processes should be agreed early on, e.g. Business Ambassador and Business Analyst to Business Visionary to Business Sponsor, and the level of empowerment agreed around decision making at each level. The Project Manager often takes responsibility for helping the team agree the boundaries of empowerment, the escalation paths and the expected timeframes for a response. On a DSDM project, getting a timely response to escalated issues is critical given the short timeframe associated with Project Increments and, in particular, Timeboxes.

At the end of a Project Increment, all requirements that have not been met are re-prioritised in the light of the needs of the next Increment. There is no automatic carry-over.

> For example:
>
> A Could Have that is not delivered in one Project Increment
>
> 1. May be reclassified subsequently as a Won't Have for the next Increment, because it does not contribute enough towards the business needs to justify its inclusion
> 2. May become a Must Have for the next Increment, if its low priority in the first Increment was based on the fact it was simply not needed in the initial Increment timeframe, but becomes critical for the next Increment timeframe

17.5 Using MoSCoW to Manage Business Expectations

The MoSCoW rules have been defined in a way that allows the delivery of the Minimum Usable SubseT of requirements to be *guaranteed*. Both the Solution Development Team and those to whom they are delivering share this confidence because the high percentage of effort in Should Haves and Could Haves provides optimum contingency to ensure delivery of the Must Haves.

The business roles can certainly expect more than delivery of only the Must Haves. The Must Haves are guaranteed but it is perfectly reasonable for the business to expect delivery of more than the Minimum Usable SubseT in the timeframe, except under the most challenging of circumstances.

DSDM's recommendation to create a sensible pool of Could Have contingency - typically around 20% of the total project/increment effort - identifies requirements that are less important or which have less impact if not delivered, in order to protect the more important requirements. This approach implies that the business can reasonably expect the Should Have requirements to be met, in addition to all of the Must Haves. It also implies that in a best case scenario, the Could Have requirements would also be delivered.

The Solution Development Team cannot have the confidence to guarantee delivery of all the Must Have, Should Have and Could Have requirements, even though these have all been estimated and are included in the plan. This is because the plan is based on early estimates and on requirements which have not yet been analysed in low-level detail. Applying pressure to a team to guarantee delivery of all Must, Should and Could Haves is counterproductive. It usually results in padded estimates which give a false perception of success. "We always achieve 100% (...because we always add significant contingency to our figures").

So, combining sensible prioritisation with Timeboxing leads to predictability of delivery and therefore greater confidence. This also protects the quality of the solution being delivered. Keeping project metrics to show the percentage of Should Haves and Could Haves delivered on each Project Increment or Timebox will either reinforce this confidence, if things are going well, or provide an early warning of problems, highlighting that some important (but not critical) requirements may not be met at the project level.

17.6 MoSCoW and the Business Vision - The Business Sponsor's Perspective

The starting point for all projects is the business vision. Associated with the business vision are a set of prioritised requirements that contribute to delivery of the vision. Also associated with the business vision is a Business Case that describes the project in terms of what value it will deliver back to the business. Depending on the organisation, this Business Case may be as simple as an informal understanding or it may be defined formally, showing what Return On Investment (ROI) is expected in order to justify the cost of the project.

The MoSCoW priorities are necessary to understand the Minimum Usable SubseT and the importance of individual requirements. The Business Visionary must ensure that the requirements are prioritised, evaluated in business terms, and delivered to provide the ROI required by the Business Case, in line with the business vision.

17.7 Making MoSCoW Work

Requirements are identified at various levels of detail, from a high-level strategic viewpoint (typically during Feasibility) through to a more detailed, implementable level (typically during Evolutionary Development). High-level requirements can usually be decomposed to yield a mix of subrequirements, which can then be prioritised individually. This ensures the flexibility is maintained, so that if necessary, some of the detailed less important functionality can be dropped from the delivered solution to protect the project deadline.

It is this decomposition that can help resolve one of the problems that often confront teams: that all requirements appear to be Must Haves.

If all requirements were genuinely Must Haves, then the flexibility derived from the MoSCoW prioritisation would no longer work. There would be no lower priority requirements to be dropped from the deliverables to keep a project on time and budget. This goes against the DSDM ethos of fixing time and cost and flexing features (the triangles diagram in the Philosophy and Fundamentals chapter). Believing everything is a Must Have is often symptomatic of insufficient decomposition of requirements.

Although the Agile Project Manager is not directly responsible for assigning priorities, they are responsible for ensuring the plans to deliver the project are realistic and achievable. Getting the appropriate balance of priorities is a key part of this, so the following tips help the Agile Project Manager understand and ensure the right priorities are being assigned.

17.8 Bringing MoSCoW and Timeboxing Together

Although the term Timebox can be used to describe the project or Project Increment, the Timeboxing practice is applied only to the lowest level Timebox used during Evolutionary Development and this is where the strength of the MoSCoW/Timeboxing combination is most powerful.

Before moving into Evolutionary Development some thought needs to be given to the use of Timeboxing for this project, for example: to determine what the default length of a Timebox should be and to what extent and with what formality the Timeboxing practice is to be used. See Tips for Assigning Priorities opposite.

17.8.1 Timeboxes - how long?

During Foundations, the Agile Project Manager should help the team agree the preferred length of the Development Timeboxes - short enough to keep the team focused, but long enough to achieve something complete and meaningful. The majority of projects choose Timeboxes of between two and four weeks, although on very short rapidly moving projects, Timeboxes can be as short as a day. Timeboxes longer than DSDM's recommended four weeks are unusual, because there is a high risk that the team becomes unfocused. Sometimes longer Timeboxes are a necessary choice, for example where the solution complexity cannot sensibly be decomposed, or where resource levels are low and team members are only available part-time. However agreeing to work with longer Timeboxes would normally be a last resort where other options to work within DSDM's recommended guidelines have proved impossible.

Tips for Assigning Priorities

- Ensure that the business roles, in particular the Business Visionary, Business Ambassador and the Business Analyst, are fully up to speed as to why and how DSDM prioritises requirements
- Consider starting with all requirements as Won't Haves, and then justify why they need to be given a higher priority
- For each requirement that is proposed as a Must Have, ask: 'what happens if this requirement is not met?' If the answer is 'cancel the project; there is no point in implementing a solution that does not meet this requirement', then it really is a Must Have. If not, then decide whether it is a Should Have or a Could Have (or even a Won't Have this time)
- Ask: 'If I come to you the night before Deployment and tell you there is a problem with this Must Have requirement and that we can't deliver it, will you stop the Deployment?' If the answer is 'yes' then this is a Must Have requirement. If not, decide whether it is Should Have or a Could Have
- Is there a workaround, even if it is a manual one? If a workaround exists, then it is not a Must Have requirement. When determining whether this is a Should Have or a Could Have requirement, compare the cost of the workaround with the cost of delivering the requirement, including the cost of any associated delays and any additional cost to implement it later, rather than now
- Ask why the requirement is needed - for this project and this Project Increment
- Is this requirement dependent on any others being fulfilled? A Must Have cannot depend on the delivery of anything other than a Must Have because of the risk of a Should Have or Could Have not being delivered
- Allow different priorities for acceptance criteria of a requirement.

    For example:

    'The current back-up procedures need to ensure that the service can be restored as quickly as possible.' How quick is that? Given enough time and money, that could be within seconds. A smarter definition would be to say it **Should** happen within four hours, but it **Must** happen within 24 hours
- Can this requirement be decomposed? Is it necessary to deliver each of these elements to fulfil the requirement? Are the decomposed elements of the same priority as each other?
- Tie the requirement to a project objective. If the objective is not a Must Have, then probably neither is the requirement relating to it
- Remember that team members may cause scope creep by working on "interesting" things rather than the important things. MoSCoW can help avoid this

Most teams choose to work to a consistent length for Timeboxes, because this allows the team to develop a feeling for what work can be done in the timeframe - the Team velocity - based on previous, similar Timeboxes.

However, there are times when it may be necessary to have a different length Timebox. For example

- To align with an external delivery date
- To allow for limited availability during a holiday period

The advantage of short focused Timeboxes is that they allow everyone, both at the team level and the project level, as well as external stakeholders, to assess on a regular basis (weeks, rather than months) the true progress - what has actually been delivered, in terms of requirements/User Stories. If progress is not meeting the expectations, they provide early warning of problems, and an early opportunity to address the problems. The earlier that problems are identified the more options there are available for addressing them.

By managing on-time/on-target delivery at the lowest level during Evolutionary Development, on-time and on-target delivery at the higher levels (project and Project Increment) can be assured. Initial MoSCoW prioritisation of the work for the Timebox and continual reassessment of what can be achieved in its agreed timeframe ensures that Timeboxes finish on time every time and deliver a working solution to meet business objectives in line with business expectations - "No nasty surprises".

17.8.2 Timeboxes - what style?

As identified in the Timeboxing chapter in Section 1, DSDM recognises two styles of Timebox:

- A DSDM structured Timebox
- A free format Timebox

As part of the planning during the Foundations phase, the Agile Project Manager should be discussing and agreeing with the project-level roles and the Solution Development Team which Timebox style is the most appropriate for this project.

17.8.2.1 A DSDM Structured Timebox

The structure within a DSDM structured Timebox is very useful to allow forward planning of the times when the Business

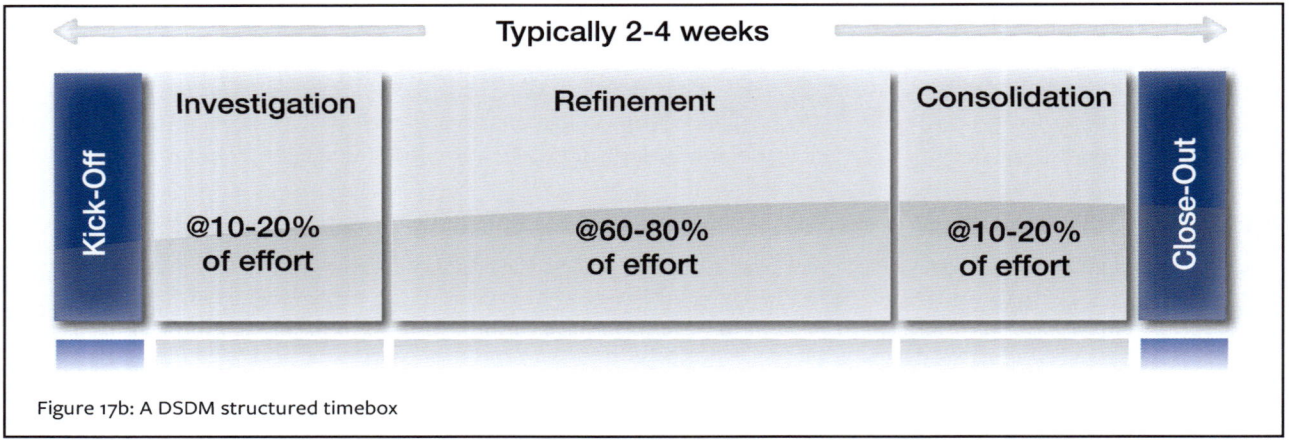

Figure 17b: A DSDM structured timebox

Ambassador will attend specific planning, feedback and review sessions. As well as these specific planned sessions, there is still an expectation of some day-to-day business engagement, e.g. attending Daily Stand-ups and timely response to urgent questions.

By projecting this structure forward to future Timeboxes, it becomes possible to schedule the various Timebox control points (Kick-Off, the three reviews, Close-Out) for all the Timeboxes in the Project Increment. Where a Business Ambassador is trying to manage a very busy diary, this can be a great help.

At any point during the DSDM structured Timebox, the whole Solution Development Team has visibility of progress and early warning if the overall Timebox objectives are at risk.

Timebox Kick-Off

The aim of the Timebox Kick-Off is to:

- Review the Timebox objectives, as outlined in the Delivery Plan, to gain a common understanding of what is to be achieved
- Ensure that it is still feasible within the Timebox to deliver what was initially expected during the Foundations phase, and to re-plan accordingly if this is no longer possible
- Where possible, agree the acceptance criteria for each product to be delivered within the Timebox
    - If it is not possible to agree this level of detail at the Timebox Kick-Off, then agreement can be deferred to the end of Investigation but, in this case, high-level acceptance criteria must be agreed until the additional detail is available (Going into a Timebox without an understanding of the acceptance criteria is extremely risky)
- Review the availability of all members of the Solution Development Team (including the business roles) to participate in Timebox activities for this Timebox
    - Commitment to delivery is based on pre-agreed resource levels at the project level. However, an individual's availability can vary between one Timebox and another, for example, due to planned time off

- Highlight any known dependencies (internal or external) that may affect this Timebox. The Solution Development Team's dependencies could be:

    - Internal - other Solution Development Teams on this project working concurrently in parallel Timeboxes

    - External - people or projects outside the team's control that may impact this project

The Kick-Off should be attended by all members of the Solution Development Team (including Business Ambassador(s)) who will be working in the Timebox as well as the Project Manager, the Technical Coordinator and the Business Visionary.

Timebox Step 1: Investigation

The aim of Investigation is to provide a firm foundation for the work to be carried out during Refinement and to clarify further the requirements and their acceptance criteria. Investigation entails the Solution Development Team jointly investigating the detail of requirements and agreeing how these requirements will be met as part of the Evolving Solution. This detailed information may be captured as part of acceptance criteria, against individual requirements, or as an elaboration of the Prioritised Requirements List.

Acceptance criteria should be confirmed as correct and providing appropriate coverage of the scope of each requirement. Whenever possible, an initial model or prototype of the solution is created to demonstrate an understanding of the requirements and to provide early visibility of the solution for assessment and feedback.

During Investigation, the entire team should work together on the full set of requirements agreed for the Timebox at the Kick-Off. It is necessary to understand the detail and priorities of the work intended for completion in the Timebox, so that informed decisions can be made later about which lower priority requirements may be dropped if necessary.

Some very early testing may be possible and is to be encouraged, but during investigation the main test focus is to work with the Business Ambassador and the Business Analyst, as well as the rest of the Solution Development Team, to clarify acceptance criteria and to start planning testing for this Timebox.

At the end of Investigation the whole Solution Development Team review the following:

- Dependencies:
    - The team ensure they understand any dependencies within this Timebox on teams working in other parallel Timeboxes on this project (concurrent teams) or elsewhere in the business, and between the requirements they are addressing

- Timebox Plan:
    - The team informally reviews the work still to be done, and agree which members of the team will be working on what. This ensures that no single individual is overloaded. This informal review validates the Timebox Plan (or highlights if the Investigation work has shown that the Timebox Plan is no longer viable, so that remedial action can be taken)

- Risks:
    - Based on the information gained from the investigation, and risks recognised for this Timebox from the Delivery Plan and risk log, the Solution Development Team analyses the risks associated with this Timebox and, on that basis, ensures an acceptable balance of requirements of differing priorities in accordance with the MoSCoW rules

The feedback from this review is captured as a Timebox Review Record (which can be as simple as a brief email, confirming what has been agreed). The investigation feedback is used to drive the next step in the Timebox - Refinement - and ensures the Solution Development Team can fully commit to achieving the Timebox objectives, based on an enhanced level of understanding.

A formal, documented review involving Business or Technical Advisors with responsibility for legislative or corporate compliance may be used as a demonstrable form of control over the Evolving Solution and provide a valuable audit trail.

Timebox Step 2: Refinement

The aim of Refinement is to complete as much of the development work as possible, including testing the product(s). Development and testing are carried out iteratively; the primary objective is to meet the detailed acceptance criteria previously agreed (at the latest, by the end of Investigation) but also to keep the focus on the current business need. The order of the work should be driven by the MoSCoWed priorities for this Timebox but should be influenced by other factors, such as:

- A sensible development order from a technical perspective
- Availability of specific resources such as Technical Advisors, Business Advisors
- Any known cross-team dependencies

Refinement ends with a review with the Business Ambassador(s) and, where appropriate, other stakeholders, such as Business Advisors who have been actively involved in this Timebox, and the Business Visionary. By this point (end of Refinement) the work for this Timebox should be nearly ready.

The review determines what actions are necessary to achieve full completion of the work according to the acceptance criteria by the end of the Timebox. No new work should be started after this point. Final feedback (fixing minor outstanding issues) requested at this time should be carefully considered and prioritised. Any significant demand for change at this point often exposes a lack of appropriate involvement of business roles previously during this Timebox - a lesson to be learned for the future.

This review would typically involve a demonstration of the product developed within the Timebox. The feedback from this review is captured as a Timebox Review.

Again, with appropriate formality, this review can be an effective demonstration of legislative or corporate compliance.

Timebox Step 3: Consolidation

During Consolidation, the actions agreed at the Refinement review are carried out, together with final testing and any work required to satisfy organisational or project standards. Examples of this could be:

- holding a peer review
- migrating code to a different environment

Any final quality control checks are carried out by the Solution Development Team to ensure all products meet the business need to an acceptable quality. Consolidation ends with a review to check whether the Timebox objectives have been met. Any products not meeting the agreed acceptance criteria by this point (the end of the Timebox) are deemed not to have been delivered. These undelivered products remain open on the Prioritised Requirements List.

Formal sign off here, or during Close-Out, by qualified advisors will acknowledge compliance of the solution with corporate or legislative needs.

Timebox Close-Out

The primary aim of the Close-Out is to record formal sign-off or acceptance of all the products delivered from this Timebox. An important secondary aim is to determine what is to be done about work that was initially part of the Timebox but was not completed. Such work may be:

- Considered for the next Timebox
- Scheduled for some point later in the Project Increment or project
- Dropped from the Project Increment or project

If overall timescales are to be met, it is important to avoid the situation where unfinished work passes automatically into the next Timebox, without any consideration of the overall priorities. A final aim of the Close-Out is to look back on the Timebox, to see if there is anything that can be learned to make the Iterative Development process and/or Timebox management process more effective in the future. This ongoing process of holding a short retrospective workshop as part of each Timebox Close-Out has a number of benefits:

- To allow the team to learn from their experiences in this Timebox
    - To recognise and build on the good experiences
    - To recognise problems and avoid repeating the same mistakes in the future
    - To define issues to be resolved in the next Timebox
- To gather ongoing information for use in the later, more formal reviews (at the end of the Project Increment and at the end of the project)

Where the Timebox has been successful and where the team is already established, this retrospective workshop can be very short. If there have been problems during the Timebox, or if this is the first Timebox with a new team, the retrospective workshop may need additional time. Depending on the time needed for the Close-Out, it may be practical and sensible to run the Close-Out back to back with the Kick-Off session for the next Timebox.

17.8.2.2   A free format Timebox

The free format Timebox reflects the style used by other popular Agile approaches such as a Scrum Sprint. A free format Timebox may be effective where the formality and structure of the DSDM structured Timebox is not possible or helpful.

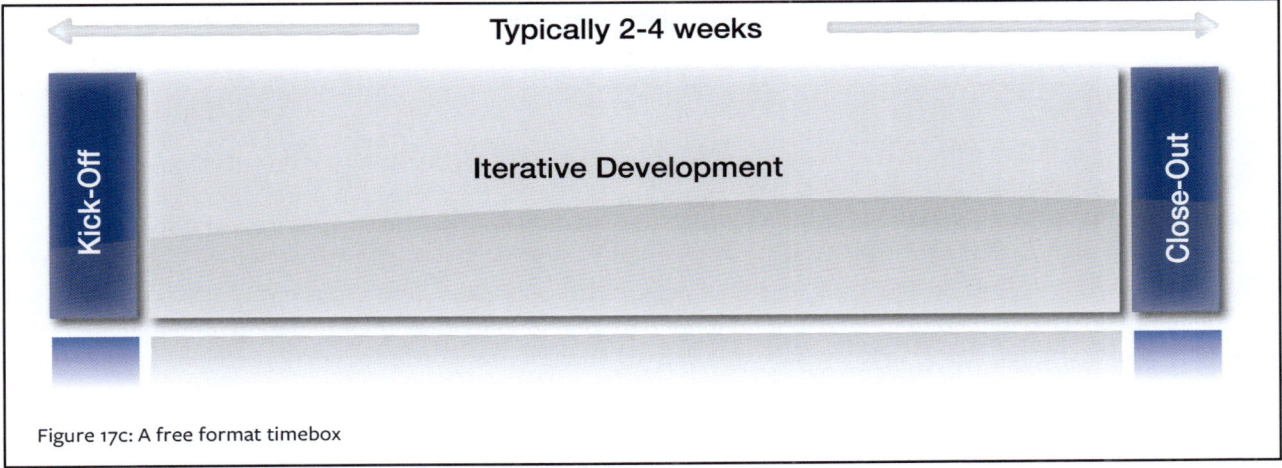

Figure 17c: A free format timebox

The free format Timebox also starts with a Kick-Off and finishes with a Close-Out. However, in between there may be any number of formal or informal review points. Typically the Solution Development Team will pick up one or more products or requirements/User Stories and evolve these iteratively until completed. Completion means a product or a requirement/User Story meets the previously agreed acceptance criteria. The Solution Development Team then pick up the next product or requirement/User Story and repeat the process. This free format style relies on the Business Ambassador being available consistently to review and provide feedback on an ongoing basis.

17.9   The Daily Stand-Up and the Agile Project Manager

As mentioned in Chapter 11, a key and integral part of all Timeboxes, regardless of the style adopted, is the Daily Stand-up. This is the Solution Development Team's opportunity to share information across the team and to do any day-to-day replanning and reorganising necessary when issues occur. However, it is important to emphasise that ongoing informal communication goes on between all team members during the day as needed, and not just at the Daily Stand-up.

The Agile Project Manager regularly attends the Daily Stand-up, primarily as an observer, to understand the progress being made and to pick up escalated issues. Other roles who also typically attend as observers are:

- The Business Visionary - in order to keep in touch with progress, to provide ongoing, visible support
- The Technical Coordinator - in order to keep up with technical decisions and pick up escalated technical issues

It is important for the Agile Project Manager to appreciate that these daily sessions are run by the Solution Development Team for the Solution Development Team, and are not for "reporting to" the Project Manager. So the style adopted by the Agile Project Manager is important.

Where the Stand-up identifies problems, the team typically agrees who needs to participate in solving any problems that arise, rather than attempting to solve the problem there and then, especially where reaching a resolution will take any more than a minute or two. It is common practice for problems to be taken off-line, which allows for follow-up discussions which are not run under Stand-up guidelines and which only involve those who are directly impacted. The follow-up discussions may sometimes need the Agile Project Manager to be involved.

A useful "best practice" for Stand-ups is where, at the end of the Stand-up, whoever is facilitating asks the observers whether there is anything that the team need to be aware of that may impact this Timebox. This enables the Agile Project Manager to pass on any important information that needs to be shared with the whole team.

As an observer, it is helpful for the Agile Project Manager to keep an eye on the style and behaviours being adopted by the team. This information may be used to feed into a retrospective.

- Is the team following the Stand-up rules - i.e.
    - Is the session informal and short? (maximum two minutes per person)
    - Is everyone answering the three standard questions?
    - Are problems being followed up afterwards? (Rather than being resolved during the Stand-up)
- Is the whole team attending on a daily basis, or are some team members missing on a regular basis?
- Is this session being focused around the Team Board, and information being updated accordingly?
- Are problems being shared (rather than hidden, in the hope they will resolve themselves)?
- Where not everyone is physically present, is this working for all parties? Teleconference Stand-ups (dial-ins) may be necessary where the team is split across multiple sites. However, for choice, this works better if groups at each site get together in a room and dial in to the groups at the other site(s). For teleconference Stand-ups:
    - it becomes even more important to use the suggested three question format to provide a simple structure for the communications
    - Formal facilitation of the Stand-up by the Team Leader may be advisable to ensure that everybody understands what is being said and is able to contribute appropriately
    - The team needs to decide how the Team Board will be used. In these circumstances, it may be an electronic version, rather than a physical area
    - Consider dialing in sometimes to see how the Stand-up is working where someone is not in the same room. People are often too polite to say they can't hear or don't understand, especially where not everyone shares the same native language

The Stand-up also provides the primary mechanism for the Solution Development Team to track progress and exert the necessary flexibility and control over themselves and their work to ensure on-time delivery of the agreed products by the end of the Timebox. It is also the primary mechanism for the Agile Project Manager to have an accurate and up-to-date picture of true progress, based on a true picture of what is happening on a day by day basis.

Daily Stand-ups are also an effective technique for the Agile Project Manager when used outside a Timebox, for example during Foundations, or in any circumstance where informal and ongoing communication needs to be embedded as part of "the way we do things".

17.10 Empowered Teams Dealing with Change Within a Timebox

Iterative Development is what enables a team to deliver a product that is genuinely fit for its intended purpose by the end of a Timebox. Converging on the accurate solution is achieved through constant refinement of the product, based on review by the business, led by the Business Ambassador and supported by the Business Analyst.

It is vital that the decisions about whether, at any given time, a solution appears right, or needs to change to make it right, are both quick and sure. If decision making is not quick and sure, there is a real risk that significant time will be lost (by waiting for decisions to be made) or wasted (as a result of decisions being overturned). It is important that all members of the Solution Development Team are appropriately empowered to handle any change that falls within the agreed scope of the Timebox objectives, without the need for a formal change control process that reaches beyond the team.

As a rule of thumb, the following scenarios always mean a change of scope and therefore need more formal management (outside the empowerment of the Solution Development Team) and would be escalated to the project-level roles:

- Changing the breadth of the solution (i.e. adding to the high-level requirements or removing Must Have requirements)
- Increasing the percentage of Must Have effort, either by introduction of new Must Have requirements, or by upgrading Won't Have, Could Have or Should Have priorities to Must Haves

However, negotiation around the detail (the depth) of the solution can generally be handled by the empowered Solution Development Team without the need for any escalation or formal approval by those outside the Solution Development Team.

Regardless of whether changes are deemed to impact scope or not, typically the Solution Development Team is empowered to operate within agreed boundaries without the need to escalate to the Project Manager or other project-level roles. The Project Manager should help to establish boundaries of empowerment by the end of Foundations and review for effectiveness on a regular basis (as a minimum, at the end of each Timebox).

> *For example:*
>
> *Following the practice of MoSCoW, dropping a Could Have requirement from a Timebox (or even from a Project Increment or project) is normally something that is reported after the event, rather than requiring permission. By comparison, significantly changing the meaning of a Must Have requirement often requires external guidance.*

However, all changes to the content of a Timebox must be agreed and accepted by the Solution Development Team as a whole, and must not be simply imposed on them or decided by one individual member of the Solution Development Team in isolation.

17.11 Summary

MoSCoW (Must Have, Should Have, Could Have, Won't Have *this time*) is primarily used to prioritise requirements, although the practice is also useful in many other areas. On a typical project, DSDM recommends no more than 60% effort for Must Have requirements on a project, and a sensible pool of Could Haves, usually around 20% effort. Anything higher than 60% Must Have effort poses a risk to the success and predictability of the project, unless the environment and any technology is well understood, the team is well established and the external risks minimal.

Timeboxing is one of DSDM's key practices and is used in combination with the practice of MoSCoW prioritisation to ensure on-time delivery. At the lowest level, the Timebox maintains focus on delivery in the short term (weeks or even days). This provides control at the lowest level, as well as a clear indication of the health of the project overall. If Timeboxes are successfully delivering the Must Haves and the Should Haves (the expected case) at the agreed time, then the estimating process is working well enough, the team is working effectively, the delivery plan is being validated and the risks are being managed. This Timebox-level confidence feeds upwards to instil confidence at the Project Increment level and the project level.

AgilePM

Timeboxing - Agile Project Manager Top Tips

- A good check for an effective Timebox Plan is to ask "How soon can the Solution Tester start testing?" and "What is the earliest that we can fully complete a User Story?" (i.e. have it developed, tested and accepted by the business). Completion of a User Story within a few days of starting a Timebox demonstrates early tangible progress
- Believe in the Timeboxes. Encourage the Solution Development Team to finish on time by prioritising what is to be done
- Never let the Timebox 'overrun'. In a worst case, insist that work stops at the agreed time and work out what is 'done' - if it turns out to be 'very little' or, worse still 'nothing', get everybody to acknowledge the failure, understand why and learn from it for the next Timebox
- Beware of the fact that, even if a Timebox has the correct proportion of Must Have, Should Have and Could Have requirements, individual skills and capabilities of team members may still make achieving the objectives difficult or even impossible
- Check Timebox progress by observing daily Stand-up meetings and enabling the team to react to any problems immediately
- Build an environment of trust and 'no blame' to ensure that the team are open about progress
- Ensure that the Timebox Kick-Off involves the right people
- Ensure that acceptance criteria for successful Timebox completion are as clear as possible at Kick-Off, and clarified further during Investigation
- Ensure that key risks which may affect the Timebox are identified at Kick-Off, and monitored during the Timebox
- Ensure that the Close-Out also performs a Retrospective of learning points to feed into future Timeboxes.

18. People, Teams and Interactions

18.1 Introduction

Collaboration and good communication are major factors in ensuring successful projects. DSDM places such importance on these that two of the eight principles highlight these topics.

Principle 3 - Collaborate

Principle 7 - Communicate continuously and clearly

Poor communication is recognised as the major cause of project failure. There are many examples of poor communication on projects; these are just some of the more common ones:

- Not defining and using shared language
- No access to the right people at the right time, particularly lack of verbal contact
- Ignoring information which is difficult to deal with or which contradicts your own view
- Key stakeholders not being identified or kept fully informed
- Appropriate communication channels not considered
- Only communicating using the written word

Poor communication on a project often results in delivery of the wrong solution. DSDM directly addresses a number of such issues which improve communication and collaboration.

A key responsibility for an Agile Project Manager is to build and support a one-team culture within the project. If this is missing, collaboration will be severely restricted. In addition, an Agile Project Manager should be focused on working with the team to put in place techniques and practices to support effective communication. Good communication requires thought, planning and commitment from the whole team.

18.2 Effective Communication

18.2.1 Communication skills and the use of terminology

Effective communication skills are essential for all those involved in a DSDM project. They underpin many of the DSDM principles and are vital for effective team-working and for ensuring the transparency that all Agile approaches rely on. It is also important to remember that face-to-face communication is as much about listening (verbal messages) and watching (body language messages) as it is about speaking. In some circumstances, a lot of information can be gained without saying a word. Like many of the soft skills, communication skills are not easy to teach or to learn; they can be worked on and improved, but they rely on a basic willingness and desire to improve communication in the first place. If this desire is absent, then communication is not two-way, but ends up more as a question-and-answer session, driven by one side or, worse still a documented statement 'sent out' for feedback and approval. This is not the DSDM way, as DSDM fully supports the Agile manifesto statement:

> *"We value individuals and interactions over processes and tools [and] customer collaboration over contract negotiation"*

The soft skills possessed by the team, and the importance of those skills, should not be underestimated. When recruiting team members, selection criteria should balance technical capability and soft skills where possible. A well-performing, communicative team can achieve far more than a team with the same technical capabilities but without these soft skills.

When selecting team members for a project or assessing the suitability of suggested participants or when considering training and coaching needs for an existing team, it is important that the Project Manager considers the practicalities of collaboration. Effective communication skills should be considered as important as the knowledge and experience individual team members may have.

Teams may benefit from some short sessions to explore the way they communicate or possibly from some behavioural coaching. In any case, the way in which the team communicates and the effectiveness of their communication, both internally and with those outside the team, should be a key part of the retrospectives held throughout the project, evaluating soft skills such as:

- Listening
- Co-operation, compromise, negotiation
- Open, honest, transparent interactions
- Nonverbal communication, e.g. body language, tone of voice etc.
- Self-awareness
- Appreciation of others, empathy

It's also important to recognise that a DSDM team brings together people who often use a different vocabulary or specialist language, based on their area of expertise. Members of the team should always try to use plain shared language, where possible. Where this is not possible, then it is good practice to maintain a glossary to define each term and its agreed definition. This simple step can avoid much confusion.

18.2.2 Planning effective communication

Effective communication does not happen automatically, especially since there are now many channels of communication to choose from.

One of the key risks is that starting to rely too heavily on technology for communication stops people from communicating effectively. Most people have experienced situations where heavy use of email starts replacing person-to-person conversation, resulting in the loss of much of the real meaning:

- Emailing the person at the next desk! This may give the perception of not disturbing them but misunderstandings and lack of clarification often cause problems later on. Some organisations address this with guidelines for email etiquette
- Being inundated with high volumes of emails, many of which are copied to a large number of people (just in case). This can result in important issues being missed

Communicating effectively actually requires some careful thought on how to take full advantage of the communication options available. It is important to identify which style of communication will give the best results in the particular circumstances and to select the most appropriate style for the situation. It is worth lightly considering such aspects as the different communities, the type and frequency of communication, the best medium and which roles are best suited to communicate with them.

> *For example:*
>
> *A solution may be delivering a significant change to a user community and such a message is usually best delivered face-to-face (if possible) by the Business Visionary, or the Business Ambassador*

Well-known techniques such as stakeholder engagement are still valuable to support decisions about communication.

> *For example:*
>
> *Identifying key stakeholders (in terms of power/influence and interest) who warrant face-to-face communication, often on a one-to-one basis*

There will also be a number of people with limited power or influence, who simply need to be "kept in the loop". For these people, simple email communication may genuinely be the most effective choice. The important thing is that such decisions are informed choices, and that effective communication is a two-way process. Even a very light and informal assessment of the most appropriate method, frequency and process for different communications helps to focus communication. It is also important to be clear which decisions need to be recorded, to ensure everyone is clear which decisions have been made, and also to ensure key decisions are communicated.

Planning effective communication is usually seen as the responsibility of the Project Manager and on an Agile project this planning becomes even more important, as it encompasses not just the external stakeholder communication, but also needs to consider the Solution Development Team's internal communication. Planning should consider the technical options available and their associated value to the project. Because this is an Agile project that relies heavily on spontaneous informal communication as well as the more formal, outward-facing communication, the Project Manager should also consider the communication skills of the team members, to understand whether they are already in place and effective, or whether some training or coaching in this area is needed.

18.2.3 Communication choices

1) Face-to-Face: Face-to-face communication will usually be the most effective way of communicating, either with individuals or with a small-to-medium sized group (in a workshop or a meeting). As well as enabling the rationale behind decisions to be fully understood, face-to-face communication allows immediate clarification of misunderstandings.
   - Allows communication using all the senses, but particularly words, tone of voice and body language
2) Conferencing - Video Conference (VC) and its variations: If those involved cannot physically get together, then a video conference is often the next most effective channel. For preference, each local group should gather in the same room, sharing one link in to the group conversation.
   - VC - Allows communication using words, tone of voice and body language (although body language communication may be limited by the field of vision of the video link, e.g. facial expression only, as well as the performance of the link which, if poor, may lead to 'blocky' images or a lag between sound and vision).
   - Teleconference - Allows communication using words and tone of voice, but excludes body language.

For preference, distributed teams should run their Daily Stand-ups around their Team Board with some kind of video link

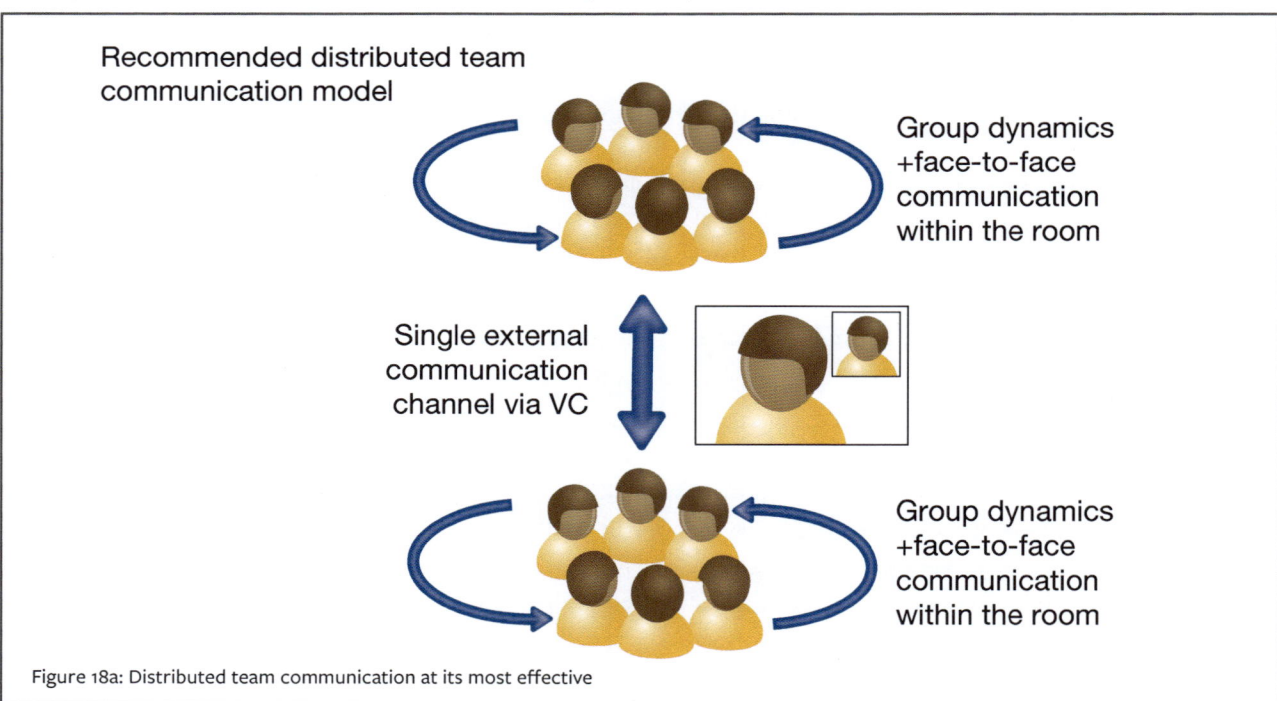

Figure 18a: Distributed team communication at its most effective

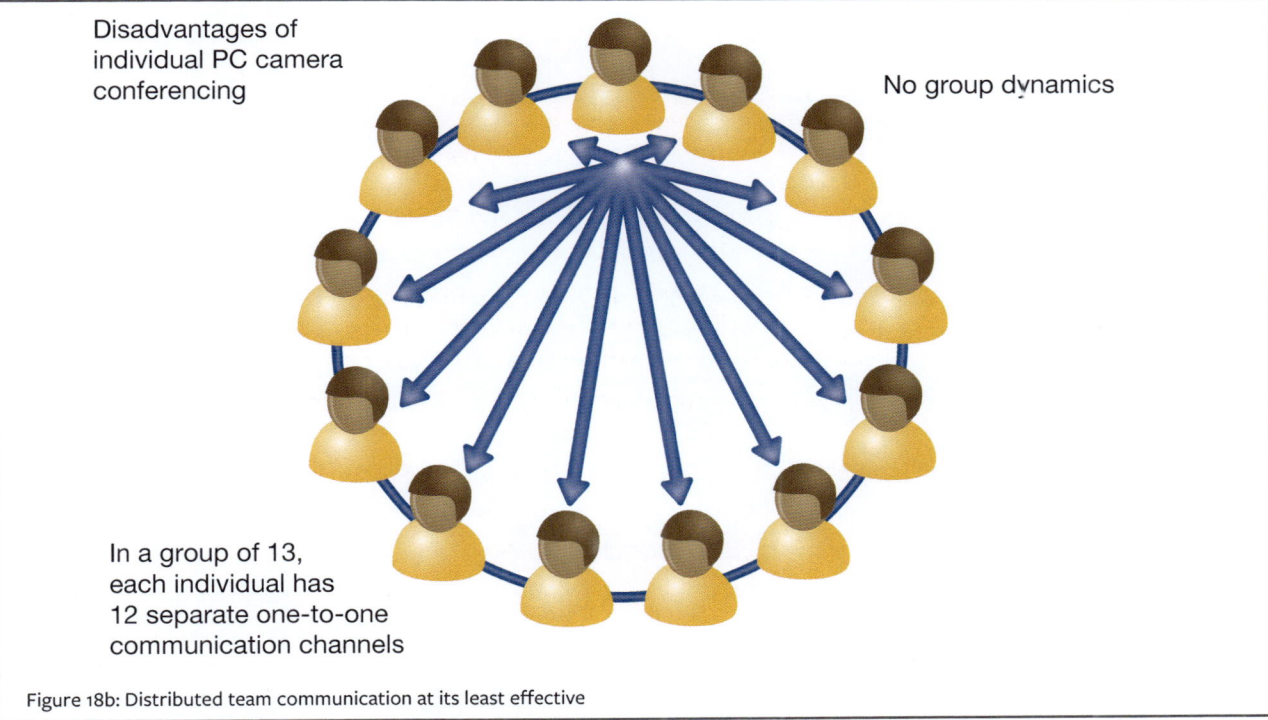

Figure 18b: Distributed team communication at its least effective

to the remote team members. Some DSDM teams will even have a live link running between onshore and offshore team members in order to simulate a single workplace. However, if these options are not possible then individuals can use headsets and video cameras on their PCs, although this is less effective than communicating as local groups.

However, where there is a large group in one location and several smaller groups or individuals all in separate locations, it may be more effective (and fairer) for everyone to dial in or VC so that everybody is working with similar constraints as regards to making themselves heard. Alternatively, consider a more facilitated session where somebody in the central location is responsible for ensuring the remote participants can participate effectively.

Whichever version of conference is chosen (video or telephone), everyone should aim to make each session as dynamic, vibrant and fun as possible, as if all team members were together. This can be done with a little thought, and it will greatly increase the real atmosphere of the DSDM style of working.

3) Chat facilities: For quick interchange of short pieces of information, this can be very effective. The sender can usually see whether the recipient is actually online and so they can expect a fast response. Most chat facilities have an automatic record feature, allowing the conversation to be saved.

- Allows communication using words
- Excludes tone of voice and body language

4) Email: Often treated (wrongly!) as the default communication channel. Email can be very effective for confirming what has been previously agreed (where the earlier discussion has used a communication channel higher up on this list). Email is also an effective channel for broadcasting information to a large group where getting people together is not justifiable, provided email best practice is followed.

- Allows communication using words
- Excludes tone of voice and body language

To be most effective, emails should remove as much of the unnecessary "padding" as is possible whilst still ensuring the message is clear and stands out. Care should be given to elements such as the email title (so that the recipient can quickly assess how relevant the content is to them) and the list of To: and Copy: recipients.

5) Collaborative workspaces: These can be very effective for communicating informally within a team.
   - Allows communication using words, models, pictures
   - Some workspace examples are project websites, intranets/extranets, Googledocs, Dropbox, Huddle; there are many others

6) Documents: These are still important in DSDM, for capturing and managing more formal information and artefacts which need to be shared and managed, for example a risk log. However, where information is volatile or needs clarification, a document would normally be the last choice for effective collaborative communication .

   A useful guideline for creating documents is "If you don't know who is going to read the document, then don't write it. And if you do know, ask them what they need it to contain".

   Where possible, documents may communicate more effectively when pictures, models and diagrams are included, in preference to relying solely on large blocks of solid text.
   - Allows communication using words, models, pictures

18.2.4 Words or pictures?

Figure 18c: "A picture is worth a thousand words"

Sometimes the most effective communication can be by drawing by a simple picture, rather than giving a verbal or written description. DSDM actively encourages the use of visualisation through the use of practices such as Modelling and Iterative Development: both practices enhance the effectiveness of the spoken or written word.

18.2.5 Ongoing day-to-day communication

Similarly to all other Agile approaches, DSDM chooses from all available options to share information in the most effective way.

18.2.5.1 Team Boards

These are also sometimes referred to as Information Radiators (IRs), Kanban Boards or Big Visible Charts (BVCs).

They are simple, easily understood, often graphical representations of key information about the project. Although they are normally used for the current Timebox, they can also be useful at the project level or even at programme level. Team Boards form an intrinsic part of information sharing. For a co-located team, these are usually held on a physical wall or whiteboard. However for a distributed team, they will have to be electronic (or both physical and electronic, if this is practical).

People, Teams and Interactions

An effective Team Board provides a summary of team progress and the current status of their work. Ideally, it should never be more than one working day out of date. It forms the focus for the Daily Stand-up.

Team Boards enable both the team members themselves and also any interested stakeholders, in particular the Agile Project Manager, to be able to see for themselves progress and other information with minimal effort. This removes the need to interrupt team members simply to find out "What's going on".

At its simplest, for a Timebox for example, the Team Board should show

- The objective for this Timebox
- The requirements or Stories that the team have committed to deliver, and which of these stories are not started, which are in progress, and which are "done". This information is usually shown by the position of the story (and potentially its associated tasks) on the Team Board. Displaying information in this way is based on the concepts of Kanban
- Any work that is currently blocked (the use of bright warning-type colours is an effective way of emphasising the importance and risk of these blocked items)
- A countdown of the time left to the end of this Timebox (to emphasise the principle of deliver on time and to keep the team focused)
- Any significant risks or issues for this Timebox and the risk owners

This simple level of information may be expanded to provide addition information. However, it is important that the Team Board does not become so cluttered that it loses clarity. Team Boards can also be used very effectively in the wider organisation, whether for tracking the progress of specific activities, or for showing the current state and progress of programmes of work.

18.2.5.2 Daily Stand-ups

The Daily Stand-up is the opportunity for the team quickly to catch up on where everyone is; to make any fine adjustments to the plan for the next 24 hours, and to flag up very early if any significant problems are starting to appear and to re-affirm that, as a team, they are still on track to deliver what they agreed to deliver at the end of the current Timebox. This session may either be facilitated by the Team Leader or preferably run by the team members themselves as a self-organising Solution Development Team.

The session is not intended as a daily report to the Project Manager, although they will usually be very interested in the discussions as an observer.

It is also sometimes useful at the end of a Stand-up for the team to ask the Project Manager if there are any project-level issues that could impact their work in the next 24 hours. The Project Manager's response should focus on risks, issues and exception. It should not become a blow-by-blow description of their normal activities.

Full details of the Daily Stand-up can be found in Chapter 11.

As part of (or following on from) the Daily Stand-up, the empowered team may decide to swap tasks around, to take advantage of a task that has finished early or to reduce the risk of a task that is taking significantly longer than expected. This demonstrates not only effective communication, but collaboration in action.

In exceptional circumstances, the information from the Daily Stand-up may also need to be reflected in the Delivery Plan.

18.2.6 Co-located teams

The ideal situation for effective communication (and collaboration) is where the team is co-located. It is always easiest to share information when other team members are sitting nearby. Wherever possible, as a minimum, the Solution Development Team should have their desks grouped together and, ideally, include one or two spare desks for business roles as and when they spend time with the team. It is also useful to be near to, or to have access to an informal area for Stand-ups or wider team conversations to avoid disturbing others who may be engrossed in their own work at that time. However, such ideal conditions are not always possible or practical, since teams may be working split across different floors, sites, towns, countries, continents or time zones.

The responsibility for organising an Agile working area often falls to the Agile Project Manager.

18.2.7 Distributed teams

In some circumstances, co-location is simply not possible or practical. Where people are based in different locations on one or more sites, then careful consideration needs to be given to methods of effective communication and how communication will work. Effective communication requires effort and planning, it does not just happen automatically with no effort.

There is already a lot of valuable guidance published on distributed team working, especially in relation to off-shoring. However, in reality the problems are similar whether the site is split across continents or just at opposite ends of a city or even on different floors of the same building. It is just that cross-continent working adds more complexity around time zones and language and cultural differences!

Despite the technology available to support distance communication, if possible, a team should plan in some early face-to-face sessions to help establish a good working relationship. This in turn ensures that video-conference or teleconference sessions later on are more effective.

18.3 Collaboration

18.3.1 What is collaboration?

Collaboration is defined as "The action of working with someone to produce something".

Collaboration is first and foremost about people. A good starting point for collaboration is the working relationships. Where there are healthy working relationships, this is where the best collaboration takes place. True collaboration, especially in a team context, is about ensuring give and take on all sides and being comfortable with this.

There are also a number of important cultural factors to consider for effective collaboration, (for example, values, beliefs and assumptions) and around personal style (personalities and behavioural preferences).

In particular, individual characteristics have a direct influence on the ability to collaborate. People who are approachable, personable, good at forming relationships, open and good natured are, typically, naturally collaborative. For others, improving collaborative behaviours may require some conscious effort or coaching. Some people prefer working in a collaborative way, for others, a collaborative style of working would not be their first choice. In order to foster a collaborative DSDM culture, it is important to recognise and accept that this style of working comes more easily to some than others and to provide support and encouragement for people and teams as they start adopt a different (DSDM) style of working.

Collaboration is about understanding and working with differences of opinion and differing views. There is demonstrable value in fostering a collaborative team culture, both in terms of building better solutions, but also in terms of motivation and job satisfaction for individuals.

18.3.2 Building effective collaboration

Certain ingredients are needed to build effective collaborative teams. Some examples of these ingredients are:

- Having mutual trust between team members
- Having mutual respect between team members
- Being open-minded as an individual
- Being approachable as an individual
- Being available when needed
- Being open to change
- Having a clear direction
- Having a consistent and stable team membership
- Having belief in yourself as an individual and belief in others
- Communicating properly and effectively (e.g. using active listening, empathy etc.)
- Being subject to effective (DSDM-style) leadership

It is very rare to have the perfect team and the perfect environment already in place. So in reality, some of these ingredients may already be in place, others may need work to improve or establish them.

In order to capitalise on the value that collaborative working brings, it is sometimes necessary to address issues within the organisation or within individuals that act as barriers to collaboration.

Some examples of these collaboration barriers are:

- Organisational structures which group similar types of skill in silos, encouraging and supporting a "them and us" culture
- Managers who have to resource their projects based around scarce resources
- Organisational focus and reward based only on personal, individual goals
- Unwillingness to concede something for "the greater good" which would impact a personal goal
- A culture of personal competition

Collaboration can sometimes find itself in direct conflict to competition. In some organisations and cultures, recognition and reward, e.g. appraisals and salaries, are based on competition and being better than others, rather than around team achievement. As a result, this encourages individual success (competition) rather than team success (collaboration). These barriers need to be addressed to foster an environment where collaboration can thrive.

18.3.3 Collaborative people

Collaboration is all about problem-solving, bringing together people with expertise in very different areas in order to find a solution to the problem. Effective collaboration works best where individuals possess T-shaped skills: on the one hand, possessing a deep knowledge of their own discipline (the vertical part of the T), on the other hand, understanding how their discipline interacts with others (the horizontal part of the T).

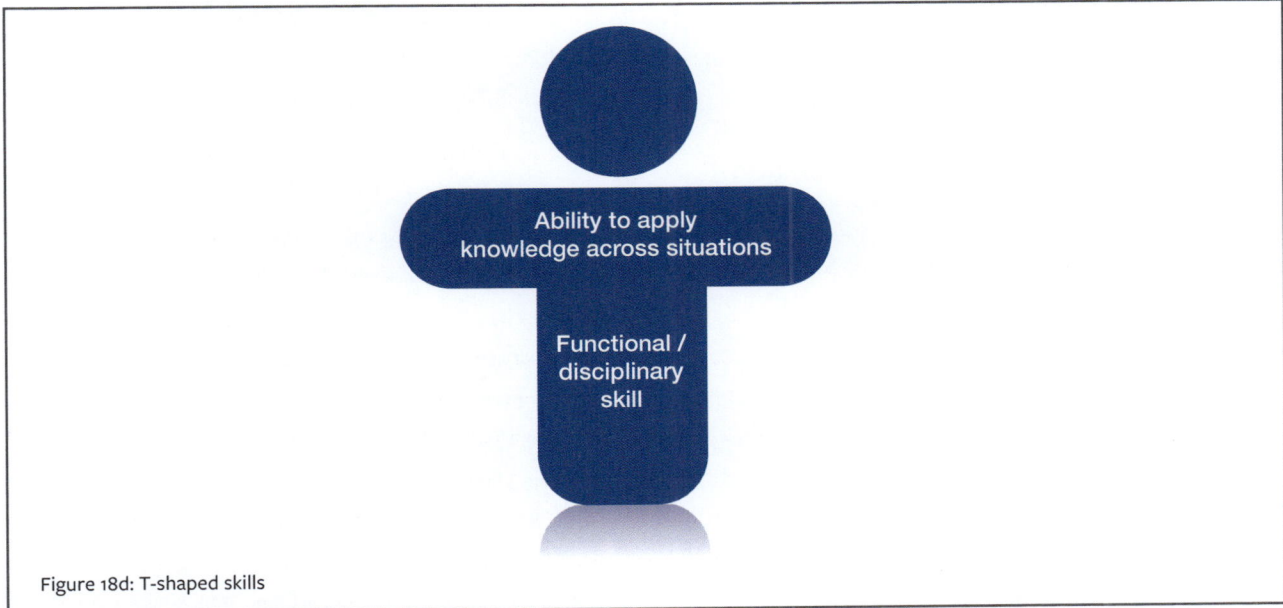

Figure 18d: T-shaped skills

Having this breadth of experience is useful in dealing with both opportunities and problems. People with this broader skillset can apply different perspectives to their thinking to help the team form a cohesive approach. An understanding of how an individual's discipline interacts with others is vital to help individual team members build a collaborative team.

18.3.4 DSDM teams

All Agile approaches place a high emphasis on the concept of "team". DSDM teams bring together people from the business and solution community to work jointly towards a single shared goal. This is a very different scenario from many traditional style projects, where the divisions, the "us and them" culture, is reinforced from day one. However, unlike most other Agile approaches, DSDM takes a wider view of the concept of "team", recognising the importance of engaging the wider stakeholders. Hence, as well as the Solution Development Team roles, DSDM identifies the roles that are focused on the overall project, and the roles that are supporting the Solution Development Team. DSDM also strongly recommends ensuring that the standard best practice on stakeholder identification and stakeholder management should form part of the lifecycle, particularly during Feasibility and Foundations activities, and will usually be driven by the Agile Project Manager. By ensuring everyone has the full picture of those involved in the project, those impacted by the project and those who will have an impact on the project, DSDM minimises the risks of nasty surprises later in the project.

This chapter focuses predominantly on collaboration for the project (based on the roles as defined in Chapter 7). However the guidance can also be applied to any external stakeholders for the project.

18.3.5 Shared team goals and ways of working

The cornerstone of team collaboration is having a single shared goal and ensuring this goal is visible to the whole team. Without a single goal, which the whole team buys into, collaboration is at risk as competing goals or personal agendas emerge.

It is also very beneficial to agree the team "norms" - the behaviours that form the basis of the team's interactions and how they expect to work together.

As part of the lifecycle, the early phases of a DSDM project and the early DSDM products are important in bringing people together and making sure that common goals are established and visible to all. Products such as the Business Case, which define and publish the business vision ("a clear and concise statement of where the business or product expect to be after the project has completed") are key to ensuring everyone on the team has the same understanding of the reason for the work and the value it will deliver to the business. This simple step alone removes much potential confusion. For many teams that are unused to a DSDM style of working, seeing this information stated in clear language emphasises DSDM's strong focus on effective communication as well as being a motivator to do a good job.

18.3.6 A culture to support collaboration

Collaboration is usually most effective where there is a supportive culture in place. This provides members of the team with the confidence and trust to be open and honest, and thus paving the way to ensure issues are raised early. When issues are raised early, solutions can be found while there are still options available. The later an issue is raised, the less choice is open to the team.

A blame culture is the antithesis of a supportive culture. Where a blame culture exists, it prevents the necessary honesty, and often results in behaviours such as:

- Spending time and effort shifting responsibility or preparing a defence in case problems arise in the future, rather than simply sorting the problem out now
- Hiding a problem, in the hope that it will somehow be resolved before anyone finds out
- Over-estimating the time needed for tasks, to avoid the perception of "failure"

A supportive culture means that there is recognition that mistakes do happen but that lessons are learnt and the team ensures that they are not repeated.

An Agile Project Manager should ensure that a supportive culture is in place so that team members are empowered to be honest and transparent. Ideally this comes down from the top level of an organisation. Where the organisational culture is less supportive, it may fall to the Agile Project Manager to foster a supportive culture at the team level and where possible, to protect the team from the external blame culture.

The DSDM practices of Workshops and Iterative Development as described in Chapter 12 also help to build and support a collaborative culture.

18.3.7 Leadership in a collaborative culture

A collaborative culture requires a particular style of leadership - facilitative and collaborative (as opposed to the authoritarian "command and control" style so often encountered on traditional-style projects). This facilitative and collaborative leadership style is promoted by all Agile approaches, and is sometimes referred to as "servant-leader". However as a "servant-leader", there is still an expectation that the leader will be an active participant, rather than a passive bystander, while always encouraging the team to be self-organising.

In particular, the DSDM roles of Project Manager and Team Leader should actively encourage, promote and support a no-blame culture and, where necessary, protect the team from external pressure, although all roles share the responsibility for making this happen. See Chapter 14 - Roles and Responsibilities - the Agile Project Manager View for more detail of the style expected from Project Manager and Team Leader.

18.4 Summary

In summary, the importance of effective communication and collaboration cannot be underestimated. It is directly linked to the whole ethos of DSDM working. DSDM came about directly because technology allowed the creators of a solution to sit alongside the requestors of the solution and to talk to one another, providing short communication loops to evolve the solution. Initially, this was often on a one-to-one basis and occurred where the creators self-selected and actively chose to work this way. But as DSDM has grown over the years, as the teams scale up, as teams involve people who have not selected themselves for this style of working, everyone needs to remind themselves of the basics of effective communication and collaboration, since it is only when communication and collaboration are really working well, that a DSDM project can succeed.

> ### People, Teams and Interactions - Agile Project Manager Top Tips
>
> - Work actively to promote effective and timely communication. It rarely happens automatically
> - Consider the communication skills and the communication challenges for the team, and understand what you can do to help improve things
> - Make full use of modern technology to support effective communication, but remind the team that where there is an element of uncertainty, spoken communication and, wherever possible, face-to-face is often the best option
> - Actively promote having a dedicated area where the team (or as many as possible) can sit together.
> - A lot of communication happens naturally when people are co-located, and a lot of information is assimilated by overhearing discussions between other team members. This can be especially useful to help a PM informally keep up to speed on what is happening day-to-day
> - Consider the "Forming, Storming, Norming, Performing" stages of team building, and see what you can do to help the team get to "Performing" as quickly as possible
> - Encourage all team members to appreciate the value of their differences, and not just their similarities. Good teams include a mixture of personalities and styles
> - Support excellent communication beyond the project team e.g. between the business roles and the wider business community: it may be that their usual day job does not have such a strong and varied communication need as their DSDM project role requires

AgilePM

19. Requirements and User Stories

AgilePM

19.1 Introduction

The importance of a well-understood, prioritised and agreed set of requirements is self-evident. However, the attempt to define a full and detailed set of requirements too early in a project often proves to be counterproductive, restrictive and wasteful. It is unrealistic to define requirements in detail at the outset of a long project. The business environment changes as time progresses; new requirements and opportunities present themselves. As the project progresses, the team understands more about the business need. Defining detailed requirements too early means either needing to change the specified requirements later, which wastes the original work, or delivering to the originally specified requirements and consequently failing to adequately satisfy the business need.

DSDM acknowledges this dilemma and proposes a better way of working. DSDM advises the capture of requirements at a high level, early in the project. Further detail is gradually elicited as the project progresses, deliberately leaving the finer details until as late as is practicable, i.e. during the Timeboxes of the Evolutionary Development phase.

19.2 What is a Requirement?

At its simplest, a requirement is a service, function or feature that a user needs.

> *For example, in a training company with its own training centre:*
> - *The Course Manager has a requirement to schedule training courses and reserve rooms, in order to make available courses visible and to ensure courses run effectively*
> - *The Training Centre Manager has a requirement to keep track of what training is running, in order to ensure appropriate allocation of trainers to courses*
> - *The Financial Accountant has a requirement to maximise the amount of time that the training rooms are in use, in order to maximise revenue from the rooms*

If the product to be delivered is a custom-built car, the requirements would be more feature-based:

- √ *The ability to move*
- √ *The ability to change direction*
- √ *A comfortable place to sit*

However, it should be noted that the following are not requirements, but solutions:

- X *An internal combustion engine*
- X *A steering wheel*
- X *Bucket seats*

DSDM projects aim to state requirements as what needs to be achieved, without tying them to a particular solution for as long as possible. So that more flexibility can be retained in how a solution is eventually provided, rather than how they will be met from a technical point of view, e.g. "the ability to move" rather than "an internal combustion engine". A solution expressed too early may constrain what can be achieved within the available time and budget.

19.2.1 Categories of requirement

The success of any solution is the product of two aspects:

- what it does (functionality, features)
- how well it performs against defined parameters (non-functional attributes, Acceptance Criteria, service levels)

19.2.1.1 Functional Requirements (FRs)

Functional Requirements express function or feature and define *what* is required: e.g.

- *"Visit Customer Site"*
- *"Obtain Conference Venue"*

The requirements do not state *how* a solution will be physically achieved.

- *"Drive to Customer Site"* is one possible solution. However, *"Fly ..."* or *"Travel by train ..."* are potential alternative solutions which may be worth consideration
- *"Build Conference Centre"* is one possible solution. *"Hire a hotel room"* is an alternative solution

Stating requirements early in the project as *what* (rather than *how*) allows room for flexibility and innovation later.

19.2.1.2 Non-functional Requirements (NFRs):

Non-functional Requirements define *how well*, or to what level a solution needs to behave. They describe solution attributes such as security, reliability, maintainability, availability (and many other "...ilities"), performance and response time, e.g.

- *responding within 2 seconds;*
- *being available 24 hours per day, every day.*

These NFRs may be:

- Solution-wide or impacting a group of functional requirements: e.g.
    - *"All customer facing functionality must carry the company logo"*
    - *"All customer-facing functionality must respond within 2 seconds to requests"*
- Applicable to a particular functional requirement. e.g.
    - *"Hire Conference Venue"* might have NFRs related to the necessary levels of Accessibility, Security, and Availability

19.3 User Stories

19.3.1 What is a User Story?

A User Story is a requirement expressed from the perspective of an end-user goal. User Stories may also be referred to as Epics, Themes or Features but all follow the same format.

A User Story is really just a well-expressed requirement. The User Story format has become the most popular way of expressing requirements in Agile for a number of reasons:

- Its focus is the viewpoint of a role that will use or be impacted by the solution
- It defines the requirement in language that has meaning for people in that role
- It helps to clarify the true reason for the requirement
- It helps to define high-level requirements without necessarily going into low-level detail too early

User goals are identified and the business value of each requirement is immediately considered within the User Story.

User Stories are often comprise three elements - the 3 "C"s:

- **C**ard
- **C**onversation
- **C**onfirmation

These are described in the following two sections.

19.3.2 User Story Format

The format of a User Story is as follows:

As a <role>

I need <requirement or feature>

So that <goal/value>

The following two examples demonstrate User Stories at different levels, but using the same format:

At a Project Level (as defined during Feasibility)
As a Marketing Director
I need to improve customer service
So that we retain our customers

At a detailed level (as defined during Foundations or possibly a Development Timebox)
As an Investor
I need to see a summary of my investment accounts
So that I can decide where to focus my attention

Choosing User Stories to define requirements demonstrates an intention to work collaboratively with the users to discover what they really need. The User Story is brief and intended to be a placeholder for a more detailed discussion later - the Conversation. Much of the detail of User Stories emerges during Development Timeboxes as part of Evolutionary Development. High-level User Stories (Epics) are broken down by the Solution Development Team into more detailed User Stories just before development commences on that group of stories. Even then, the User Stories are not intended to be full specifications of the requirements. Fine detail may not need to be written down at all, but may simply be incorporated directly into the Solution as part of the work within a Development Timebox.

The User Story format helps to ensure that each requirement is captured in a feature-oriented, value-oriented way, rather than a solution-oriented way.

In DSDM projects, User Stories are recorded in the Prioritised Requirements List (PRL).

This is the equivalent of a Product Backlog in Scrum.

19.3.3 User Story - The Card

From the PRL, User Stories are often presented on physical cards, for planning purposes and to help the Solution Development Team monitor progress.

The Front of the Card

On the front of the card, the following information is typically displayed:

- A unique "Story Identifier", usually a number or reference
- A clear, explicit, short name or title
- The User Story in the format:

    As a <user role>

    I need <requirement>

    So that <business reason/value>

- This section states:

    who the primary stakeholder is (i.e. the role that derives business benefit from the story)

    what effect the stakeholder wants the story to have

    what business value the stakeholder will derive from this effect

Requirements and User Stories

The Back of the Card
On the back, the "Confirmation" area contains:

- Acceptance Criteria (the test criteria), which are written as questions that expect an answer "Yes"

These Acceptance Criteria define, at a high level, the test criteria which will confirm that this User Story is working as required. These are not intended to be the full test scripts, but will be used to create all the appropriate test scenarios and test scripts during Development Timeboxes, as necessary.

For User Stories at the highest level (sometimes called a Project Epic), the acceptance criteria may be used to define the aims of the project using criteria that may be measured after the project has completed (as part of the Benefits Assessment).

Project Acceptance Criteria Example:

- *Is Customer retention improved by 20% within two years?*
- *Is Product range increased by 10% within 5 years?*
- *Has speed of dispatch improved to within 24 hours of time of order for 99% of in-stock items within 6 months?*

User Story Example:

Story Identifier: *STK001*

Story Name: *Customer Order*

Description: **As a** *Customer,*

I need *to place an order,*

so that *I can have food delivered to my house.*

Confirmation: **Acceptance Criteria** *examples:*

Functional:

- *Can I save my order and come back to it later?*
- *Can I change my order before I pay for it?*
- *Can I see a running total of the cost of what I have chosen so far?*

Non-functional: Availability:

- *Can I place an order at any time (24/7/365)?*
- *Can I view the order at any time (24/7/365) up to and including delivery?*

Non-functional: Security:

- *Are unauthorised persons and other customers prevented from viewing my order?*

19.3.5 Well constructed User Stories

Bill Wake's **INVEST** model provides guidance on creating effective User Stories:

Independent - Stories should be as independent as possible from other stories, to allow them to be moved around with minimal impact and potentially to be implemented independently. If any stories are tightly dependent, consider combining them into a single user story

Negotiable - Stories are not a contract. They are "placeholders" for features which the team will discuss and clarify near to the time of development

Valuable - Stories should represent features providing clear business value to the user /owner of the solution and should be written in appropriate language. They should be features, not tasks

Estimable - Stories need to be clear enough to estimate (for the appropriate timeframe), without being too detailed

Small - Stories should be small enough to be estimated. Larger "Epic" stories should be broken down into smaller, more detailed User Stories as the project progresses. The smaller stories should still follow the INVEST criteria

Testable - Stories need to be worded clearly and specifically enough to be testable

A well-written User Story is clear, concise and complete. Some simple checks are:

- It does not combine, overlap or conflict with other User Stories
- It conforms to organisational and project standards and policies where applicable
- It is traceable back to the business needs expressed in the Business Case and project objectives
- Where several User Stories relate to the same feature, but for different users, they are cross-referenced to each other

19.4 Requirements Through the DSDM Lifecycle

Projects need:

- a clear project objective
- a statement of the business vision
- a Business Case, agreed with key stakeholders

These form the anchor for the deliberate evolution of the more detailed requirements, iteratively and incrementally, as the project progresses. As the hierarchy of requirements emerges in expanding detail, as the project unfolds, each requirement/User Story must always be traceable back to the original vision.

19.4.1 Requirements Activity during Feasibility

All projects begin with an idea and an expectation of benefits to give a return on investment. The Business Analyst ensures that the Terms of Reference (which is sometimes vague or unclear) is expanded to provide a clear project objective, a business vision and an outline of the Business Case. The highest level Epic User Story is the objective of the project. The User Story format can be effectively used to clarify:

- Who needs this? (Do we have the right Business Sponsor?)
- Why do they need it? (What is the key business value expected or needed)
- What are their expectations? (What are the high-level acceptance criteria)

The User Story format also helps to identify the key stakeholders with whom to gain agreement for the requirements.

In Feasibility, the User Stories (sometimes called Epics or Themes) should constitute a small number of clear statements - just sufficient to scope the project, to identify whether it is worth proceeding further and to establish likely costs and benefits achievable. DSDM recommends typically fewer than 10 Requirements/User Stories at this point.

Some of the critical non-functional requirements (see above) may be evident from the outset, when the project objective is established, and these need to be captured here because they may constrain some of the project choices. However most of the non-functional requirement detail emerges later.

Even at this high level, User Stories help to focus on the value of what is required.

> *For example:*
>
> *"As a Human Resources Manager, I need a better way to deal with employee records, so that employee history can be tracked including their training and career moves."*
>
> *is a far more effective way of defining what the business needs, than the vague but technically constraining statement:*
>
> *"The organisation will implement a human resources system."*

The User Story format helps to bring out the real objectives of a major change.

19.4.2 Requirements activity during Foundations

During Foundations, more understanding of the requirements is needed, sufficient to clarify the scope of the project, prioritise, estimate and formulate a realistic Delivery Plan. This is normally achieved through a series of Workshops, some focused on defining requirements (the Business Visionary, Ambassador and Advisors agreeing the next level of requirement detail or prioritising requirements), some using the requirements to help plan development (the Solution Development Team estimating the requirements, or working with the Project Manager to create the Delivery Plan).

During Foundations, the high-level Epic or Theme stories established in Feasibility are now broken out into simple User Stories (functional and non-functional). User Stories defined by the end of Foundations in a DSDM project must be specific enough to estimate and small enough to fit into a Development Timebox (typically 2-4 weeks work). As a guide DSDM recommends typically fewer than 100 Requirements/User Stories by the end of Foundations.

This is not the lowest level of breakdown that the project will achieve but, by the end of Foundations, User Stories need to be just sufficient to allow for estimates of work to be done and to plan a schedule of Development Timeboxes for the first Increment of the project.

During Foundations, User Stories are assembled into a Prioritised Requirements List (PRL). The focus is on describing the business need embodied in each User Story, in a way that does not constrain unnecessarily how the requirement will be achieved.

Key non-functional requirements should also be considered and documented during Foundations. It may be difficult or impossible to accommodate such requirements if they are discovered too late in the project.

The PRL is baselined at the end of Foundations, to give a clear checkpoint for the set of requirements which was used for planning. In this way, new requirements which emerge during development are clearly identified, and their impact can be assessed.

19.4.3 Requirements activity during Evolutionary Development

At the outset of each Development Timebox, the User Stories from the PRL allocated to that Timebox are further investigated. These are broken down into more detailed User Stories which are small and clear enough for the team to work from. The detail is only elaborated one Timebox at a time, and thus the complexity of the requirements is managed. Also, since fine detail is only elicited immediately before that element of the solution is created, this avoids time being wasted on developing detail on all areas up front ("analysis paralysis") and ensures that requirements always reflect current thinking.

During Development Timeboxes, the detailed requirements emerge iteratively. Where appropriate, the Business Analyst captures the emerging detail within the PRL, working collaboratively with both the Solution Development Team and project-level roles to help retain the project's focus on value and priorities.

New requirements may emerge which were not identified during Foundations. The Business Analyst facilitates the consideration and impact analysis of these and records their inclusion or otherwise in the project, based on discussions with the Business Ambassador, the rest of the Solution Development Team (typically when such requirements represent depth and detail associated with higher level requirements) and/or the Business Visionary (typically when a new requirement is at a higher level, because it may indicate a change to project scope). The role of the Solution Tester is invaluable during these discussions, to help define effective acceptance criteria.

19.5 Summary

Requirements evolve and emerge in a DSDM project. Analysis of the detailed requirements is deliberately left as late as is sensible, to avoid unnecessary rework and to manage complexity. Because of this, it is important to obtain agreement to a high-level, baselined set of prioritised requirements in the PRL by the end of Foundations. This gives scope, direction and an appropriate degree of control for the project to evolve the detail whilst allowing change to be embraced and controlled.

Requirements - Agile Project Manager Top Tips

- Ensure requirements come from the right people: The Business Visionary (owner of the process) provides the high-level requirements, the Business Ambassador(s) and the Business Advisor(s) (the real end users of the solution) provide the detail.
- Beware of too much detail too early. Ignoring DSDM's guidance of typically less than 10 Requirements/User Stories by end of Feasibility and typically less than 100 Requirements/User Stories by end of Foundations may indicate an inappropriate level of detail and, if so, introduces a risk to the effective use of DSDM on a project.
- Ensure all prioritisation of requirements is reflected in the project objectives.
- Use workshops for agreeing requirements: workshops enable all stakeholders to agree on requirements and their priorities.
- Ensure there is an agreed requirements baseline by the end of Foundations - without this it is impossible to control scope.
- New requirements may need to be incorporated into the solution or the PRL throughout - this is all part of iterative development. Changes to the baseline (the breadth) need to be managed more formally than expansion of details (the depth).
- The PRL can also be used to capture progress (such as highlighting requirements that have been accepted). Some PRL templates allow this to be used as a Burn-down chart - a visible graph showing the expected rate of requirements completion necessary to achieve the deadline. This has the advantage of making any slippage extremely visible as soon as it happens, so that action may be taken if necessary or, as a minimum, in order to highlight that action may soon be required.

20. Estimating

20.1 Overview

Agile estimating is a different style of estimating for the Project Manager to work with, compared with project estimating for a sequential style of development (Analysis, Design, Build Test - often called "traditional" or "Waterfall"). Agile projects are incremental, so estimates made early in the project will be based on limited knowledge and will necessarily be adjusted during the project as understanding of the required solution deepens and the productivity of the project team is proven.

An estimate may be for the size of a product or requirement or for effort to deliver it.

Estimates can be used for several purposes: to evaluate a Business Case, to assess feasibility, to plan project schedules and costs or to communicate with stakeholders. Estimates may also influence prioritisation (*"How big??! In that case, it is a Won't Have"*).

An estimate is a forecast of how much it will take to deliver a specified requirement (objective) in terms of cost, effort and duration or, conversely, how much of the full set of requirements can be satisfied for a given cost, effort, competence or timeframe. It is important to define and understand the assumptions used to create an estimate and the risks associated with the estimate.

Estimating in DSDM can use any of the techniques used in other project approaches but there are four key points to consider:

- Estimates always need to include a level of contingency to cover the risk associated with unknown factors. In DSDM, contingency is provided by applying MoSCoW prioritisation to the scope of features to be delivered
- Estimates are only as precise and accurate as is necessary for their purpose at a given point in the lifecycle
- Wherever possible, the people delivering the project outputs related to a set of requirements should create the estimate for that delivery
- Estimates need to be re-validated throughout the project as the understanding of the requirement deepens and as the team's actual velocity is proven. At that point adjusted estimates are used to influence future plans in terms of how much can be achieved, but without altering time and cost

20.2 Coping with Uncertainty

> *"The person who claims to be able to estimate the impact of the myriad [project and design] decisions at the outset is either a prophet or not very well informed about the intrinsic nature of software development"*
>
> **Steve McConnell - Software Project Survival Guide**

There will always be uncertainties on a project, and it is important to accept this and have strategies in place for coping with them. This is a better way of working than spending significant amounts of time trying to remove all uncertainty - an approach that is likely to fail, and which formed the basis of the traditional style of project management.

As uncertainty decreases, so estimate confidence and estimate precision increase. So, for example, the level of confidence in estimates for the next Timebox to be worked on is significantly higher than the level of confidence in a Feasibility view of "How big is this project?", and the styles of estimating and the way the estimates are presented will be very different.

Estimators often deal with uncertainty by considering risks and using assumptions - these are informed or educated guesses about factors that may influence an estimate (up or down!). A good estimate will state all assumptions that were used as its basis, preferably before quoting any numbers, since it is not realistic to separate the assumptions from the estimate.

> *Examples of assumptions:*
>
> *"Based on the assumption that software [x], that we don't know, will behave in a similar way to software [y], that we **do** know, then the work will take [bottom range - top range]"*
>
> *"Based on the assumption that we will deliver Increment 2 with the same team as Increment 1, then ..."*

If there are questions about an estimate, it is usually the assumptions that need to be challenged, rather than the end figures or the estimator. And where major assumptions have been made, these present a risk to the project and probably merit some early project activity to validate whether they are correct or not.

Some common sources of uncertainty are:

- The expected volatility of business needs changing high-level requirements during the life of the project
    - Low-level change is expected, but always within the agreed baseline. Changes to high-level requirements (i.e. true change of scope) risk changing the basis for the project as a whole
- Unknown team or key individuals (whatever their previous experience)
- Level of knowledge/experience of individuals within the team
- Difficulty/ease of communication within the team (affected by location, etc.)
- Low ability to "protect" project team members from other responsibilities (impacts productivity)

Other possible sources of uncertainty could be working with new technology or not having a full understanding at this point of the rate at which the team can deliver.

For any significant area of uncertainty identified on a project, first estimates should include some time/effort assigned to develop an approach to mitigate it in the short term and to eliminate it in the longer term.

Always record the assumptions that are made against the areas of uncertainty, so that the estimating decisions and assumptions can be revisited as the project progresses and the uncertainties are removed.

20.3 Styles of Estimating

Estimating best practice suggests that the accuracy of estimates can be improved by estimating using more than one technique and estimating using multiple people (ideally those who will be doing the work). Two common styles of estimating are 'top-down' (also known as 'estimating by analogy') and 'bottom-up' (also known as 'estimating by decomposition').

20.3.1 Top-Down estimating

Top-down estimating is where the visible features of a product are used to estimate its size. The estimate draws on the skill and experience of the estimator who has done something similar (something analogous) previously, to provide the time element. Typically, items of similar size are grouped together to help validate the time element of the estimate. The time estimate can be applied from either the perspective of how much can be delivered within a certain time, or how long will it take to deliver x features.

Different techniques may be applied to this top-down style of estimating. Techniques common in Agile estimating include T-Shirt estimating and Story point estimating.

> **T-shirt estimating**
> This assigns a T-shirt-style sizing to requirements, e.g. S(mall), M(edium), L(arge), XL (eXtra Large) etc. This is a very quick and easy technique that is best used when relatively little is known about the item being estimated

> **Story point estimating**
> This is a consensus-based technique (formally known as wide band Delphi), which uses group discussions to assign a relative size to a story /requirement. This is a more sophisticated and time-consuming technique that requires a better understanding of the item being estimated but it does generate more precise results. A version of this estimating technique, that uses specially styled playing cards is described in Appendix C

> *T-shirt estimating example*
>
> *A set of stories to be delivered are grouped as Small, Medium, Large or eXtra Large. After this an estimate of effort is associated with each size, typically in days or months. Then this number is used to multiply up the effort e.g.*
>
> - *Small = x (6 hour) days*
>   - *15 Small requirements / stories equates to approximately x * 15 days effort*
> - *Medium = y (6 hour) days*
>   - *10 Medium requirements / stories equates to approximately y * 10 days effort*

Top-down estimating is relatively quick and easy to do, and is the standard estimating practice for estimating during early lifecycle phases. The expectation for top-down estimating is that not every grouping will exactly meet the sizing applied to that category, but that the law of averages will even things out - some may be slightly over, others will (hopefully) be slightly under.

Either before or after grouping, an estimate of effort/time needs to be associated to each size group. This can be done in two ways:

Estimating by Velocity is typically used with Story points. Velocity is based on a team's previous performance (in terms of the number of story points they can deliver in a Timebox) and uses that information to project forward what can be expected in the future. However, it is important to recognise that Velocity cannot be compared across different teams and that, if the team members change, the Velocity will need to be reset and recalculated.

> *For example*
>
> *If an established team has been delivering an average of 20 story points per Timebox (i.e. their Velocity is 20 points), and the next Increment is planned to be 5 Timeboxes, then the expectation is that this team can deliver about 100 story points in the next Increment and plans can be built based on that assumption*

Where the velocity of a team is not known that velocity will itself need to be estimated:

> *For example*
>
> *To estimate velocity for a new team: In Timebox Planning, the team take the highest priority story, break it down into the activities required to deliver it and estimate the effort required. This process continues until the team agrees the Timebox is full. The total value of story points then becomes the predicted velocity for the team. This velocity will be checked at the end of this and every subsequent Timebox*

Estimating by Example is used for T-shirt estimating, but can also be used for Story Point estimating, where Velocity is not available (e.g. it is a new team or there is new technology). The team take a small number of small requirements/stories (typically 2 or 3), and as a group break them down into tasks and estimate the tasks (i.e. they use bottom-up estimating on a small number of stories). They then add up the tasks so that they can associate actual expected effort with a requirement/story of a particular size. This is repeated for the other chosen stories, and then the average is calculated as the time/effort example for this size.

> *For example*
>
> *(T shirt): the average time expected for a Small requirement/story is 7 hours (calculated as an average of 8 hours, 6 hours, 7 hours). The team agree Medium equates to 2 x Small, Large equates to 3 x Small)*

20.3.2 Bottom-Up estimating

Bottom-up estimating is where each component is broken down into individual elements, effort is estimated against each element, and then the effort for all elements is added up. This decomposition may break down work into a series of tasks (Work Breakdown) or may break down a product into a series of sub-products (Product Breakdown).

> *For example*
>
> *Work Breakdown - A requirement to "Create a new screen for our web site" might split into tasks such as*
>
> - *Check corporate design standards for web screens (2 hours)*
> - *Design screen (5 hours)*
> - *Create test data (2 hours)*
> - *Test screen (2 hours) etc*
>
> *which are then added up to show 11 hours effort is needed*

> *For example*
>
> *Product Breakdown - A requirement to "create a web shop for classic car club" would involve breaking the 'web shop' product into the components that would make that up such as a 'parts database', a 'customer database', and 'order entry form', a 'credit card payment interface' etc. These sub-products can be further broken down if required. For example, the 'parts database' could be broken into a per part 'part number', 'description', 'price', 'stock level' etc. The effort associated with creating these sub-products at the lowest level of the breakdown can then be estimated and added together in order to show the total effort needed*

Bottom-up estimates are the most precise way of estimating, since each task is estimated separately. The top-down estimate and bottom-up estimate for the same piece of work will probably differ but that is not a problem as one style can validate the other in line with the estimating best practice guidance to estimate using more than one technique.

Bottom-up estimating can be very time-consuming and requires a good understanding of what needs to be done (sometimes supported by historical data regarding speed of task completion). The time needed to estimate an entire project bottom-up in the early phases would make this an expensive option, and since early estimates are often based on a lot of assumptions, the estimate appears very precise but is probably completely inaccurate.

20.3.3 Which style?

The choice of style depends very much on the position of the project in the lifecycle. Typically top-down estimating is done in the early lifecycle phases (Feasibility and Foundations) and bottom-up is done in Evolutionary Development (during Timebox Planning). It is common practice in DSDM to pull forward the bottom-up estimate for the first planned Timebox into the end of the Foundations phase in order to use the bottom-up estimates for that subset of the work to validate the earlier top-down estimates.

20.4 The Estimating Cycle

Estimates are carried out at all stages of a project, initially to help planning. Throughout the project, these initial estimates should be validated and revised to give increasing precision based on emerging detail, the validation of assumptions and actual measures of project performance. DSDM expects early estimates to give a broad picture, sufficient only to support the decision on whether or not to proceed. Realistically they cannot lay down a precise shape for the project since estimates are expected to change as more information becomes available.

Initial estimates during Feasibility will be based on the limited information known about the project at this stage, but are also based on experience of similar solutions in different projects. In Foundations, as more becomes known about the detail of the project, the estimates can be refined based on that knowledge, and are used to fix the Time and Cost. Depending on the knowledge and experience of the team and the size of the project, these may be fixed for the whole Project at this point or it may be fixed for the first one or two Increments with the expectation of revisiting Foundations when better knowledge and experience is available within the organisation and the team. Later, as some of the solution starts to be developed (during Evolutionary Development) actual results and measures of velocity can be used to refine estimates even further.

> *Example 1: On a project where the level of confidence in the Foundations estimate is high, then it is reasonable to fix the estimate for the project*
>
> *Example 2: On a project where the level of confidence in the Foundations estimate is lower (more uncertainty than usual), it makes more sense to use the estimate to fix the Increment and review the project estimate at the end of the Increment*
>
> *Example 3: In some organisations, a budget is allocated to a project in advance, sometimes at the beginning of the financial year. In this circumstance, the Foundation estimating is then used to work out what can realistically be delivered within the budget. Although this seems an odd way round to do things, in reality it is equally effective and all the guidance provided elsewhere in DSDM still applies*

Estimates are not static. They should always be reviewed at intervals throughout a project to reassess their validity based on actual events and experience, such as further detail being elicited, risks manifesting or going away, velocity (speed of delivery) being higher or lower than expected, assumptions proving valid or invalid, unexpected events occurring, team availability changing, change requests being formally raised and so on. In DSDM, the Cost (in terms of people allocated to the project), Time and Quality are fixed, so the focus is on validating what will be delivered within the agreed timeframe, with the agreed resources and to the agreed level of quality.

20.5   Estimating Throughout the Lifecycle

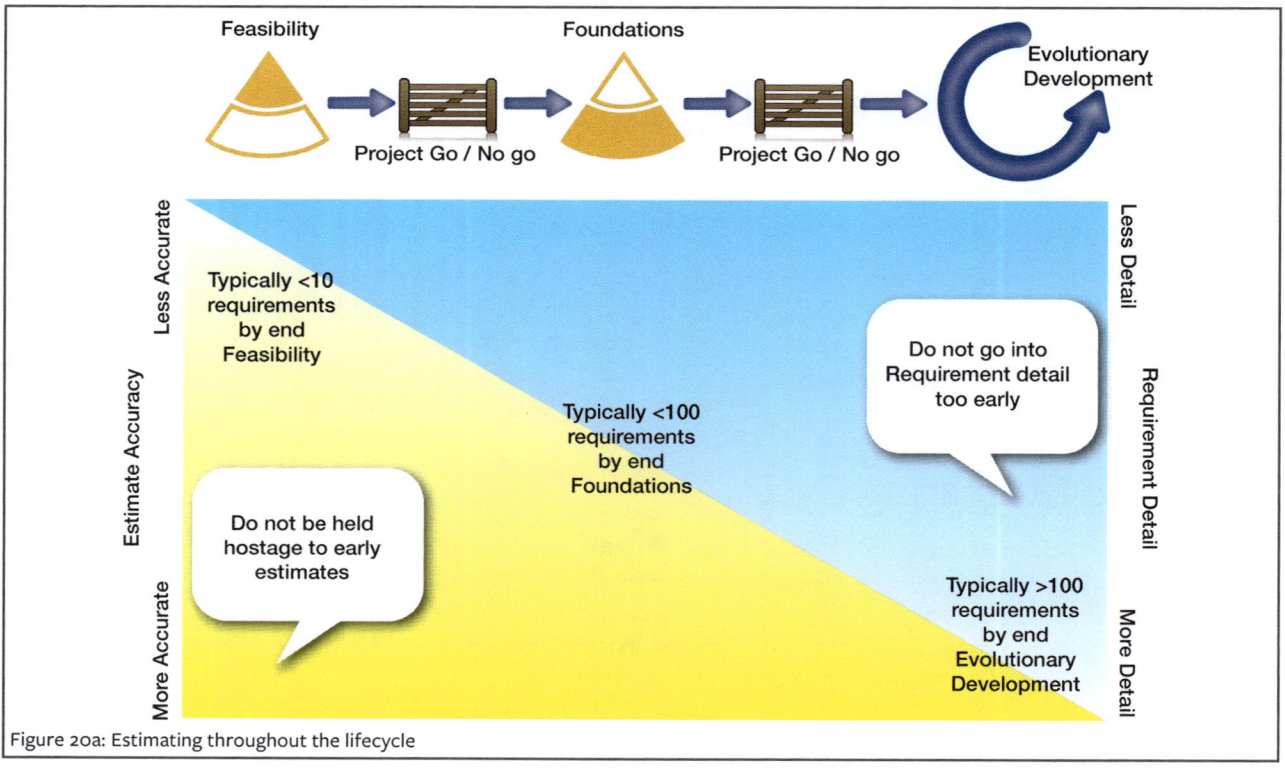

Figure 20a: Estimating throughout the lifecycle

20.5.1 Feasibility

This early in the project, the requirements are high level and few in number (typically fewer than 10). The purpose of an estimate at Feasibility is to provide outline costs and timescales to support the project Outline Business Case.

Estimating is done top-down, typically using a time basis, rather than a points basis, since decisions here will be based on "Roughly how much?" and "Roughly how long?" Since there are only a small number of overarching requirements and a high degree of uncertainty, the estimate at this point cannot be precise. Additionally, the balance of priorities within requirements is often not enough to cater for this level of uncertainty (all Must Haves at Feasibility is very common). This means it is more sensible to present the estimate as a range of values for both cost and duration.

> *For example: a figure of between 100 and 200 days/£100,000 to £200,000*

Ideally, the lower end of this range should be enough to build confidence in the cost/effort needed to deliver at least the Must Have requirements.

During Feasibility, a detailed estimate for the work of the next phase (Foundations) is also produced

20.5.2 Foundations

During Foundations, more detail becomes available about the requirements (typically requirements have increased from fewer than 10 to up to 100). This additional detail provides more information for estimating (see diagram above) and reduces the range of uncertainty in the estimate, but the estimate is still typically top-down. Now the estimate is likely to be more accurate, and the level of accuracy should be enough to fix time, at least for the first Increment, as this will be balanced by the prioritisation of the in-scope requirements. Some projects may be able to provide more precise estimates, depending on the size of project, the experience of the team and the client, but most projects come out of Foundations with some level of uncertainty.

The purpose of estimating at this stage is to revisit the Business Case and to produce the Delivery Plan. For the Business Case, the confidence in the estimate must be enough to enable a firm go or no-go decision on the project. For the Delivery Plan, the estimate must have enough detail to give confidence in the delivery approach and to allow a credible Delivery Plan to be produced.

20.5.3 Evolutionary Development

During this phase the purpose of estimating is to define exactly what will be delivered within the immediate Development Timebox. The estimates for the Increment and for the project are reviewed and validated, based on experience gained on the project.

The estimating session for a Development Timebox takes place at the start of each Timebox and is carried out by the Solution Development Team.

At this point, the team is estimating the requirements to be delivered in this Timebox and therefore their knowledge and confidence should be significantly higher than during Foundations. Since the amount of work being estimated is limited (typically 2-4 weeks work only), it is realistic and sensible here to do bottom-up estimating, estimating the tasks in hours potentially based on which team member is doing the work) to provide the Timebox estimate. Since there is less uncertainty at this point, the MoSCoW prioritisation of the Timebox requirements should provide any necessary contingency.

Bottom-up estimates created during Evolutionary Development provide the basis for the Timebox estimate and therefore drive the Timebox Plan.

20.6 Summary

In DSDM, the precision of estimates and the level of confidence increase as the knowledge of the requirements increases and the uncertainties decrease. During the early lifecycle phases (Feasibility and Foundations), a top-down approach to estimating is more appropriate, whereas during Evolutionary Development, bottom-up estimating becomes possible since more detail is available.

AgilePM

Estimating - Agile Project Manager Top Tips

- It is reasonable (and acceptable) to challenge an estimate - i.e. to question the assumptions that form the basis for the estimate, since they may be based on a misunderstanding. It is NOT reasonable (or acceptable) to challenge the final figures and ask for a smaller number (for example in order to force more work to be done in the time)!

- Estimating for small pieces of work is more likely to be precise

- Encourage the practice of providing a range where being precise is risky. This is very typical of early estimates at which point it is better to estimate something as, say, 5-10 days and be accurate (by delivering within that range) than it is to estimate something as, say, 7 days (being artificially precise) and be proven inaccurate when delivery takes 8 days

- Always ensure the team who will do the work create the estimate - they have a vested interest in creating a valid, realistic estimate and will be more committed to achieving it

- Encourage the team to compare their estimates to actuals, to help them identify estimating problems. The AgilePM can then use facilitative techniques to help the team resolve these problems

- The best estimates happen when estimating is done by the whole Solution Development Team. The group discussions start to highlight omissions and misunderstandings and help to create a firm agreed base for the estimate

- Re-estimation happens throughout the project. Use MoSCoW prioritisation to remain on track

- Do not allow the desire to protect initial estimates to prevent change from occurring. Learning occurs as the project progresses and freezing the scope just means the project may miss many of the stakeholders' key requirements

- Protect the team from external pressure to provide more certainty in their estimates than is possible in the early stages of a project. Otherwise the estimates become inflated to cover risk of "being wrong". (MoSCoW is how DSDM deals with uncertainty)

- When using estimates to calculate elapsed time to complete, remember to allow for "non-productive" time, e.g. dealing with emails, attending non-project meetings, etc. A typical starting point is to assume 4/5th of a working day is spent on productive work

21. Project Planning Through the Lifecycle

21.1 Introduction

Chapter 9 - Project Planning and Control describes DSDM's:

- Three Project Planning Concepts
    - Outcome-based planning
    - Planning to sensible horizons at the right level of detail
    - Plan and re-plan based on best available estimates
- Six Testing Concepts (that project plans need to accommodate)
    - Testing integrated throughout
    - Collaborative testing
    - Repeatable testing
    - Prioritised testing
    - Independent testing
    - Test-driven development
- Four Tracking and Control Concepts (referencing baselined plans)
    - Timeboxing and outcome-based measurement
    - Transparency of process and progress
    - Responding to change
    - Management by exception

These sets of concepts are interrelated and also related to:

- DSDM Products specifically:
    - The Business Case, the Prioritised Requirements List and the Solution Architecture Definition which provide strategic direction for the project
    - The Development Approach Definition and Management Approach Definition which shape the strategy for how project work will be carried out
    - The Timebox Review Records and Project Review Report that describe progress in the terms of value delivered, in the context of the plans created to do this
- DSDM Practices specifically:
    - MoSCoW Prioritisation
    - Timeboxing
    - Iterative Development
- The responsibilities associated with the DSDM roles:
    - At the project level (for direction and oversight)
    - At the Solution Development Team level (for day-to-day application)

21.2 Planning in a DSDM Project

Strategic planning for the project starts in the Feasibility phase with an initial outline of the project management and solution development approaches supported by a possible timeline for delivery. Assuming a preliminary judgment that the project is feasible, these outlines are gradually refined throughout the Foundations phase to generate high-level plans and agreed ways of working that form the basis of the commitment to delivering what the business needs when it needs it.

Plans always need to evolve to meet changes in real-world circumstances. This may be as a result of shifting business needs. Alternatively, as requirement and solution detail emerges over time, the understanding of what is possible and what is necessary to deliver a valuable business outcome may change.

Project Planning Through the Lifecycle

The following sections describe likely planning activities phase by phase. Although the Project Manager may not be responsible for all of the planning described, a key responsibility of the role is to ensure that all plans align with the high-level plans to deliver what the business needs, at the time agreed and within agreed costs.

21.3 Planning Activities Phase By Phase

The following diagram describes at a very high level the focus of planning activity in each phase of the project. This planning activity is described in more detail in the rest of this section.

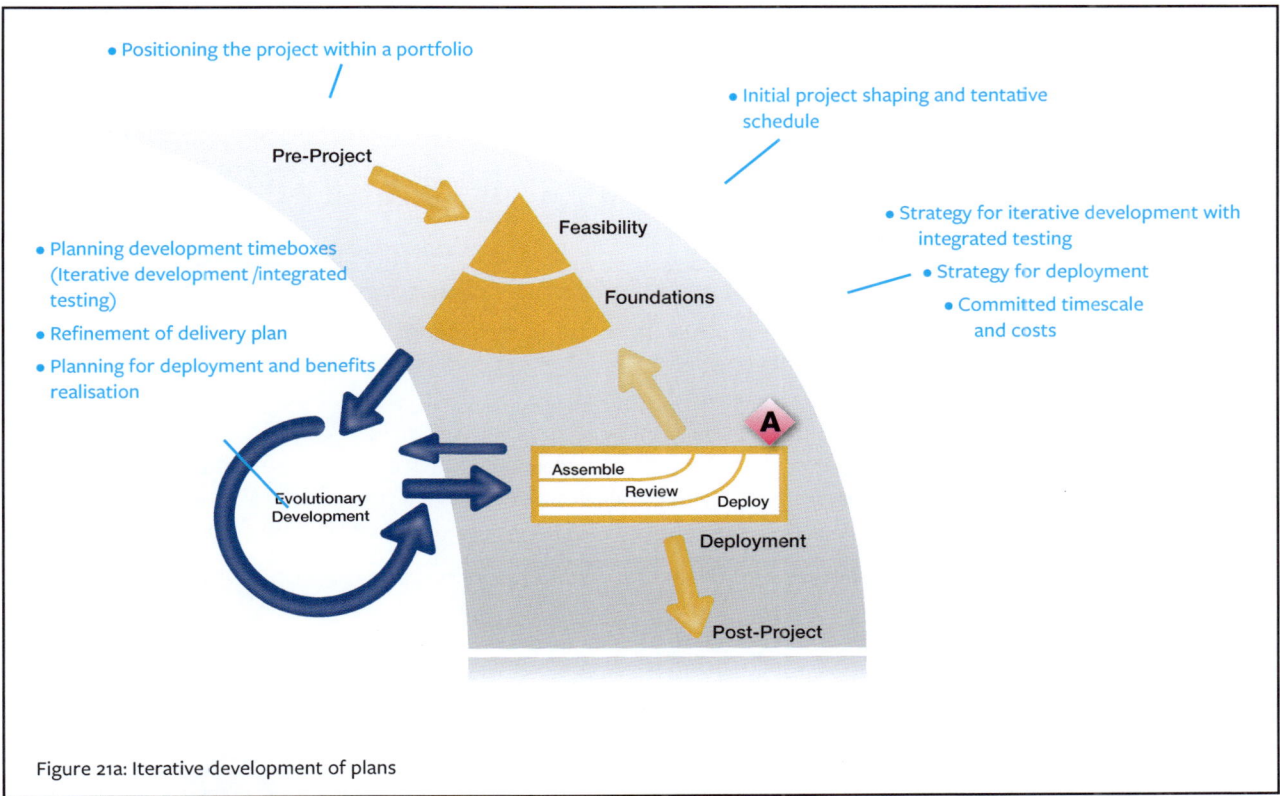

Figure 21a: Iterative development of plans

21.3.1 Planning Pre-Project

Planning during Pre-Project is carried out at the programme/portfolio level and is focused on whether and when the Feasibility for the project will be assessed - based on the individual merits of the proposed project - and ensuring that the resources required to carry out the Feasibility assessment are available to do the required work.

21.3.2 Planning during the Feasibility phase

During Feasibility, a high-level investigation is carried out. Typically, at this point, there are a small number of requirements (fewer than ten), the solution is only an outline and there is still a lot to be discovered about the project. However, even with this level of information, it is both possible and sensible to plan in detail for the next phase, Foundations. It is also possible to provide an approximation of the size and duration of the overall project, based on what is known at this point, but this can only be an educated guess. At this point, the Delivery Plan will describe the next few weeks (the Foundations) in detail, provide a very high-level outline for the first Increment and perhaps list the proposed dates for Project Increments further into the future.

The detailed plan for the Foundations phase will include the timescale, the deliverables, the resources and the facilities needed. It is very useful to record some detail of Facilitated Workshops, (dates, participants, etc.).There is not sufficient information available yet to make detailed planning possible for the Evolutionary Development and Deployment phases, so there will be no detail about the number, duration and focus of the Timeboxes even for the first Project Increment. Instead, this first cut of the Delivery Plan will probably simply state that the Evolutionary Development and Deployment phases will be of the order of x-y weeks/months, with a likely resource profile of z (Solution Developers, Business Ambassadors, Business Analysts and Solution Testers). At this point, given the level of information available, a significant margin of uncertainty is to be expected.

The business may have key dates in mind that reflect strategic business plans, so the Delivery Plan should also include an outline of what each of the proposed Project Increments are expected to achieve and any hard deadlines for them. It may not be possible to meet these deadlines and, given the very limited information known about the requirements and proposed solution for the project, it is not realistic to make any sort of commitment to delivery dates until the investigation during the Foundations phase is complete.

The answers to questions in the Project Approach Questionnaire (PAQ - see Appendix B) will have an impact on how the project will be managed. Any special approaches to the project including any tailoring of the DSDM approach arising from the PAQ assessment are included in early drafts of the Management Approach Definition or Development Approach Definition. More detail on Tailoring can be found in Chapter 24.

21.3.3 Planning during the Foundations phase

During Foundations, the team takes investigation to the next level of detail. By the end of Foundations, understanding of the requirements is a lot clearer. Each of the very high-level requirements from the Feasibility phase will have been expanded into more detail, so that typically requirements now number in tens (typically, still less than 100) and the overall MoSCoW priorities can be agreed. Since more information is now known about the requirements, the uncertainty is reduced and the accuracy of the estimate of work increases. However, a range may still be provided unless a fixed price estimate is required. In addition, more information about the business and technical background has been clarified. The foundation for the project is now a lot better understood and therefore it should be possible to create a version of the Delivery Plan with some committed dates.

In the Foundations phase, planning focuses on three areas:

- Creating a schedule of Timeboxes for the first Project Increment along with resources required
- Defining the approaches to be used across the project for developing, and controlling the development of the solution
- Agreeing a strategy for deployment. The Delivery Plan is baselined at the end of the Foundations phase and the delivery date for at least the first Project Increment is committed

As well as describing the number and likely duration of the Timeboxes, at least for the first Project Increment, the Delivery Plan also provides information on the probable focus for each Timebox, as well as the resources required to evolve the solution. The Delivery Plan does not provide the low-level detail of objectives and tasks for individual Timeboxes, that comes later, on a Timebox-by-Timebox basis as each Timebox is reached.

The detailed plans for deployment of the solution are left until later in each Increment but the strategy for Deployment and the high-level impact of, for example, business organisation change and training in the use of the new solution needs to be agreed at this point.

21.3.4 Planning Timeboxes as part of the Evolutionary Development phase

Timebox planning is carried out at the beginning of each Timebox and represents the lowest level of planning within a DSDM project. The Solution Development Team members are responsible for Timebox planning with plans being based on the objectives and outcomes agreed at the Kick-off of each Timebox. Timebox Plans are based on task-level estimates that emerge as a result of detailed investigation of requirements and the decisions made on how these should be fulfilled. The plan itself is typically captured on a Team Board (or perhaps electronically where team members are not co-located) and will indicate who is responsible for doing what work to: achieve the objectives of the Timebox, and to generate the agreed outcomes.

The Team Leader is responsible for ensuring that all the work is covered by the plan and that resources are sufficient to do the majority of the work agreed. The Team Leader is also responsible for bringing to the attention of the Project Manager any significant issues that may arise as the Timebox progresses, especially if these impact on the agreed outcomes.

Timebox duration is fixed at the Kick-Off - before the detailed planning is carried out. Therefore it is important that the requirements to be addressed are appropriately MoSCoW-prioritised to ensure that there is sufficient effort associated with the Could Have requirements (for the Timebox) to allow this work to be deferred if necessary. The contingency provided by the Could Have requirements ensures a coherent Solution Increment will be delivered by the agreed and immovable Timebox end-date.

21.3.5 Planning for deployment

As the detail of the solution emerges during the Evolutionary Development phase of the project, the plans for deployment of the solution can be considered in more detail. Deployment involves everything needed to transition the solution (or partial solution) into live operational use. The scope of the deployment activity varies considerably depending on complexity of the solution being deployed, the number of people impacted and the process used to deploy it. The Delivery Plan is updated with these deployment activities as they become clear. Care needs to be taken to ensure that plans for deployment are agreed far enough in advance to reserve the necessary resources. This may include anything from the scheduling of rooms and individuals for training to ensuring access to a computer room on the 'go live' night and should always include roll-back options, where appropriate, in case of significant, unexpected problems.

21.3.6 Planning benefits assessment activity, Post-Project

As the plans for the deployment of the solution become clear, the activities needed Post-Project to measure the benefits the solution will provide can also be planned. As the project will have closed down by this point, measurement of benefits is an activity that is owned by the Business Visionary: it is the Business Visionary who has responsibility for *owning the wider implications of any business change from an organisational and business process perspective* and *promoting the translation of the business vision into working practice*. In reality, a Business Analyst associated with the project can be involved with the planning of this activity whilst the project is still running and may also be involved with the actual measurement after it has closed down.

21.3.7 Incremental planning - revisiting the Foundations phase between Increments

The incremental nature of a DSDM project means that it is often sensible to revisit the Foundations phase at the end of each Project Increment, following the back-arrow within the DSDM process (marked as **A** in the planning activities diagram) to:

- Check that the project as a whole remains viable and should therefore proceed to the next Increment (based on validated actual effort and an updated, more informed view of the Business Case)
- Firm up plans for that Increment

The latter will involve a check on the validity and priority of requirements for the upcoming Increment and the scheduling the Timeboxes (as described above in Planning during the Foundations phase). It may also involve quickly revisiting the Management Approach (including a review of roles and responsibilities) and the Development Approach to check that these are still appropriate.

21.4 Summary

As an activity, planning in a DSDM project follows all of the DSDM Principles. Every plan in DSDM needs to:

- *Focus on the business need* - i.e. the outcome being planned
- Demonstrate that what is being planned can be *delivered on time*
- Be evolved with the *collaboration* of all involved with executing it
- Be sufficiently well considered in order to *never compromise quality*
- Be built incrementally - in line with sensible levels of detail appropriate to different planning horizons - from high-level but firm strategically aligned foundations
- Be subject to continuous iteration as it is aligned and realigned with changing project circumstances
- Continuously and clearly communicate sensible predictions of what will be delivered when
- Form the basis for measuring actual progress against what was predicted and act as a demonstration of control over the work being done against baselines taken prior to appropriate replanning

Planning - Agile Project Manager Top Tips

- Remember that planning activities in DSDM should be highly collaborative to bring in the expertise of those executing the plans and to improve their buy-in to them. This is particularly important for the Delivery Plan
- Timebox Planning is not your responsibility - that is owned by the Solution Development Team. The most you need to do is review the Timebox plan to ensure that it is properly aligned with the agreed timebox objectives at the outset and remains so
- Any tools used to support planning activity should not work against or in any way constrain effective DSDM planning
- When planning, always check to ensure that work identified is adding real value to the project

22. Never Compromise Quality

22.1 What do we mean by Quality?

DSDM has a principle that states

 Never compromise quality

It is important to understand what this principle actually means and how it works in practice on a DSDM project.

A simple measure of quality could be "Does the solution meet the business need?" But although this is a key measure, it is not the only measure of solution quality. In the majority of projects the technical quality of the solution is equally important and needs to be at the appropriate level. Delivering a project that is technically fragile introduces a risk to the business, makes future enhancement a problem, and increases the cost to support the solution in the longer term.

For larger or more regulated organisations, there may be an additional dimension to quality, where compliance with internally defined standards and practices is required in order to demonstrate control over product development and service delivery. And for some, meeting an external quality standard such as ISO or CMMI is mandated and formally audited on a regular basis. However the need to meet internal or external formal quality standards and the use of DSDM are fully compatible, although this usually involves collaboration with the members of organisation's Quality team.

It is always important to remember that delivering quality is not about simply following a process blindly in order to tick the right boxes. DSDM, like all Agile approaches, values individuals and interactions over processes and tools, and recognizes that it is the people - the roles on the project - that drive a quality solution, through their professionalism and their skills.

One way to deliver quality solutions consistently and predictably is to use a process that reflects recognised best practice for the type of solution and the specific circumstances for this project. The reasoning behind this is sound, since best practice processes are built on a base of successful projects and lessons learnt. Therefore following a best practice process should guide a project team to do the right things at the right time, to involve the right stakeholders and to ask the right questions. This in turn drives up the quality of the solution.

Guidance on quality therefore needs to consider two distinct areas:

- Solution Quality
    - Does the solution meet the business need?
    - Has it achieved the standards set for it? e.g.
        - Does the time to respond fall within the (defined) acceptable levels?
        - Is it usable? e.g.
            - Does it support the users of the solution carrying out their daily tasks?
            - Can a visually impaired person use it effectively?
        - Can it be supported? e.g.
            - Has the appropriate support documentation been delivered?
            - Does the agreed level of maintainability match the planned life expectancy of the solution?
- Process Quality (Quality Management)
    - Does the project follow the accepted best practices?
        - These are set at the organisation level and may range from informal guidelines through to fully defined and audited ISO or CMMI processes and procedures
    - Can this be demonstrated?
    - Does the project remain under governance?

For the purposes of this guidance, Process Quality refers to organisation-level quality standards.

DSDM addresses both strands of quality:

- By embracing the DSDM Philosophy, Principles, Process and Practices, delivery of a solution that meets business expectations is assured. Acceptance of properly defined standards (appropriately documented) by all individuals who fully embrace the responsibilities associated with their role ensures that agreed standards are achieved
- Following a DSDM approach (appropriately tailored, as required) provides the defined and predictable process demanded by those organisations where compliance to defined quality standards is needed.

22.2 Solution Quality

There are two key dimensions to Solution Quality; the first related to the scope of the features delivered, the second related to the technical quality of what is delivered. Together, these dimensions determine whether the solution created by the project is fit for purpose.

22.2.1 Scope of features delivered

For most traditional approaches, delivery of anything less than 100% of the requirements is seen as a quality failure since an expectation of 100% requirements was set from the start as soon as a fully detailed specification was signed off. By comparison, in DSDM the quality of the solution or Solution Increment is judged on whether, and to what extent, it meets the business need.

In DSDM, requirements are prioritised using the MoSCoW prioritisation practice - categorising requirements as Must Have, Should Have, Could Have and Won't Have this time. Provided the MoSCoW rules are properly applied to create a realistic balance of effort for Must, Should and Could Haves, a quality expectation in terms of the anticipated feature content of the solution is set by the end of the Foundations phase.

A solution meeting only the Must Have requirements will be viable but is unlikely to deliver the value the business expects. The quality of that solution would therefore be considered less than that expected from the perspective of completeness and value.

A solution meeting the Must Have and Should Have requirements is the most likely outcome and should represent a solution of the expected quality, in terms of completeness and value.

A solution that additionally includes some Could Have requirements will be exceeding expected quality in terms of completeness and value.

22.2.2 Technical Quality of the solution delivered

In DSDM, quality is about delivering a solution that is fit for purpose, i.e. delivering a working solution to meet the agreed acceptance criteria. Fitness for purpose will vary from project to project, but once agreed at the end of Foundations, it becomes the level that the project must achieve in order for the solution to be accepted as fit for purpose. Downgrading or even removing acceptance criteria, even to meet the deadline or budget constraints, contradicts the principle to never compromise quality and, as such, should only ever be a very carefully considered option approved by ALL the project-level roles.

Without an agreement of what standard must be achieved, it becomes difficult to identify when a product is 'good enough' and various problems may ensue, because the delivered solution fails (either actually, or debatably) to meet the business need. These problems will include one or more of the following:

- The delivered solution has the wrong functionality
- The delivered solution has an unacceptable number of flaws
- Ongoing support becomes expensive, risky and time-consuming
- The delivered solution is unnecessarily complex and puts the project timescales at risk
- The solution is deemed unusable by the business, since it prevents them from carrying out their day-to-day activities

There should be open discussions on Solution Quality in the early phases of the project so that all roles on the project have a shared understanding of what standard must be achieved. In this way, an area of potential conflict is avoided and Solution Quality forms part an integral part of all plans.

22.2.3 Maintainability - A key decision

Maintenance is a fact of life since all businesses have to deal with change and the solutions that support the business have to align to new ways of working. So although maintenance happens after the project moves into support, it has to be considered from the very beginning of the project. Solutions with poor maintainability result in a higher TCO (Total Cost of Ownership) as they:

- take more resources to maintain
- take longer to change and cost more to change
- are more likely to introduce further errors with change
- will be unreliable
- may slow or even prevent the development of future enhancements
- are a risk to the business

Therefore, if one of the business goals is a maintainable solution, building in maintainability to the level agreed ensures the solution will achieve this goal. An initial assessment of maintainability objectives may be made during Feasibility but DSDM mandates that a final decision be made during Foundations as to which of the maintainability objectives described below applies to this project.

As for all key non-functional requirements, once the decision on maintainability has been made, the risks of the chosen approach must be defined and a risk management strategy agreed.

The maintainability decision, taken at the start of the project and formalised at the end of Foundations, should be reaffirmed at all major milestones of the development.

In a DSDM project, there are three possible choices of maintainability objectives. The three levels are set out below.

22.2.3.1 Maintainability is a required attribute of the initial delivered solution

The priority here is for a supportable solution from the first Project Increment. This means that each Solution Increment that is to be deployed needs to provide the required functionality in a robust way and to ensure the components can be fully supported before it is accepted and released to the business.

> *For example:*
>
> *A project is delivering part of a corporate strategic programme (planned to support core business for several years). As each Solution Increment is deployed, it is handed over to the Customer Services Team and needs to meet the usual corporate standards and to include all the appropriate support documentation.*

22.2.3.2 Deliver first, re-engineer later

The business priority here is to implement a working solution quickly. However because the solution will have a long life and must therefore be maintainable in the longer term, the business is prepared to pay for subsequent (behind the scenes) re-engineering after deployment.

This means a greater development cost than building for maintainability first time, but gives a quicker initial delivery. It will also produce a lower lifetime ownership cost than struggling for years with maintenance problems. This option is often the choice where time to market is critical, for example, in releasing a new product into a fast moving market or a new process to satisfy a fast moving business. For this option, it is important to ensure sizing and funding has been agreed for the project as a whole and an appropriate portion of that funding is protected to allow for the later re-engineering work. If this later re-engineering work does not happen, for example where the Phase 2 is cancelled, then the solution becomes a short-term, tactical one, but by default rather than by choice.

> *For example:*
>
> *A soft launch of a product (Deliver first): A new product is being launched at the Annual Business Show in November although it will not be offered for sale to the wider public market until April. The launch solution will only need to accept a limited number of customers, so corporate performance standards will not be applicable. The launch solution will only be used on standalone laptops, so it will not be linked in to the corporate network, and will not need to pass the corporate security tests. A subsequent Project Increment (Re-engineer later) will start in January to enhance the new product and integrate it into the corporate systems. This second Project Increment will ensure it meets all the appropriate corporate standards and is robust enough to handle the high demand before the April deadline.*

22.2.3.3   Short-term, tactical solution.

The target here is to deliver a solution as early as possible. Acceptance will not consider maintainability, since it is agreed and formally recorded that this is a one-off or temporary solution, and on a defined date it will either be removed from use, or it will be replaced - before maintenance costs become a problem.

The short-term solution should always be seen as nothing more than a stopgap.

> *For example:*
>
> *An organisation is moving from an old computer system to a new one. On the day before the new system goes live, all customer bank account information from the old solution needs to be migrated to the new one. To do this conversion, a one-off data migration application is developed.*

It is particularly important that any decision to deliver a short-term tactical solution is documented and the life expectancy of the solution formally agreed - the date at which the solution will be removed. Without this formal agreement, there is a tendency for such solutions to live on and become long-term solutions. Sometimes this option is even treated as a cheap way of getting a solution. However, the reality is it may appear to be relatively cheap to deliver, but it will be very expensive to support. When a solution outlives its life expectancy, this presents a major risk and significant potential expense to the organisation.

22.2.4   How DSDM helps to build quality solutions

One of the key factors for ensuring the solution will meet the business need is for the business to actively "own" the solution. Projects are often wrongly described as "an IT project", where in reality it is a business project that is being delivered using IT. DSDM's full set of business roles - Sponsor, Visionary, Ambassador and Advisors - ensure that the project always has access to the wider business viewpoints:

- The financial view (budget and business case) - Business Sponsor
- The big picture, the future of the business and project context view - Business Visionary
- The day-to-day view - Business Ambassador
- The business specialists - Business Advisors

The DSDM Practices and techniques also help drive the quality of the solution:

- DSDM's clearly defined set of Roles and Responsibilities ensures the right people are engaged from the start and involved throughout the process
- The use of Facilitated Workshops allows for effective collaboration between groups of people in order to achieve consensus on decisions that drive the project in the right direction. In particular, Workshops ensure the appropriate business roles help to build a good set of requirements with agreed project MoSCoW priorities. Workshops also support team estimating and planning, which in turn ensure plans to deliver the project are owned by everyone on the project (rather than a perception that plans are owned by the Project Manager)
- The use of Modelling and Workshops, together with Daily Stand-ups and Team Boards support collaboration and effective communication, which are vital to ensure convergence on the right solution

- The combination of DSDM's practices of Timeboxing and Iterative Development ensure that the Evolving Solution is constantly validated against the business need

22.2.5 Quality across the lifecycle

During a DSDM project, there are key points in the early stages (up to and including Foundations) where quality decisions need to be made. The reason for making these decisions early is so that everyone involved in the project clearly understands what is and what is not acceptable. These decisions will affect estimates, plans, resources (numbers and skill profiles) and timescales.

Feasibility
 Set early expectations
	• Agree any general high-level acceptance criteria, particularly where these are non-standard
	 • Start considering the level of maintainability for the solution
	   - This is because the life expectancy of the solution has a major effect on the required quality and will affect the estimates
	   - It is important not just to consider the development cost, but also the Total Cost of Ownership (TCO) which typically includes the support and maintenance costs for a number of years. This has a significant effect on the Business Case for the project
	 This information forms part of the Feasibility Assessment. So by the end of Feasibility, there is already an early understanding of the appropriate Solution Quality acceptance criteria

Foundations Confirm and refine early expectations	• Expand the high-level acceptance criteria to provide more detail *This information will be represented in the Prioritised Requirements List as non-functional requirements and acceptance criteria on functional requirements* • Make appropriate architectural decisions to ensure these are met *This information is captured in the Solution Architecture Definition (if required)* • Agree an appropriate strategy for review and testing activity *This information is captured in the Development Approach Definition (if required)* By the end of Foundations, the quality expectations and overall acceptance criteria have been agreed at least for the first Increment with high-level acceptance criteria agreed for later Increments (if it is appropriate to defer the detail on these until later)
Evolutionary Development Meet expectations	• Agree the objectives for each Timebox before starting any development work in the Timebox *This ensures that the quality of the Timebox deliverable is pre-determined and agreed by all roles* • Agree the acceptance criteria for the individual requirements that are to be developed in this Timebox *This reduces the level of subjectivity during acceptance* • Make sure that testing is fully integrated during the Timebox - on a requirement-by-requirement basis *This reduces the risk of late feedback. It also focusses on progress being measured on completion of requirements (rather than completion of tasks)* • Wherever possible, make sure testing happens during development of the requirement (rather than after development of the requirement has been completed) *This supports the testing concept of 'testing integrated throughout'. The earlier a problem is identified, the easier, cheaper and quicker it will be to fix it*

Evolutionary Development Meet expectations	• Make sure that both Technical and Business Testing happens before the end of the Timebox *This ensures the right people are involved at the right time and allows ongoing acceptance of completed requirements* • At the end of the Timebox, check that the Timebox Objectives have been met *This ensures that focus is not just at the micro-detail level and that the rationale for the work is also considered as a measure of success*

22.3 Process Quality

22.3.1 Why is this needed?

All organisations want to be able to deliver quality solutions consistently. But in order to achieve this consistency, there needs to be an underlying project process in place that is effective and supports best practices which fit the situation for each project and which have been proved to lead to a successful outcome.

Ensuring projects follow the appropriate current best practice, tailored where appropriate for specific situations:

- helps guide a project to do the right thing at the right time
- avoids omissions and oversights
- brings in lessons learnt from previous experience

This is the rationale behind Process Quality - consistent delivery of quality solutions.

22.3.2 The simple view

So with this in mind, the simple view of Process Quality is

- Say what you do
- Do what you say
- Prove it
- Improve it

The following Table shows how the DSDM supports this.

Process Quality statement	How DSDM addresses this
Say what you do (Planning for Quality)	During the Foundations phase decisions on how the project will be governed and managed and the strategy for how the solution will evolve are agreed. Where appropriate the following products may be created to formally define the approach: Management Approach Definition: - Defines roles and responsibilities and project governance Development Approach Definition - Describes the review and testing strategy and any standards such as those for design and development that need to be applied
Do what you say	DSDM assumes that all participants in a project will act professionally in the best interests of the organisation as a whole and of the project in particular. In an environment of empowered collaboration, members of the team will self-organise to achieve agreed objectives The team should always do everything they can to make plans and progress against those plans visible to all. Team Boards, Daily Stand-ups, Timebox reviews and end of Timebox demonstrations provide this transparency
Prove it	Timebox Review Records may be created where there is a need to keep a formal, auditable record of all relevant feedback during Timebox reviews, with appropriate checks and a record outcomes of agreed actions being carried out during subsequent reviews and, by default, at the end of each Timebox
Improve it	Timebox and Project Retrospectives (where appropriate, documented in Timebox Review Records and Project Review Records respectively) form the basis of in-project and organisation-wide learning

22.3.3 Predictability

One of the key considerations with regards to Process Quality is predictability. An effective project process should allow for the status of the key variables of Time, Cost, Quality and Features to be known and compared with what is expected. Based on this knowledge, the future status of these variables should also be predictable.

By default DSDM fixes time, cost and quality whilst allowing the scope of the features delivered to vary. For the project as a whole the on-time, on-budget delivery of a solution built to the agreed level of quality is an expected outcome. Therefore, considering the project as a whole it would have failed to meet expectation if it delivered late, cost more than agreed or delivered a solution that was not fit for purpose.

22.3.3.1 Delivery on time

As time is fixed by default in DSDM, delivering late would represent a failure of the process and thus a quality issue. This is a particularly important quality consideration as failure to deliver on time could seriously impact the value of, or even undermine the whole rationale for, a project. For example, a wedding dress delivered the day after a wedding might be the most fantastic, even perfect, creation but if it isn't available on the wedding day it is pointless.

On-time, incremental delivery, Timebox by Timebox, provides a focus for project teams to deliver on time and thus achieve an early return on investment, and in turn this helps avoid unnecessary gold-plating the solution.

22.3.3.2 Delivery on budget

As cost is fixed by default in DSDM (in terms of fixed team size for a fixed duration), spending more than budgeted on delivering the solution would represent a failure of the process and thus a quality issue. Agreement during Foundations of the resource levels that are sufficient to staff productive Timeboxes and fixing that level for the duration of the project typically covers the aspect of cost that is most likely to vary. For other costs, such as the provision of infrastructure, it is important to ensure sufficient contingency is allowed to deal with issues such as price increases, exchange rate fluctuations, etc. since these are often outside the control of the project.

22.3.3.3 Predictability of what will be delivered

The incremental approach allows less important features to be descoped from an early delivery, and to be considered for inclusion in a later delivery where appropriate. At the beginning of the project and of each Project Increment, the scope of the solution is defined by the Prioritised Requirements List and a sensible length of time and level of resource is agreed for delivery of this scope. The Delivery Plan indicates which requirements are expected to be met in the Evolving Solution by the end of each Timebox. As the project progresses, if actual achievement does not match what is expected, the business roles decide which of the lower priority requirements will be descoped or deferred to a future Project Increment in order to meet the agreed deadline. The requirements expected to be met in the solution delivered at the end of each Project Increment is likely to change Timebox by Timebox but is always under control, allowing plans for deployment, with the implementation of any necessary workarounds, to be appropriately refined.

22.3.4 The level of Process Quality formality

For some organisations, Process Quality is simple and informal. However, for others, process quality is formally assessed and may be a mandatory or regulatory process with regular checks and full external independent audits.

Process quality and quality-related activities are sometimes perceived as adding bureaucracy and overheads. This should not be the case provided that the organisation's approach to quality is:

- flexible enough to allow the solution to evolve using DSDM's Agile process and practices
- robust enough to ensure, and prove, the solution has evolved in the right way to meet the needs of the business

The emphasis for DSDM projects is to:

- focus on the business need
- deliver on time
- never compromise quality

An unnecessarily high degree of ceremony or bureaucracy in quality-related processes will distract from this.

Provided that:

- the use of DSDM on this project has been an informed choice
- the choice is validated by completion of the Project Approach Questionnaire (PAQ) at the end of Foundations to identify areas where this project does not have DSDM's Success Factors in place
- the PAQ has been completed collaboratively with the appropriate Project Level roles
    - As a minimum the Project Manager, the Business Visionary and the Technical Coordinator
- the risks identified are being addressed and where necessary the DSDM approach has been tailored

the application of DSDM for this project should be used to assess how the project is following the process that has been agreed for it.

This allows a DSDM project to be able to demonstrate without any additional overhead that:

- the correct process is being followed
- the appropriate deliverables are being produced
- everyone knows who is responsible for what
- all parties know what happens next

Following a DSDM process ensures consistent delivery of Solution Quality because:

- The emphasis remains on keeping the project focused on delivering a fit-for-business-purpose solution
- True fitness for purpose is achieved through constant review with the business representatives - irrefutable proof that this will deliver what is needed (compared with traditional-style validation which relies on compliance with a previously approved and signed-off specification)
- There will be fewer formal changes. Most change is in the detail and is accommodated within the process itself
- There is ongoing refinement of requirements and the Evolving Solution as the business needs change, understanding deepens and the opportunities presented by the Evolving Solution become apparent

See The Agile PMO Pocketbook, published by the DSDM Consortium, for additional information.

22.3.5 Quality Reviews

Projects may need to be reviewed from time to time in order to determine their compliance with the organisation's procedures, practices and standards. For DSDM projects, such reviews must not result in unnecessary rework or wasted effort (e.g. producing additional records for the sole purpose of satisfying a quality reviewer or ticking a box).

Another focus of a Quality Review could be to assess the health of a project, based on whether it is following DSDM recommended best practice. This can be used effectively to identify projects at risk and allows measures to be put in place to get them back on track, or in extreme circumstances to put them on hold or stop them. This may be formalised, for example as a Gateway Review, with a Go/No-Go decision, based on the review outcome.

Some key questions to consider when reviewing a DSDM project include:

- Is there sufficient business involvement to support the approach?
- Is the team empowered?
- Is the lifecycle being followed?
- Are the products being produced that the project said it would produce?
- Is feedback from review and testing activity being properly incorporated?
- Are priorities being adhered to?
- Are Timeboxes being respected?
- Is configuration management appropriate and effective?

22.4 Summary

DSDM identifies two areas of quality to be addressed - Solution Quality and Process Quality. The iterative, incremental, change-friendly approach that DSDM defines, when properly controlled using MoSCoW prioritisation and Timeboxing, should naturally lead to the delivery of a quality Solution. Agreeing the maintainability level for each project is a key decision to ensure that the Solution Quality level to be achieved is both understood and planned for from the early phases. This ensures that every feature delivered is good enough to support the business need. An integral part of DSDM quality is the understanding that delivering less than a 100% solution is acceptable provided the business needs are met, whereas delivering late is not acceptable.

Quality - Agile Project Manager Top Tips

- Compromising quality is never acceptable nor in the long term does it save time
- Quality is built-in, not bolted on. It is very hard (time-consuming and expensive) to include quality retrospectively - planning for the appropriate level of quality from the start avoids surprises later
- Constant discussion with all stakeholders and acting on the feedback helps to improve quality.
- Quality is not an absolute; it must be determined project by project.
- Quality solutions are best delivered by skilled empowered people working as a team collaboratively to achieve a shared objective
- Ensure that control is demonstrated by the whole team and each individual, and not just applied on their behalf by the Project Manager. Individual and collective
- Ensure the project has individuals covering all DSDM roles and responsibilities, and make sure that everyone understands that they are empowered. This is the starting point for delivering a quality solution
- Use the DSDM products such as the Management and Development Approach Definitions and the Timebox and Project Review Records, formally where necessary, as the basis for quality planning (saying what you do) and showing compliance with that plan (proving you do what you say)
- Where necessary ensure that products intended to form an audit trail, such as Timebox Review Records, are directly related to the work being done in the Timebox and are created at the time, not in retrospect

23. Risk Management

AgilePM®

23.1 Introduction

The main motivation for project risk management is to ensure a successful project outcome and to reap greater benefits by having the confidence that you can manage the risks associated with more creative solutions. Some key benefits are:

- Enabling improved decision-making for this project:
    - regarding the project's Business Case
    - regarding resources needed
    - keeping attention focused where it is needed
- Supporting improved decision-making for future projects and for programmes and portfolios
- Demonstrating and encouraging control and responsibility
- Supporting governance and decision-making for larger or more complex enterprises
- Improving predictability
- Increasing confidence

In addition to risk events (an event or set of circumstances that, should it occur, will have a positive or negative effect on achievement of one or more of the project objectives), the PRAM guide[1] defines Project Risk as also encompassing other sources of uncertainty and offers the following definition:

"Project risk is the exposure of stakeholders to the consequences of variations in outcome"

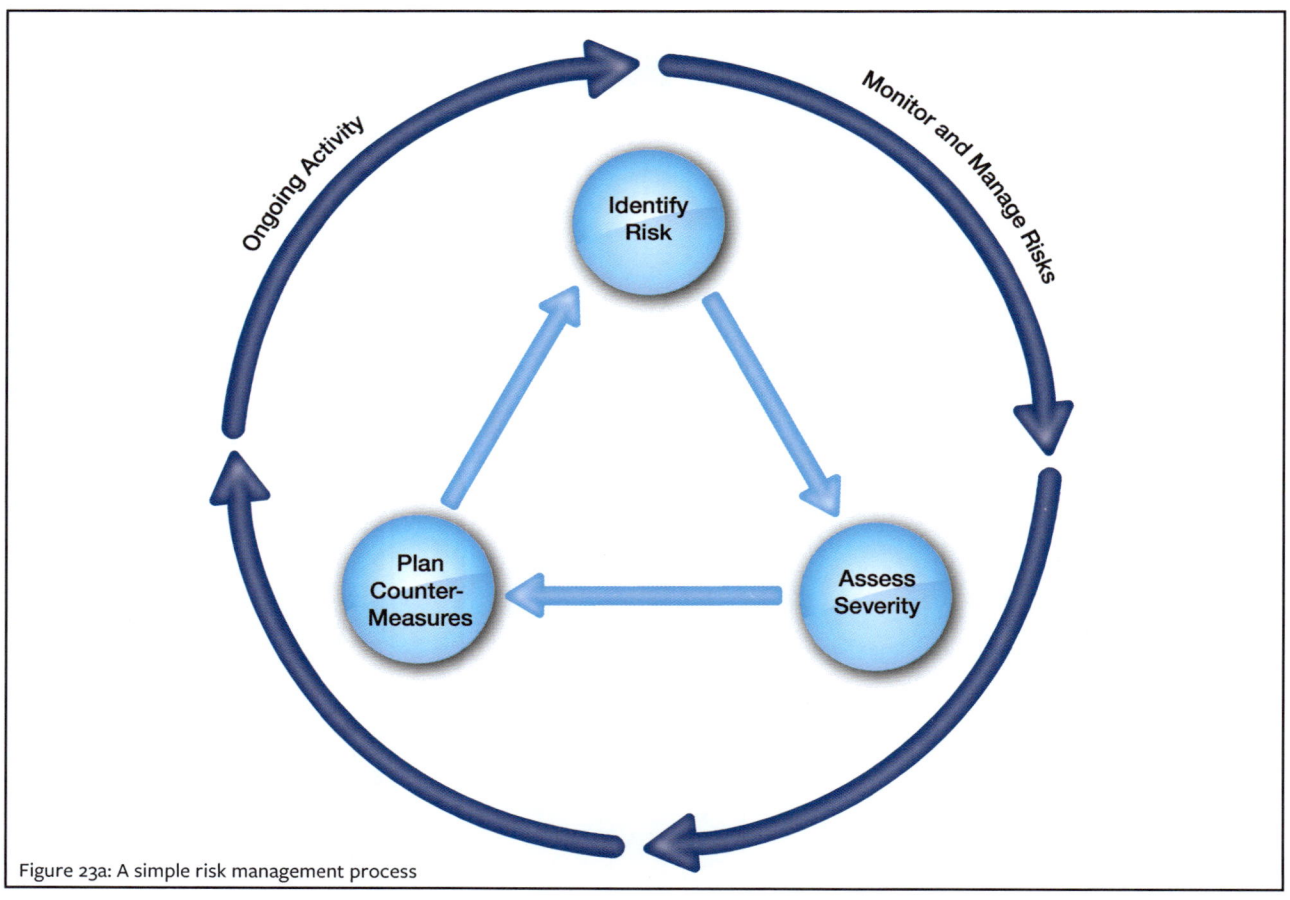

Figure 23a: A simple risk management process

[1] Project Risk Analysis and Management Guide, APM Publishing, 2nd Ed., 2004

Risk Management

The field of risk management is well-established, and its best practice is as important for a DSDM project as it is for any other style of project. Extensive risk guidance is generally available and so is not repeated here.

As with other project management processes, it is important that the tools and techniques chosen for risk management do not impede agility. The generic, iterative risk management process of the following steps fits well with DSDM's Agile Project Management:

- Identify the risks
- Assess the probability (likelihood) and the impact of each risk to determine its severity
- Plan proactive and reactive countermeasures as appropriate for the severity determined
- Monitor and manage the risks appropriately throughout the project

What is considered a risk will be influenced by the style of the approach chosen and the risk appetite of the individuals and the organisation(s) involved: for some, living with high risk is a fact of everyday life, some organisations are extremely risk-averse, but for most, careful risk management enables greater creativity and a higher probability of delivering the benefits.

When running a project, two major risk areas should be considered:

1. Risks to achieving the project objectives (address these according to existing risk management best practice)
2. Risks relating to the approach chosen

For 2 (above), the key areas of DSDM which greatly assist reducing the risk of an unsuccessful DSDM project are assessing, monitoring and managing the ISFs (Instrumental Success Factors), the PAQ (Project Approach Questionnaire and adherence to the Principles (see Chapters 4, 5 and Appendix B). DSDM's early Feasibility phase is where these are initially considered. In Foundations, they are reassessed as the project team work towards using these tools to reduce the risks which threaten the success of the DSDM Project. Key risk areas include:

- levels of business involvement and commitment
- team skills, ability and availability
- clarity of vision without defining detail too early
- maintaining focus on delivering on time by varying the features

Although there is a strong focus on identifying the risks and what to do about them during Feasibility and Foundations, it is critical that risks are managed throughout the project. New risks are likely to arise and those already identified may change. In the key tools mentioned above (the ISFs, the PAQ and the Principles), the prompters point towards aspects of the project which can change rapidly and need to be managed carefully.

Once a DSDM project moves into Evolutionary Development, DSDM naturally allows a cadence of risk management activities within its structure because best practice recommends a consideration of risks for each specific Timebox, as part of the Timebox Kick-Off. At this point, identification of new risks will trigger the risk management process described above. There is also an opportunity here to reassess the severity of risks previously identified and, where necessary, to refine planned countermeasures.

There is often a perception that risk management is solely the responsibility of the Project Manager. However, while the Project Manager is accountable for maximum effectiveness of risk management, individual risks will have named owners, often people performing roles at the project level. All members of the Solution Development Team(s) on a project should be aware of currently identified risks and plans to mitigate them and also be alert to new risks, bringing them to the attention of the Project Manager as appropriate.

Ultimately the risk of the project not delivering as expected is "owned" by the business, since effective operation of their business depends on successful delivery. Therefore it is important that the Business Visionary and Business Sponsor are kept informed about and, where appropriate, take ownership of key risks that they are best placed to manage.

23.2 Project Risk

Major sources of risk for Agile projects are:

- The working environment in terms of enabling individuals to work together effectively
    - To minimise risk in this regard, the working environment must support collaboration and cooperation of team members to the extent required by the agreed approach to building the solution
- The competence and professionalism of individuals involved in the project
    - There is a risk to the project if individuals are unwilling or unable to do the job expected of them to an agreed standard and in an agreed way. Note that this applies as much to those involved on the periphery of the project as it does to those involved day-to-day
- The behaviour and style of those managing the project
    - To mitigate risk, expectations of management (whether senior management from the business or supplier side, or project management) must be realistic and the style of management must align with the capabilities of the team, incorporating appropriate levels of empowerment and control
- The inability to accurately and appropriately describe the business need to those building the solution
    - To mitigate risk, requirements need to reflect the full scope (the breadth) of the project at the outset but without defining the detail too soon (if the project is to be time and cost limited). The requirements need to be expressed at an appropriate level of detail at an appropriate time in the project lifecycle in line with the project approach
- Lack of clarity on overall business vision - resulting in ineffective iteration, wasted work and potential loss of business opportunity
    - To mitigate this, DSDM requires the Business Visionary to bring clarity and consistency of vision to the evolving project at key points and to be significantly involved in guiding the project's direction
- The inability to validate the implementation of requirements as the project proceeds
    - However well it appears that requirements have been expressed, it cannot be assumed that they have been understood. To mitigate risk in this area, it must be assumed that initial interpretation of requirements is likely to be flawed and mechanisms need to be in place to check interpretation as the project proceeds (not just at the end)
- The lack of appropriate contingency to counter such things as imperfect understanding of the business need at the outset, inaccuracies in estimation, staff sickness, extreme weather events, etc.
    - Without contingency, the project is almost certain to be compromised. It is important to understand that time, cost, quality and the scope of features to be delivered cannot all be fixed. Assuming that allowing quality to vary is not an option, in order to protect the agreed time and budget constraints of an Agile project, contingency must be provided in terms of the 'outcome expected' (i.e. allowing for a reduced scope of features to be delivered)
- Inflexible requirements
    - Inflexible requirements present a source of risk in terms of contingency (see above) but also in terms of effective expectation management. With flexibility of the feature set providing the ability to deliver on time and budget, an initial expectation of fixed and detailed requirements often results in disappointment and a sense of failure if some are changed or not delivered
- Change - other types
    - Change to the business need (in particular to scope and timescales), change to the project personnel (swapping people in and out, changing their levels of availability and ability to interact with others etc.) and change to the project environment (physical or technical change and changes to standards and practices) all introduce risk to the project and its outcome

- The project approach, which should be right for the project and followed by the project participants
    - Risk in this area can be mitigated by coaching and mentoring of individuals and teams
- Ineffective monitoring and governance
    - Those with responsibility for effective governance and monitoring should behave with integrity and professionalism and ensure that project processes give the necessary information, when needed in order to meet those responsibilities. 'Filtered' and potentially misleading information provided to those with governance responsibilities and inappropriate responses to such information are both equally significant sources of risk to a successful project

Although not all risks identified in these areas can be managed at the project level, it is recommended to at least consider each of them when assessing risk.

23.3 How DSDM Helps Mitigate Project Risk

The DSDM project approach has been designed to mitigate risk associated with approaches that preceded it:

- The traditional 'Waterfall' approach to development that existed first (where detailed analysis of the business problem, detailed requirements definition, detailed solution design, building the whole solution and lastly acceptance testing define the sequential project lifecycle)
- The RAD approach that emerged later (an effective approach including many of the current Agile concepts but which was often undermined by lack of professional discipline and thus delivered poor quality outcomes)
- Purely solution development focused Agile approaches that have no consideration of the full concept of a project and the associated governance needed by many larger more highly regulated - or at least more highly scrutinised - organisations

The following table shows some typical project risk scenarios and how using DSDM can reduce these risks.

Typical Project Risk Scenario	Why risk is reduced by using the DSDM approach
The business representatives are not sure exactly what they want	It is unusual to be absolutely certain of solution detail in the early stages of the project: being unsure of exactly what is needed is typical. Flexibility in early expectations is desirable for an Agile project since collaboration between the most appropriate members of the business and technical communities enables evolution of the detail from the high-level baseline created during Foundations. DSDM prompts this emerging business understanding, by: - focusing on continuous and clear communication (workshops, modelling, Timeboxing and Iterative Development.) - appointing appropriately skilled business representatives to cover the specific responsibilities of defined Business Roles e.g. - Business Visionary - for clarity of direction and vision throughout the project
- Business Ambassador - for ongoing detailed input
- See chapter 14 for details on these roles and responsibilities

Typical Project Risk Scenario	Why risk is reduced by using the DSDM approach
Uncertainty in the business or a volatile marketplace is causing the business representatives to change their minds	DSDM sees change as a fact of life and embraces an appropriate level of change to positively harness its power. The team ensures the solution is correct at the point of delivery and it works the way the business needs it to work. Since there is no detailed, signed-off specification at the start and because the lowest level of detail is agreed only at the last responsible moment, many 'changes' do not actually affect the project at all
	Change is often encompassed within Timeboxes and focused with MoSCoW prioritisation. The cadence of Timeboxes and Iterative Development aligns with the cadence of managing lower level risks. It is important that any risks identified at the lower (Timebox) level which also pose a risk to higher levels (e.g. project) are escalated to the Project Manager and possibly higher e.g. Programme, Portfolio or organisation level
	The boundaries of what can be changed informally should be agreed in the early phases of the project. Therefore everyone is clear what they are empowered to change and what they are not. Where a significant change is suggested, e.g. introducing additional Must Have requirements that alter the balance of Must Have effort or widening the scope of the project, the impact of this change poses significant risk to the success of the project. For this reason, major change needs to be escalated to the project-level roles for discussion. Ultimately it can only proceed with the approval of the Business Visionary (and possibly Business Sponsor, if the Business Case is impacted). Such significant changes are usually managed through more formal change control
	As things become clearer, further opportunities may surface, which can be exploited by the project, since a DSDM project is not formally bound by a rigid specification which was signed off some time ago. Also addressing detail only when necessary may save resources if business circumstances necessitate project closure prior to delivery
	In terms of risk, in addition to looking for what might go wrong, it is worth checking if there is the opportunity within the uncertainty to take some actions to achieve greater results
Not having all the detail agreed at the start, (particularly regarding requirements and design)	In addition to the points made earlier in this table, DSDM's principle of 'Build Incrementally from Firm Foundations' applies. The firm but high-level foundations for the project are laid in the Foundations phase. These include technical and business areas ensuring Enough Design Up Front (EDUF) to allow the project to move safely forward
Unwillingness to commit to final sign-off	DSDM defines roles and responsibilities, including business roles. All roles are involved throughout the project. Using Development Timeboxes and the associated testing and reviews, both the technical and business representatives accept the Evolving Solution incrementally. Therefore achieving final sign-off poses a lower risk, since this is simply the final step in a gradual process

Risk Management

Typical Project Risk Scenario	Why risk is reduced by using the DSDM approach
Not positioning projects for a successful outcome	The overall project approach should be suited to the type of project and the organisation in which it is to run. It is also advisable to consider tailoring of the approach to properly align it with project-specific circumstances
	DSDM defines Instrumental Success Factors - the elements needed to ensure a DSDM project is positioned for success. Once these have been considered, the Project Approach Questionnaire identifies potential risks to successful DSDM, so that the appropriate action can be taken right from the start during Feasibility and Foundations Key considerations are: • Acceptance of the DSDM approach • Strong business ownership, commitment and direction • the level of maturity and skills the teams have in using DSDM. Teams with little or no experience of DSDM may significantly increase the likelihood of success with some level of training and coaching support • A supportive environment (technical, business and organisational)
Schedule risk (e.g. late delivery, budget overruns etc.)	DSDM's whole approach is designed to deliver the right solution on time. Therefore for a DSDM project, having a fixed deadline is seen as a benefit, rather than a risk. A fixed and immovable deadline encourages everyone to stay focused on what is truly important: focusing on the business need and delivering on time
	Contingency, in the form of MoSCoWed features ensures the deadline remains achievable
	DSDM helps manage schedule risk by having frequent reviews with the appropriate stakeholders through Timeboxing. This enables corrective feedback which does not disturb the flow of the project
	DSDM also recommends a similar approach to cost management: as with fixed deadlines, Timeboxing and MoSCoW prioritisation are used for focus once the financial model has been defined in the early stages

23.4 Risks To Be Considered When Using DSDM

The table above illustrates that successful DSDM relies on certain practices which, if missing or misused, can introduce risks. DSDM also assumes a default set of behaviours and discipline and professionalism from project participants.

Risks to DSDM should be assessed in the early phases of the project and monitored throughout. DSDM's Project Approach Questionnaire (PAQ) supports risk identification through a series of questions which assess how the DSDM Principles will be applied, and whether the Instrumental Success Factors (ISFs) are in place. Typically this is completed by the project-level roles before the end of Feasibility and then reassessed immediately before the end of Foundations. The PAQ enables project teams to work on the areas highlighted during Foundations to improve the environment for a successful DSDM project.

See Chapter 24 on tailoring the DSDM approach for more detail regarding risks to successful DSDM and suggested actions to mitigate these risks.

It is usually appropriate to run a Risk Analysis workshop early on in the project. In addition, the same technique can be used at any appropriate time, such as the beginning of a Timebox where iterative risk management can support Iterative Development and at the points where significant change is proposed to better understand the implications of that change.

23.5 Summary

Choosing the right approach is a key factor in reducing project risks. DSDM directly addresses many of the common risks for projects, including the most frequently cited ones of missing fixed deadlines (a major business concern) or having unclear or volatile requirements (perceived as a problem when developing a solution). Using DSDM ensures on-time delivery of a fit-for-purpose solution. DSDM's Project Approach Questionnaire provides an effective starting point for creating a clear, shared understanding of project risks and their mitigation. It also helps highlight where the DSDM approach should be scaled (up or down) and where tailoring is appropriate, to gain the maximum benefit from using DSDM.

Risk - Agile Project Manager Top Tips

- Use the Project Approach Questionnaire (PAQ) to identify risks to the DSDM process
- Ensure the PAQ is completed collaboratively, as a minimum with the Business Visionary and the Technical Coordinator
- Ensure the answers given are realistic, and not overly optimistic or pessimistic
- Monitor behaviours to ensure they are in accordance with the DSDM Principles. Breaking any of the Principles poses significant risk to the success of a DSDM project
- Ensure the whole team is aware of the key risks - make them visible (perhaps on the team wall). In DSDM, risks affect everyone and should not just be seen as a Project Manager's concern
- At the Timebox Kick-Off meeting, highlight any risks that are particularly relevant to this Timebox and consider handing ownership of the relevant risks to the Team Leader for the duration of the Timebox
- Encourage Solution Development Teams to consider risks at planning and review sessions
- At the end of a Timebox (maybe formally in the Timebox Close-Out session), consider taking ownership of new and outstanding risks back to the project-level roles

24. Tailoring the DSDM Approach

24.1 Introduction

This chapter is drawn from the experiences of practicing DSDM consultants. It describes some typical ways that DSDM has been adapted or tailored to meet circumstances that they have encountered. Hence each of the suggested actions is tried and tested but not necessarily to the same extent or with the same rigour as the rest of DSDM as described in this handbook.

This chapter is also closely linked to the Risk Chapter.

24.2 The Project Approach Questionnaire (PAQ)

The Project Approach Questionnaire is used to identify areas where a project or its environment is not ideally suited to the DSDM approach. It can be used to negotiate changes to reduce risk and to improve the probability of success. Where changes cannot readily or quickly be made or if too much change would be required to be accommodated at once, the PAQ can be a useful guide to the tailoring of DSDM to suit individual project needs. If, on collaborative completion of the PAQ, everybody either Strongly Agrees or Agrees with every statement, then the risk associated with using DSDM to manage the project is low. Tailoring is probably not required and DSDM as described in Section 1 of this handbook should work effectively.

Disagreement with any of the PAQ statements poses a risk to DSDM. In some cases, simple corrective action is all that is required to deal with the risk. In other cases, the risk raised may not be as easy to resolve and, in this circumstance, trying to use DSDM without an element of tailoring may introduce additional risk.

In the following section, each of the statements in the PAQ and their importance to the success of the approach are explained. Where appropriate, hints and tips are provided to help resolve issues raised by disagreement with that statement.

There have been many examples of special configurations of DSDM, often created for blue-chip companies. Some of these are published as case studies. Ways of dealing with new challenges will be made available as part of the growing number of case studies available at www.agilebusiness.org

It should be noted that tailoring options may be interim solutions, to avoid imposing too much change for the team at one time. At a later stage, it may be possible to deal with the initial problem so that tailored elements can be better realigned to DSDM.

One final point to note is that some risks or issues raised through the use of the DSDM PAQ may actually have a root cause that has nothing to do with the approach.

For example:

Statement 3: *"The business vision is clearly stated and understood by all members of the project team"*

If the consensus is that the business vision is not clear and/or not understood, arranging a session for the Business Visionary to share his/her vision and answer any questions mitigates the risk of evolving a solution that is not aligned with the business vision

---

For example:

Statement 5: *"The requirements can be prioritised and there is confidence that date and cost commitments can be met by flexing the scope of what is delivered"*

If the consensus is that a very high proportion (or all) of the requirements are genuinely "Must Have" - according to the MoSCoW rules - the DSDM approach will need significant adaptation to cope with something that contradicts a fundamental underpinning of the way it was designed to work

---

> *For example:*
>
> *Statement 12: "The Solution Development Team members have the appropriate collective knowledge and skills to collaboratively evolve an optimal business solution"*
>
> *If the team doesn't have the skills required to build the solution, then regardless of what approach is chosen, the solution is highly unlikely to be built successfully*

24.2.1 The Project Approach Questionnaire Statements

Statement 1

"All members of the project understand and accept the DSDM approach (Philosophy, Principles and Practices)"

If the consensus response disagrees with this statement, it is probably because some stakeholders have not been trained (if they are participants) or briefed (if they are less actively involved). It is important that the project team fully understand the implications of this statement: this means everyone performing project-level and Solution Development Team roles. Occasionally, stakeholders who are fully informed about the DSDM approach still disagree with it, but this is extremely rare. The impact of this disagreement and any action to be taken will depend very much on the power and influence of that stakeholder.

Suggested action
Organise training and briefings as required. Consider using DSDM Accredited Training Organisations or experienced DSDM practitioners certified to Advanced Practitioner level or above to assist where necessary.

Statement 2

"The Business Sponsor and the Business Visionary demonstrate clear and proactive ownership of the project"

Senior business ownership of any project is essential. Without this, a project is likely to be starved of essential business resources (day-to-day jobs being deemed more important by default). This results in major issues that can't be dealt with by the project team remaining unresolved. Such unresolved issues either cause a project to stall or leave it exposed to high-risk assumptions or workarounds. A committed Business Sponsor who really cares about the project is almost always willing and able to push for significant issues to be resolved where senior management action is needed.

The Business Visionary is responsible for making sure that all parts of the business impacted by the business vision understand and buy in to the vision and remain aligned with it. Managing business stakeholder expectation on a proactive and ongoing basis is key to the success of projects with a wide business impact.

Suggested action
There really is no workaround for a weakness in business ownership and vision. If all negotiation and coaching efforts to actively engage at least the Business Visionary fail (i.e. if these critical roles simply refuse to engage in their project), the only technique to be applied here is necessarily harsh, and that is to refuse to start work on that project until the issue is addressed and, instead, to work on a project that does attract the right business ownership and commitment to success. Commercial and political considerations are likely to dictate whether putting a project on hold due to lack of ownership is a realistic option. However, for projects where the organisation responsible for building the solution and the sponsoring organisation belong to the same company, the argument of "the greater good of the company as a whole" may carry some weight.

With regard to managing business stakeholder expectation, a strategy for communication that the Business Visionary believes will meet the need and is happy to play an active part in, should be considered as part of the Management Approach agreed during Foundations and enacted as the project proceeds. Stakeholders should also be invited to attend demonstrations of the Solution Increments at the end of each Timebox where this helps manage their expectations. (See Statement 16)

Statement 3

> *"The business vision driving the project is clearly stated and understood by all members of the project team"*

All day-to-day project decisions at all levels in the project should be checked against the business vision. Even if the decision seems small or insignificant simply considering:

> *"Does this help move us closer to achieving the business vision?"*

often avoids wasting precious time and effort. If the answer is "Yes, it helps" then the decision is valid. If it is "no" or "not sure" then a follow up question of "So why are we doing this here and now?" should be asked. For anything likely to take up more than a couple of hours, it is always advisable to quickly consult an appropriate business or technical authority to understand why this is needed. Without a clear statement and common understanding of the business vision the thought/ questioning process cannot happen and there is serious risk that time and effort will be wasted working on things with limited or peripheral value.

Suggested action

Speak to the Business Visionary, or arrange a session for him/her to share their vision with the team and with other stakeholders and answer any questions. This should be all that is needed to set the scene for the thought and decision-making described above. It is an explicit responsibility of the Business Visionary to "communicate and promote the business vision to all interested and/or impacted parties" and to ensure that the project remains aligned to it by "monitoring progress of the project in line with the business vision". Consider creating a simple poster to place above the Team Board to help keep the vision visible to all.

Statement 4

> *"All project participants understand and accept that on-time delivery of an acceptable solution is the primary measure of success for the project"*

There are two key considerations associated with this statement.

The first consideration relates to the business driver behind the project and the importance from a business perspective of on-time delivery. Most businesses under most circumstances want to understand at the outset what a project is going to cost and how long it is going to take. These are very reasonable demands as the cost and the date that benefits will start to accrue have a direct impact on the Business Case for the project. Overrunning budget and, particularly, time, to any significant degree could seriously damage the Business Case or even the business as a whole if a critical deadline is missed.

The second consideration relates to the control of the project. Even if the first consideration is not important, working to a genuinely fixed end date for a project, or at least for a Project Increment, provides an anchor for the combined practices of MoSCoW Prioritisation and Timeboxing which form the primary mechanism of control over timely delivery of the solution. It also keeps the Iterative Development practice properly focused on the business need by discouraging a desire for perfection through iterations with progressively diminishing business value.

Suggested action

Even if there is no hard business deadline for delivery of the solution, it is usually better to plan and resource a project on the assumption that there is. Without a delivery target that everybody buys into, the project risks losing focus and running out of control. A good question to ask if there is no specific deadline date is 'what would be the impact of delivering this project/

increment by date x?' and keep repeating with different dates. Sometimes there will be a significant impact with a certain date chosen, that perhaps was not immediately obvious.

Statement 5

"The requirements can be prioritised and there is confidence that cost and time commitments can be met by flexing the scope of what is delivered"

This statement is closely related to Statement 4, as it is the ability to flex the scope of what is delivered that allows a DSDM project to guarantee an on-time delivery.

Every effort should be made to follow the MoSCoW rules for prioritisation of requirements but it is worth remembering that even if the top-level requirements (that make up the Prioritised Requirements List baselined in the Foundations phase of the project) suggest the rules are being broken, it is possible that flexibility exists in the detail of those requirements.

> *For example:*
>
> *A Must Have requirement to "manage an appointment diary" is likely to break down into sub-requirements to "make", "change" and "cancel" appointments. At this lower level, it is likely that the ability to make and cancel appointments would be Must Have whereas the ability to change an appointment would have a lower priority as there is an obvious workaround (cancelling the original appointment and making a new one).*

Suggested action

If all efforts to find sufficient contingency in the scope of the requirements fail, consider adding more "traditional"-style contingency based around time and cost. In practical terms, this would involve:

1. Creating one or more 'contingency Timeboxes' that are added to the end of the project

    The *committed* timescale for the project includes the contingency but the Delivery Plan should clearly reflect an earlier target delivery date that does not include the contingency

2. Managing the project in the normal DSDM way once development starts

However, instead of de-scoping the least important requirement to protect the *target* delivery date if that becomes necessary, the requirement is pushed out to the first available contingency Timebox

If using this tailoring suggestion, everybody's focus must remain on the end date and this target end-date must be treated as if it were the real delivery date. Without this focus, the attitude of "It doesn't matter too much because we can always put it in the contingency Timebox" risks the contingency being used up too quickly and carelessly. Again, asking the question about the impact (particularly business impact) of the later delivery date can help to focus on the target date.

Statement 6

"All members of the project team accept that requirements should only be defined at a high level in the early phases of the project and that detail will emerge as development progresses"

Defining detail too early in a project causes more problems than it is intended to solve. All Agile approaches exploit the concept of emerging detail to allow the best solution to evolve. Discussion of detail of a high-level requirement may help confirm an understanding of that requirement and help estimate the effort to fulfil it. However, it will also provide a false sense of security as the majority of change to requirements in a project happens in the detail. The reality is that detail defined too far in advance risks being inaccurate when the work on the detail is due to start. This inaccuracy may be as a result of a subtle shift in business need. It may be due to a deepening understanding of what is or is not possible, based on what has happened up to this point. It may be due to earlier assumptions proving to be untrue. For this reason, DSDM advocates deferring detailed investigation and detailed decisions to the last responsible moment.

Suggested action

Hold early discussions at whatever level of detail is needed to help drive out a shared understanding but do not capture that detail. Have the discussion again closer to the time. Subsequent discussions will probably be shorter as people refresh their memories of what was discussed previously. But these also offer an opportunity to change that detail without being constrained by what was previously assumed or wasting time having to formally change what was previously formally, and pointlessly, defined and agreed.

Statement 7

> *"All members of the project team accept that change in requirements is inevitable and that it is only by embracing change that the right solution will be delivered"*

The DSDM philosophy that "best business value emerges when projects are aligned to clear business goals, deliver frequently and involve the collaboration of motivated and empowered people" underpins the validity and importance of this statement. It is important to ensure that the project remains focused on the fundamental need and business vision that justified the investment in it. However, beyond that, the project team needs to embrace any change needed to deliver optimum business value within constraints of fixed timescales and cost. "What we thought we were going to do" is irrelevant when considered in the light of "what we need to do now to build a valuable solution".

Suggested action

If commercial arrangements dictate that a 'fixed price for a fixed specification' model should be applied to the project rather than a more collaborative approach, it is important to recognise that, at the working level, this will not be a DSDM project. Under such circumstances, all that can be done is to segment the project into small deliverable chunks and to ensure the supplier is focused on, and is paid to deliver, only what is specified in each chunk. The specification of detail for any given chunk should be left to the last responsible moment and should be informed by what has already been delivered together with the very latest thinking on what is needed. The later chunks in the project should reflect the least valuable features of the product being built by the supplier. Arrangements with the supplier(s) should allow for any changes that may be needed to the product they have built 'to specification' in an early chunk to be traded off against later work. This will, at least, force a change-tolerant incremental approach that will help mitigate the risk of losing control of timescales and/or costs.

Statement 8

> *"The Business Sponsor and Business Visionary understand that active business involvement is essential and have the willingness and authority to commit appropriate business resources to the project"*

In a DSDM project, there is no detailed specification upfront (compared with a traditional project approach where a detailed specification is created by contributions from many business representatives). On a DSDM project, without ongoing guidance from the business roles to explain the current business need, those developing the solution can only guess at the detail of what is needed and this would result in a significant risk of delivering a solution that does not meet the business need. In DSDM, active business involvement means that business roles (Business Ambassadors and Business Advisors) must be involved throughout the project, often on a day-to-day basis, sufficient to:

1. Provide detailed guidance on the meaning of requirements
2. Understand team plans for the Evolving Solution
3. Provide feedback on each step towards delivering a fit-for-purpose solution, acknowledging what is right and explaining what is not

Involvement of Business Ambassadors and Advisors at the time detail is needed cannot be negotiated away, but there is room to negotiate on how much involvement might be needed and the frequency and form that might take is discussed under the next statement (Statement 9).

Suggested action

The first and best course of action is to try to secure the necessary Business Ambassador and Advisor time. It is helpful to agree up front the amount of time and the level of commitment expected, at least for the Business Ambassador. This helps inform the business about the level of commitment that is expected and tests that commitment.

> *One example:*
>
> *During Evolutionary Development, Business Ambassador to:*
>
> - *Attend Daily Stand-ups (15 minutes) every day whenever possible.*
> - *Be available at 9.30 each morning on phone to answer questions (maximum 20 minutes).*
> - *Be available 2-3 days every 2 weeks to attend (in person or on webinar) Timebox events (Kick-Off, Close-Out, Reviews)*

It's important to stress that projects cost money and the single biggest cost is usually paying for the time of the people engaged in building the solution. Business resources are critical to the success of the project and should be budgeted for in exactly the same way as the other members of the Solution Development Team. This means that the Business Sponsor may need to pay for somebody to carry out some of the day-to-day responsibilities of a Business Ambassador in order to give them the time they need to spend on this project. It is normally the case that the best person to take on the Business Ambassador role - the main day-to-day business decision-maker on the project - is someone who is very valuable to the business area concerned. This means that negotiating commitment of their time needs careful planning and advance preparation. The answer often lies in other members of the business area picking up key responsibilities whilst handing off responsibilities most easily delegated to somebody more junior. Some businesses choose to delegate simple but time-consuming tasks to a temporary staff member, hired only for the duration of the project but treated as part of the project cost.

If it is genuinely not possible to allocate business resources to work collaboratively with the rest of the Solution Development Team on an ongoing basis, then it may be worth considering the approach described in the "Specification-led DSDM projects" tailoring white paper available at www.agilebusiness.org

Statement 9

"It is possible for business and solution development members of the Solution Development Team to work collaboratively throughout the project"

Statement 8 dealt with business roles being allocated and available to the project as needed to guide the detailed development of the solution. This statement addresses the issue of those roles, and the rest of the Solution Development Team, being able to work in a collaborative way.

With regard to business engagement in the Iterative Development process, it would be ideal if the business roles were ready, willing and able to engage in face-to-face conversation with the technical solution development roles immediately and whenever their guidance is needed. This 'instant access' would optimise the efficiency and effectiveness of the Iterative Development practice, by minimising the risk of evolving the solution in the wrong way and having to rework it to make it right. However, such access is rarely achieved and, in reality, may not represent effective use of business resources, as it implies they must be co-located with the rest of the team and do little more than sit and wait to be engaged in development or testing activity. There is also a risk that by being removed from their business colleagues, the Business Ambassador may lose touch with day-to-day happenings in their business area. While some exceptional projects do require a full-time Business Ambassador commitment, the majority of projects require active involvement for a maximum of 50% of their time, and usually it is significantly less than 50%. The amount of Business Ambassador time should, therefore, be agreed on a project-by-project basis.

What is actually needed is reasonable access throughout the day. This may be perhaps face-to-face (or by telephone or on video conference) at the Daily Stand-up and for a short period afterwards with availability on the telephone for the rest of the day. On occasional days in a month, more intense collaborative activity may be needed, for example in workshops to discuss the detail of requirements towards the beginning of a Timebox or to carry out end-to-end business acceptance testing (allowing for iterative issue resolution) towards the end of a Timebox.

With regard to collaborative working, more generally, it is important that all roles are able to work collaboratively on the Evolving Solution. It is important to ensure that the working environment can support this - ideally by allowing team members to be co-located in the workplace and in less ideal circumstances by providing technology to simulate this.

Suggested action
If access to business resources presents a challenge in terms of time, e.g. where a Business Ambassador is available for a limited number of hours a week, try to formalise the structure of the Timebox so that intense engagement during the Investigation and perhaps Consolidation steps can be planned. Also agree a short period in each day, ideally around the Daily Stand-up, when Solution Developers and Testers can interact with the Business Ambassador.

If access to business resources presents a challenge in terms of geography, e.g. where business resources are in a different building, town, country or even continent, then technology to assist in collaboration will be needed. Video and teleconference facilities are an obvious place to start but other tools are available to help with collaborative working, such as collaborative modelling tools or a virtual Team Board that all can see and interact with.

In extreme, but not uncommon, circumstances - for example when working across time-zones more than 4 hours apart, special tailoring of roles and responsibilities to deal with communication may be required. The case study on "DSDM projects with off-shore development" is available as a tailoring white paper from www.agilebusiness.org

Statement 10

> *"Empowerment of all members of the Solution Development Team is appropriate and sufficient to support the day-to-day decision-making needed to rapidly evolve the solution in short, focused Timeboxes"*

A framework of empowerment underpins the DSDM way of working. It is important that members of the Solution Development Team have the knowledge and experience necessary to make day-to-day decisions about how the Solution should evolve and that they are empowered to do so. If members of the team have to keep referring out to 'higher authorities' to make or approve such decisions, the efficiency of the Iterative Development practice will decrease, the effectiveness of Timeboxing will be seriously compromised and the promise to *Deliver on Time* will be put at risk.

Suggested action
There is no effective workaround for disagreement on this statement. A way must be found to establish a framework of empowerment even if this takes some time to achieve. The 'higher authorities' will need to engage more actively in the project in the first instance with the intention of gradually handing decision-making power to the team as they gain competence and confidence to assume that responsibility.

Statement 11

> *"The DSDM roles and responsibilities are appropriately allocated and all role holders understand and accept the responsibilities associated with their role"*

DSDM has carefully defined roles and responsibilities. One person may hold more than one role and one role may be shared between more than one person. It is useful to use DSDM role names and descriptions, particularly with business roles, as the title re-enforces their main responsibility. When agreeing people for roles it is important to review the responsibilities associated with that role and the skills required, in order to get the best fit.

Suggested action

Formal training in DSDM is recommended for all roles. Those people actively working on the project on a day-to-day basis, typically the Project Manager and all members of the Solution Development Team, should attend a DSDM Practitioner course. Roles less actively engaged should attend a DSDM Foundation course. Both training courses explain to each individual the responsibilities of their role in the context of the other roles and the DSDM approach to the project. It is also important to ensure the person in the role understands and is comfortable with what is expected of them on a project-by-project basis.

In some cases, it may be sensible to transfer one or more responsibilities from one role to another to help achieve a good fit of responsibilities to a given individual.

> *For example:*
>
> *If the best person to fulfil the majority of the Business Visionary responsibilities is more junior in the organisation than would normally be expected, it may be appropriate to transfer responsibilities such as "owning the wider implications of any business change from an organisational and business process perspective" and "ensuring business resources are available to the project as needed" to the Business Sponsor.*

Under certain circumstances it may be appropriate for one person to hold more than one role. For example, in a smaller project it might be appropriate for the Business Visionary and Business Ambassador roles to be held by the same person. Sometimes, the person holding the Technical Coordinator role will play a more 'hands on' role in developing the solution - in which case the individual concerned may also be a Solution Developer.

A DSDM coach - somebody with real practical experience of using DSDM in a variety of circumstances - can help with agreeing the best people for the roles and helping individuals understand and properly fulfil their roles, and tailoring the roles as required.

Statement 12

"The Solution Development Team has the appropriate collective knowledge and skills (soft skills and technical skills) to collaboratively evolve an optimal business solution"

DSDM works best in circumstances where all team members are experienced and empowered to shape the solution and where they have the necessary soft skills to communicate and negotiate effectively with their teammates. Ideally, solution roles will be technically multi-skilled - willing and able to work across all solution development disciplines (analysis, design, build and test). A key characteristic of an effective collaborative team stems from the ability and willingness of team members to support each other.

Suggested action

With regard to technical skills, at the project level there are no general workaround options to suggest, except to "make the best of what you have". However in some circumstances bringing in a specialist contractor with additional responsibility for skills transfer as well as getting the work done may prove a valuable option. Where work can only be done by a single individual, try to ensure it is broken down to a level where something tangible can comfortably be delivered in a Timebox. For example, avoid putting a single 10 man-day task into a 10 working day Timebox.

At the organisation level, if DSDM (or any other Agile approach) is being adopted as the default way of working on projects, effort should be made to invest in people; through training and time for personal growth, encourage project workers to become more multi-skilled over time. The value of training and coaching soft skills where these are weak also represents an excellent investment in people because, as well as being essential in an Agile project team context, these skills can be valuably applied much more widely.

Statement 13

"Solution Development Team members are allocated to the project at an appropriate and consistent level sufficient to fully support the DSDM Timeboxing practice"

By default, DSDM assumes that the Solution Developers and Solution Testers are allocated full time to a project at least for the duration of a Project Increment. Where individuals are not full time on a project, it is assumed that the work of the project is always their top priority. Where the Solution Development Team is made up of part-time individuals for whom other work takes priority, it is very difficult to make the Timeboxing practice work.

Suggested action

Where resources are only available part-time, first try to secure formal agreements as to how many hours per day, per week or per Timebox they will spend on the project. Ideally agree specific times, e.g. 9:00am to 12:30pm Monday through to Thursday. Where multiple team members are part-time, try to synchronise agreements in order to allow team members to work collaboratively.

Agree objectives and schedule the work in Timeboxes to match availability of resources: be careful not to overcommit, especially in circumstances when availability may be unpredictable. In cases where resource availability is very unpredictable, do not commit to a delivery date, just agree to try to meet a target. If this is unacceptable to the Business Sponsor, make it their problem to negotiate a more appropriate resource profile; perhaps by using contract resources.

Try to make the work as granular as possible: the smaller each piece of work, the more likely it will get finished within the boundaries of the Timebox. Avoid the temptation to make the Timeboxes longer as this dilutes what little focus on delivery there is.

Statement 14

"Tools and collaborative working practices within the Solution Development Team are sufficient to allow effective Iterative Development of the solution"

Collaboration and empowerment underpin DSDM's Iterative Development and Timeboxing practices.

Suggested action
Whenever appropriate, face-to-face communication should be encouraged at all levels. The supporting practices of Facilitated Workshops and Modelling play a significant part in making this effective.

Where teams are not co-located the suggestion offered for Statement 9 applies, i.e. using technology to assist in collaboration, and considering additional roles to focus on communication.

Statement 15

"All necessary review and testing activity is fully integrated within the Iterative Development practice"

The rationale for this statement is comprehensively covered in Chapters 9 (Planning and Control) and 12 (Iterative Development). The essence of the guidance provided is to start thinking about how the solution will be tested as early in the lifecycle as possible and defining and executing a strategy for testing that gets as close as possible to delivering fully tested Solution Increments at the end of every Timebox.

Suggested action
Where fully integrated testing cannot be achieved - perhaps due to challenges of integrating the outputs of two or more

Tailoring the DSDM Approach

Solution Development Teams or where testing is carried out by a separate off-shore team - it may be sensible to set up a parallel stream, ideally made up of dedicated resources, focused on testing and fixing any defects that may emerge as a result of that testing. Timeboxes in the testing stream would be offset from those in the main development stream so that the output of the Development Timeboxes that have just finished would be the input for a testing Timebox that is just about to start. As much testing as possible should still be carried out by the original development teams and the Technical Coordinator will need to be actively engaged to ensure that solution and test design across teams is compatible. This should lower the risk of significant rework emerging from defects discovered by the integration/testing team.

Statement 16

"Project progress is measured primarily through the incremental, demonstrable delivery of business value"

The primary output of each Timebox should be a demonstrable increment of the Evolving Solution. Every effort should be made to ensure that this is the case. If it is, then measurement of progress is both easy and fully transparent with all interested stakeholders able to see tangible progress as a result of the work of the Timebox.

The demonstration of the Solution Increment at the end of a Timebox is an excellent way of keeping all stakeholders informed of progress and provides them with a real opportunity to understand in detail how they will be impacted by the solution once it has been deployed.

Suggested action

In most cases, if Solution Increments cannot be demonstrated, it is as a result of a poor strategy for Iterative Development or poor application of the Timeboxing practice.

In the rare circumstances where it is genuinely not possible to deliver a demonstrable Solution Increment, think about what can be demonstrated. It is vitally important that all stakeholders have confidence that the project is moving towards a successful conclusion and is on track to deliver a valuable solution in the timeframe and for the budget agreed. Do whatever is necessary (within reason) to achieve this.

> *For example:*
>
> *An early Timebox was proving the ability to communicate with a new customer located several hundred miles away, so that financial transactions could be transmitted in a subsequent Timebox. The early Timebox transmitted a simple "Hello" message which was then printed at the remote site, as proof that the communication channel was now in existence.*

Consider making the demonstrations at the end of each Timebox open to anybody who is interested in what is happening in the project and, where appropriate, use it as a way of helping keep stakeholders on board.

Statement 17

"There are no mandatory standards or other constraints in force that prevent the application of the DSDM Philosophy and Practices on this project"

This can relate to internal mandatory standards, external (regulatory) standards or commercial arrangements.

Internal standards: These often cause problems in the early adoption of DSDM or of Agile practices in an organisation, where there is an assumption that a linear process will be followed, supported by specific documents

External (regulatory) standards: Although there should be no conflict between an external regulatory standard and DSDM, in reality there will usually be an additional overhead on a DSDM project in terms of governance and proof of compliance.

Commercial arrangements: Many organisations assume that the "fixed price for a fixed specification" model is the best foundation for a commercial agreement as it appears to transfer the risks associated with the project to the supplier organisation. For many projects, this transfer of risk is an illusion as all of the risks and issues associated with the traditional Waterfall way of working - which the DSDM approach was designed to address - are actually exaggerated by this commercial framework. Whilst it is true that there may be somebody to pursue for compensation when a project goes wrong, such litigation is extremely rare as 'blame' for failure can rarely be put exclusively on one party to the agreement. The end result is still that the business "loses", since it has lost time and still does not have a viable business solution to the problem.

Suggested action

Compliance with standards: Actively engage the Quality group that own and audit these standards in order to understand the reasoning behind them and to open discussions about how DSDM may provide the necessary answers while using a different approach. It is important to understand where there may be options, and where no compromise is possible.

Commercial arrangements: Consider the DSDM Principles, Practices, Roles and Responsibilities. If any of these are seriously undermined by commercial agreements, then the DSDM approach may not be the best approach to use for the project. Whilst the 'fixed price for a fixed specification' model for project is flawed, it is well understood, and trying to force DSDM to work under the restrictions imposed by it are likely to make the project even more risky than it would otherwise be. For many organisations, the procurement team are only set up to deal with a traditional style contract, and simply do not have the mindset or the willingness to take on the risk associated with a different style of contractual relationship, even where it should directly benefit the organisation.

At time of first printing of this handbook in 2014, work has been going on for some time to evolve an effective Agile UK contract framework but this is a work in progress. Work has also been done in Denmark to create a contractual framework entirely based on a DSDM approach. Check www.agilebusiness.org for resources and links to other sources for contractual models available that suit your project.

24.3 Summary

DSDM is a flexible framework for building and delivering business solutions. The advice above describes ways of tailoring DSDM to overcome issues where the project or the environment in which it exists is not ideally suited to the Agile (empowered, collaborative, iterative, incremental) way of working. In the majority of cases where issues are identified, what is really needed is a change of mindset of those involved rather than a customisation of the project approach. The full value that can be gained from using DSDM will not be achieved if too many compromises are made so every effort to get buy-in to the approach, with all that that entails in terms of working practice, should be exhausted before starting to adapt it.

Tailoring - Agile Project Manager Top Tips

- Always ensure the PAQ is completed collaboratively, as a minimum with the Business Visionary and the Technical Coordinator, as well as the Project Manager
- When completing the PAQ, encourage everyone to be realistic, rather than overly optimistic or overly pessimistic Ensure the PAQ is completed initially towards the end of Feasibility (where Feasibility takes place) and then follow up with the mitigation actions. Reassess the PAQ with the same people towards the end of Foundations, to see how (or if) the situation has improved.
- Keep an eye on the PAQ throughout the project. If any of the statements looks as though it is starting to become false, take immediate remedial action. Tailoring the method after Foundations is possible but a severe risk to project success.
- Use the PAQ to drive appropriate tailoring of the DSDM approach, which should be documented in the Management Approach Definition (MAD).
    - It is the responsibility of the Project Manager to ensure the risks to the effective use of DSDM are assessed in the early phases of the project, and that appropriate action is planned and any necessary tailoring of the approach is implemented.
    - Although the PM is ultimately responsible for getting the PAQ completed, it is always a collaborative activity involving other project-level roles.
    - Consider how the use of DSDM will integrate with existing methods in use in the organisation. Information on the integration of DSDM and PRINCE2 and DSDM (AgilePM) with Scrum is available at www.agilebusiness.org
    - Where team training is DSDM is needed, consider organising this as a team event. It helps build relationships and usually allows the training to consider any specific project issues relating to DSDM.
    - Although the PAQ is formally considered at Feasibility and Foundations, the PM should continue to assess whether the Instrumental Success Factors (ISFs) are still being met. Behaviours change since early enthusiasm for "doing the right thing in the right way" sometimes lessens over time. It is usually the case that a timely reminder of best practice (the ISF) is sufficient.

AgilePM®

Appendix A
Glossary

AgilePM

Term	Abbreviation	Detail
80:20 rule		A rule of thumb stating that 80% of consequences stem from 20% of causes. Also known as the Pareto Principle; it advocates pragmatism on a DSDM project. The value of the Pareto Principle is that it reminds you to focus on the 20% that matters.
Agile		A style of working where requirements and solutions evolve through collaboration between self-organising, cross-functional teams. Agile promotes adaptive planning, evolutionary development and delivery, a time-boxed iterative approach and encourages rapid and flexible response to change.
Agile Manifesto		The Agile Manifesto defines the approach and style that is fundamental to all Agile approaches. It was created in 2001, at a summit attended by representatives of all the Agile methodologies.
Benefits Assessment		A DSDM Product. It describes how the benefits have actually accrued, following a period of use in live operation.
Business Case		A DSDM Product. Baselined at the end of the Foundations phase, it provides a vision and a justification for the project from a business perspective.
Bottom Up		A style of estimating. Using this approach, each component is estimated individually and then the estimates are summed to find the total effort.
Burn-Down Chart		A publicly displayed chart or graph counting the number of features/requirements remaining [work remaining] or time needed to complete the outstanding work [time remaining] for the current Increment or Timebox. When the Burn-down is showing Time Remaining, team members always re-estimate time to complete, rather than simply subtracting time spent from the original estimate. Time remaining is more commonly used at Timebox Level. Work remaining is more commonly used at Increment level. Burn-down is useful for predicting when all of the work will be completed, based on the current rate of progress [Velocity]. It also highlights whether the current plan looks achievable or whether it may be necessary to de-scope features. (This information can also be presented as a Burn-up Chart, showing work/time completed)
Burn-Up Chart		A publicly displayed chart showing features / requirements that have been completed and the value earned so far.
Big Visible Chart	BVC	See Team Board
Cycle		DSDM defines Iterative Development as an informal cycle of "Thought, Action, Conversation"
Delivery Plan		A DSDM Product. It provides a high-level schedule of Increments for the project and, at least for the first/imminent Increment, the timeboxes that make up that Increment.
Development Approach Definition	DAD	A DSDM Product. Baselined at the end of the Foundations phase, it provides a definition of the tools, techniques, customs, practices and standards that will be applied to the evolutionary development of the solution.

Glossary

Term	Detail
Deployed Solution	This is a baseline of the Evolving Solution, which is deployed into live use at the end of each Project Increment.
Deployment	The DSDM lifecycle phase which focuses on getting the solution (or part of it) into operational use.
Development Timebox	A fixed period of time, part of Evolutionary development, where development and testing of the Evolving Solution takes place. Typically 2-4 weeks long. See Timebox
Done	A common term used in Scrum - an item is "Done" (completed) when it meets all the criteria that have been defined for it ("Definition of Done".) Done is binary - an item is either Done or Not Done.
Evolutionary Development	The DSDM lifecycle phase used iteratively and incrementally to investigate the detailed requirements and evolve them into a viable solution
Evolving Solution	A DSDM Product. It is made up of all appropriate components of the ultimate solution together with any intermediate deliverables necessary to explore the detail of requirements and the solution under construction. At any given time, such components may be either complete, a baseline of a partial solution, or a work in progress. They include, where valuable:- models, prototypes, supporting materials and testing and review artefacts.
Feasibility	The DSDM lifecycle phase which gives the first opportunity for deciding whether or not the project is viable from a technical and/or business perspective.
Feasibility Assessment	A DSDM Product. It provides a snapshot of the evolving Business, Solution and Management products as they exist at the end of the Feasibility phase. It may be expressed as a baselined collection of the products or as an executive summary covering the key aspects of each of them.
Fit for Purpose	Something that is good enough to do the job it was intended to do
Foundations	The DSDM phase to establish firm and enduring foundations from the three perspectives on a project of business, solution and management.
Foundations Summary	A DSDM Product. It provides a snapshot of the evolving Business, Solution and Management products as they exist at the end of the Foundations phase. It may be expressed as a baselined collection of the products or as an executive summary covering the key aspects of each of them.
Function / Feature	See Requirement
Increment	An element of the Evolving Solution, comprising a collection of one or more features which, as a group, have meaning / value for the Business. One or more Increments may form a Release.
Increment Timebox	Timeboxing can be applied at increment level and an Increment Timebox comprises the time fixed by the sum of the Development Timeboxes for this Increment. See Timebox

Term	Abbreviation	Detail
Information Radiator	IR	See Team Board
Instrumental Success Factor	ISF	A key behaviour or style of working that is seen as instrumental to position DSDM projects for success. Where these factors cannot be met, they represent a significant risk to the DSDM approach.
Iteration		1. A general term for working in a cyclic way, where several attempts are made in order to get a more accurate or beneficial result. 2. One cycle of development and testing which takes place (one or more times) inside a Development Timebox and which finishes with a Review. 3. XP Iteration equates to a DSDM Timebox
KanBan Board		See Team Board
MoSCoW		A DSDM prioritisation technique, mainly used on requirements although also useful in other areas (such as Testing). M stands for Must Have, S stands for Should Have, C stands for Could Have and W stands for Won't Have This Time.
Management Approach Definition	MAD	A DSDM Product. Baselined at the end of the Foundations phase, it reflects the approach to the management of the project as a whole and considers, from a management perspective how the project will be organised and planned, how stakeholders will be engaged in the project and how progress will be demonstrated and, if necessary, reported.
Management by Exception		Within the framework of empowerment promoted by DSDM, Management by Exception is an approach whereby day-to-day management of the work required to evolve the solution is left to the Solution Development Team. If at any point the Solution Development Team thinks that they are unable to meet the commitments they have made regarding the scope or quality of what will be delivered, they refer to one or more of the Project-level roles for direction.
Minimum Usable SubseT	M.U.S.T	The minimum set of requirements needed to deliver a usable solution - the "Worst Case" basic deliverable. The Minimum Usable SubseT is defined as the Must Haves. Provided the (MUST) MoSCoW rules are properly applied, delivery of the Minimum Usable SubseT is guaranteed.
Planning Poker		Planning poker is a consensus-based technique for estimating using sets of numbered cards. It is typically used to estimate effort or relative size of stories.
Post-Project		The DSDM phase which takes place after the last planned Deployment. It is used to assess the business value delivered by the project.
Pre-Project		The DSDM phase where the initial idea or imperative is formalised in order to initiate a project.
Principle		A 'natural law' which acts as an attitude to take and a mindset to adopt on a DSDM project.

Glossary

Term	Abbreviation	Detail
Prioritised Requirements List	PRL	A DSDM Product. Baselined at the end of the Foundations phase it describes the requirements that the project needs to address and indicates their priority with respect to meeting the objectives of the project and the needs of the business.
Project Approach Questionnaire	PAQ	The DSDM questionnaire, based on the Instrumental Success Factors which helps flag potential risks to a successful DSDM project.
Project Governance Authority		A panel of corporate decision makers who decide whether projects should proceed or not.
Project Review Report		A DSDM Product. Updated at the end of each Increment it: Captures the feedback to confirm what has been delivered and what has not; captures learning points from the retrospective focusing on the process, practices employed and contributing roles and responsibilities; where appropriate it describes the business benefits that should now accrue through the proper operation of the solution delivered by the project up to this point. After the final Project Increment a Project Retrospective, in part informed by these Increment reviews, is prepared as part of the closure of the project.
Project Timebox		Timeboxing can be applied at Project level and a Project Timebox comprises the time fixed by the sum of the Increment Timeboxes for the Project. See Timebox
Prototype		A piece of work that demonstrates how a given objective can be or has been achieved or to prove a concept.
RACI		A responsibility Assignment Matrix, describing participation by roles for completing the DSDM Products. R=Responsible, A=Accountable, C=Consulted, I=Informed
Release		A collection of Features (developed and tested elements of the Evolving Solution) being deployed into operational use. A Release may comprise one or more Increments
Requirement		Something the ultimate solution needs to be able to do (Functional Requirement) or do to a certain level (Non-functional requirement). Similar words: function, feature, User Story.
Retrospective		A facilitated workshop to look back on a recent event and to assess what went well and what could be improved.
Return on Investment.	ROI	The concept of an investment of some resource which yields a benefit to the investor
Solution Architecture Definition	SAD	A DSDM Product. Baselined at the end of the Foundations phase, it provides the design framework for the solution.
Scope		A description of what the solution will do and what it will not do. This could be a list of features and/or a description of areas of the business which may or may not be affected.
SCRUM		One of the Agile approaches, with a strong focus on the Team management process. Scrum's focus is on a flexible, holistic product. development strategy

Term	Abbreviation	Detail
Servant-Leader		Servant-Leader is the style of leadership that Agile projects aspire to, in particular from the Project Manager and Team Leader roles. A servant-leader shares power, puts the needs of others first and helps people develop and perform as highly as possible
Stakeholder		A person, group, organisation, member or system who either affects or is affected by actions taken by the Project or the Team
Story		See User Story
Story Points		A relative unit of size, used for estimating, planning and tracking in an Agile project.
Test Driven Development	TDD	An approach whereby a test is written before the solution is built, thus ensuring the requirement is understood and testable. TDD aims to encourage simple designs and inspire confidence. It is most commonly applied in an IT environment but is now gaining interest as a technique outside IT.
Team Board		A large graphical representation of Project / Timebox information kept plainly in sight within an Agile team's shared workspace. It shows anyone who views it information they care about, and thus avoids the need to keep asking the team for information. This ensures more communication with fewer interruptions. Team Boards can contain most types of charts used in Agile development. Burn down charts, task boards, planning boards and storyboards are among the possibilities. An information radiator is usually hand-drawn or printed but can also include computer-generated charts and electronic displays. (Sometimes called Information Radiator, Big Visible Chart or KanBan Board)
Terms of Reference	ToR	A DSDM product created Pre-Project. It is a high-level definition of the over-arching business driver for, and top-level objectives of, the project.
Timebox		A fixed period of time, at the end of which an objective has been met. The objective would typically be a deliverable of some sort. Typically Timeboxes operate at development level, but timeboxing can also be applied at project and increment level. A timebox is managed by adding or removing content in order to meet the timebox objective and the deadline. (See also Sprint [Scrum] and Iteration [XP])
Timebox Plan		A DSDM Product. It is created for each Development Timebox. It elaborates on the objectives provided for that Timebox and details the expected deliverables, along with the activities to produce those deliverables and the resources to do the work. The Timebox Plan is created by the Solution Development Team and is often represented on a Team Board as work to do, in progress, and done.
Timebox Review Record		A DSDM Product. It is created for each Development Timebox, capturing the feedback from each review that takes place during that Timebox. It describes what has been achieved up to that point together with any feedback that may influence plans moving forwards. Where appropriate, e.g. in a regulated environment, it may provide a formal auditable record of review comments from expert Business Advisors and other roles.

Term	Abbreviation	Detail
Top-Down		A style of estimating using approximate sizings and groupings. For example, estimating 10 small components at typically one day each, 20 medium components at typically three days each, three complex components at typically five days each. These groups are summed to give an approximate estimate for a solution where the low level detail is probably still unknown.
Total Cost of Ownership	TCO	The cost of the whole life of a project and its product, including support (rather than just considering the development cost).
Transparency		This describes openness, communication, and visibility. Transparency means operating in such a way that it is easy for others to see what actions are being performed and what progress is being made.
User Story		A requirement expressed from a user point of view and with associated acceptance criteria. The usual format is: As a <role> I need <requirement / Feature> so that <benefit to be gained>
Velocity		Velocity uses story points to provide a simple measure of the rate at which a team delivers business value. Velocity (initially estimated but soon validated by the team's track record of delivery) is used for forward planning. E.g. In an Increment of 4 x 2 week Timeboxes, a team with a velocity of 25 points can confidently plan to deliver about 100 points. NB A velocity score is individual to a team (their velocity signature) and should not be used as a comparative measure across teams
XP	eXtreme Programming	One of the Agile approaches with a strong focus on technical (IT) development techniques. XP is intended to improve software quality and responsiveness to changing customer requirements.

Appendix B
Project Approach Questionnaire (PAQ)

AgilePM

DSDM Project Approach Questionnaire (PAQ)		Collective opinion				
Ref	Statement	Strongly Agree	Agree	Neutral	Disagree	Strongly Disagree
1	All members of the project understand and accept the DSDM approach (Philosophy, Principles and Practices)					
2	The Business Sponsor and the Business Visionary demonstrate clear and proactive ownership of the project					
3	The Business Vision driving the project is clearly stated and understood by all members of the project team					
4	All project participants understand and accept that on-time delivery of an acceptable solution is the primary measure of success for the project					
5	The requirements can be prioritised and there is confidence that cost and time commitments can be met by flexing the scope of what is delivered					
6	All members of the project team accept that requirements should only be defined at a high level in the early phases of the project and that detail will be emerge as development progresses					
7	All members of the project team accept that change in requirements is inevitable and that it is only by embracing change that the right solution will be delivered					
8	The Business Sponsor and Business Visionary understand that active business involvement is essential and have the willingness and authority to commit appropriate business resources to the project					
9	It is possible for the business and solution development members of the Solution Development Team to work collaboratively throughout the project					
10	Empowerment of all members of the Solution Development Team is appropriate and sufficient to support the day-to-day decision making needed to rapidly evolve the solution in short, focussed Timeboxes					
11	The DSDM roles and responsibilities are appropriately allocated and all role holders understand and accept the responsibilities associated with their role					
12	The Solution Development Team has the appropriate collective knowledge and skills (soft skills and technical skills) to collaboratively evolve an optimal business solution					
13	Solution Development Team members are allocated to the project at an appropriate and consistent level sufficient to fully support the DSDM Timeboxing practice					
14	Tools and collaborative working practices within the Solution Development Team are sufficient to allow effective Iterative Development of the solution					
15	All necessary review and testing activity is fully integrated within the Iterative Development practice					
16	Project progress is measured primarily through the incremental, demonstrable delivery of business value					
17	There are no mandatory standards or other constraints in place that prevent the application of the DSDM Philosophy and Practices on this project					

Appendix C
Estimating using Planning Poker® and Velocity

AgilePM®

Introduction

Planning Poker is also known by some as Scrum Poker, but for correctness should probably be called Estimating Poker as it is used for the process of estimating rather than planning.

Although the term 'poker' is used there is no gambling or risk taking associated with the technique which is based on sound scientific reasoning and has proven to be both reliable and accurate. It is true that a casual observer of an estimating session is likely to see a group of serious looking people sat around a table each holding a hand of cards and concentrating intently on 'the game' but that is really where the poker analogy begins and ends.

Planning Poker was created and first described in 2002 by James Grenning and later popularised by Mike Cohn in his book Agile Estimating and Planning and cleverly combines a number of estimating techniques .

Both James and Mike were contributing authors to the Manifesto for Agile Software Development. Planning Poker® is a registered trademark of Mountain Goat Software LLC.

The Cards

A typical deck of cards contains enough playing cards for four estimators. Multiple decks and partial decks can be used to support the number of estimators contributing in the session.

Each set of cards (analogous to a suit in a normal card deck) typically contains cards with a range of values from zero to 100 and also contains two special cards.

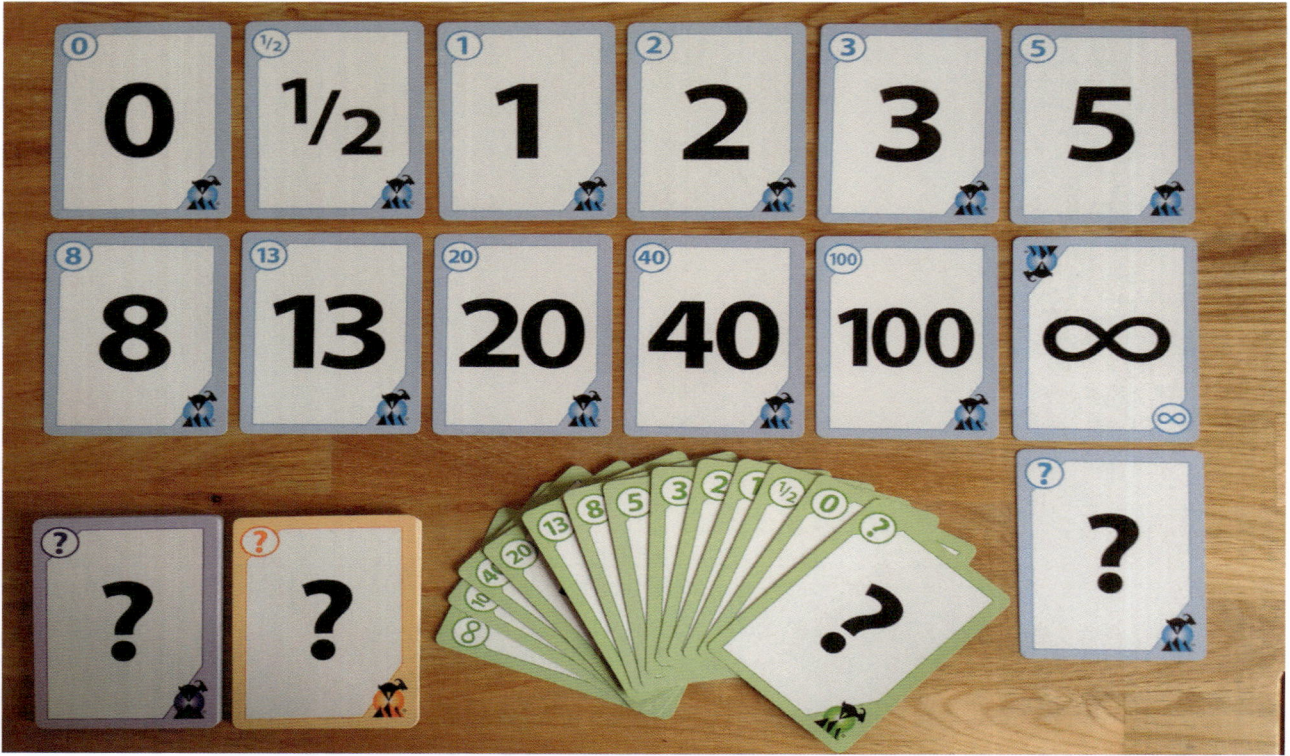

The numbers on the cards represent a non-linear progression of values based on the Fibonacci sequence - where each new number in the series is a sum of the previous two.

The numeric cards are used to convey an estimate in terms of story points, the special '∞' card is used to express an estimate that is greater than 100 story points and the '?' card is used if an estimator is unable to provide an estimate.

Electronic versions of Planning Poker cards (e.g. mobile phone apps) also exist.

Story points

Story points are used to provide an estimate for a user story that is indicative of the effort required to fulfil that story. Very importantly, it is deliberately not time-based in the first instance. This allows for individuals of differing skill and experience within a group to all make a contribution to the collaborative estimating process.

> *For example - consider painting the walls in a room*
>
> *Asking a professional decorator and an amateur decorator for an estimate of how long it will take to paint a wall to a reasonable standard will lead to very different estimates based on skill and experience. The professional would naturally base his estimate on how long it would take him to complete the task - perhaps 30 minutes. The amateur would base his estimate on how long it would take him to complete the task - perhaps 90 minutes. Whilst each estimator could try and place themselves in the position of the other (the professional estimating for the amateur and vice versa) the results are likely to be inaccurate as neither has the actual skill and experience of the other on which to base the estimate.*
>
> *That said, it is very likely that both the professional and the amateur would be able to agree that it would take roughly twice as long to paint 2 similarly sized walls as it would to paint one wall.*

A second advantage to estimating effort without directly relating it to time is psychological. Many people are, quite rightly, very wary of putting a figure in hours or days to a task for fear of being 'held to their estimate'. Under such circumstances they are more likely to inflate their estimate in order to 'protect themselves' from any criticism that may come from their estimate proving inaccurate. This fear often stems from the estimators experience of the inappropriate behaviour of the receivers of the estimate, which makes it a difficult obstacle to overcome.

Estimating in story points is an easy way to remove that fear.

Why use a non-linear range of values?

Typically the larger and more complex a task is, the more difficult it is to estimate precisely. This is because there are often more variables to consider in the estimate and more potential unknowns.

> *For example - preparing a cup of coffee for a friend*
>
> *If asked to estimate how long it would take to prepare a cup of coffee for a friend, making use of the ingredients and equipment visible and available to you in your home, you could expect to provide a reasonably precise estimate for what is a relatively short, simple, self-contained task. Perhaps 4 minutes +/- 1 minute would be a reasonable estimate.*
>
> *If asked to estimate how long it would take to prepare a cup of coffee from a specific blend of coffee beans, using a specific type of milk and supplemented by a specific flavouring syrup that are not all visible and available to you could only expect to provide a much more vague estimate because you would have to consider buying/gathering the ingredients and there is a lot more uncertainty in that. Will one local shop have all the ingredients required or will a trip to several shops be needed? How long will it take to travel to the shop(s)? What if the car doesn't start or the bus is late? etc. Perhaps 2 hours +/- 1 hour would be a reasonable estimate*

The second estimate in the example above is not only a larger estimate for a bigger task (120 minutes compared to 4 minutes) but also has a much wider range of values (60 minutes compared to 1 minute) to reflect a lack of certainty around the complexity of the task.

Why use playing cards?

The main reason for using playing cards is to prevent the estimators consciously or unconsciously influencing each other. Each estimator can consider the problem and then present their estimate when they are ready without being influenced by somebody who has arrived at a conclusion more quickly and made their opinion known. Typically a more experienced person will arrive at an opinion quicker than a less experienced person who may need longer to think things through. Also typically, a less experienced person will naturally be led by somebody they believe is more likely to be right. Keeping an opinion 'secret' - by holding on to the card until everybody is ready to show theirs improves the power of group estimating and provides more honest estimates.

Playing the game

All members of the Solution Development Team, including Business Ambassadors should participate in the estimating session which should be run as a Facilitated Workshop, typically facilitated by the DSDM Team Leader. Business Advisors expected to make a significant contribution to the detail of stories should also attend with any other Advisors ideally contactable if required. A neutral facilitator is not needed for this workshop. The Project Manager may find it useful to observe the estimating session in order to gain an understanding of the assumptions and design considerations behind the estimates and to help with subsequent high-level planning. The Project Manager should not, however, participate in the estimating process or try to influence the estimators as this will lead to a lack of real ownership of the estimates by the team.

Part 1 - the baseline story

Planning Poker uses comparative estimating - with each Story being estimated by comparison with a baseline story.

> *To extend the previous painting example:*
>
> *If the story "As a home owner, I want this wall painted so that it complements my new carpet" is worth 1 story point and was used as the baseline story.*
>
> *Then by comparative estimating, the story "As a home owner, I want all four walls in this room repainted so they complement my new carpet" could be estimated as 3 story points because*
> *although it would take approximately four times the effort to paint four times the number of walls the brushes etc. would only need to be cleaned once.*

Similarly "As a home owner I want all the walls in my house painted so that they complement my new carpets" could be estimated at 40 story points.

Typically the baseline story is selected:

Either as the story from the current Prioritised Requirements List for a project that the Solution Development Team believe will take the least effort to fulfil

Or as a default story used across projects that everybody understands would be a relatively straightforward to deliver.

> *An IT systems example of a sensible baseline story might be:*
>
> *"As a customer, I want to provide my address and other contact information so that you can send me the items I have purchased, inform me of the progress of my order and contact me in the event of any issues arising" - a story that would require a simple form to capture and validate the data, the provision of a database table and the functionality required to store the data in that table.*

Part 2 - generating the estimates

Having agreed on a baseline story, and typically assigning it a story point value of 2, the group estimate each of the other stories in turn. They do this by following the following steps which are carried out collaboratively with all disciplines (analysis, development and test) participating.

1. The Business Ambassador (or Business Advisor where appropriate) selects a story to be estimated and reads it to the group, providing any further contextual and detailed information that they believe is relevant.

2. The estimators consider the story and ask questions where detail and context may be absent or unclear - as this is done in a group environment any additional clarification benefits the team as a whole.

3. Having fully understood the requirement, the estimators briefly discuss what they think needs to be done to fulfil the story. Naturally, high-level design considerations will feature in this discussion and there is also the opportunity to agree any key assumptions used for the estimate. Both of these may be noted against the Story, particularly if they will be useful for high-level planning

4. After a few minutes of discussion (typically 2 or 3 minutes) the facilitator (typically the DSDM Team Leader) will ask the estimators to select a card from their hand and to hold it out in front of them *face down*

5. When everybody has selected a card the facilitator requests that they are turned face up and the estimates are considered

    - Where the values presented are with one on the scale (e.g. a collection of 3s and 5s or a collection of 5s and 8s) the higher value is attributed to the story. (Note: given the uncertainty at this point, dealt with by the non-linear number series, it is not appropriate to use a value not represented by a card)

    - If there is another story to be estimated the process loops back to step 1, otherwise the process ends

6. Where there is a wider range of values (e.g. a collection of 3s, 5s, 8s and 13s) the facilitator will ask one of the estimators with the lowest value to explain why they believe it is so straight-forward, and one of the estimators with the highest value to share their thoughts on what makes it so relatively large or and complex

This triggers a further conversation and leads to wider understanding for one or more estimators and potentially clarifies additional assumptions which are noted. Then the process loops back to step 4. This iterative refinement of estimates is the Wide band Delphi technique

Part 3 - normalising the estimates

Once all the stories have been estimated, the Story cards are arranged on the table grouped by story points (i.e. all the 1s together, all the 2s together, all the 3s together etc.) and each estimator checks to see if the stories in each group are of similar size. If, on reflection, any stories stand out as being different in size (noticeably bigger or smaller than the rest) then the group decide whether it might be appropriate to amend the story point estimate for that story and move it to a different group. E.g. if one 3 point story looks bigger than the rest then the group compare it to the stories with an estimate of 5 and decide whether it needs to be re-valued as a 5 or left where it is as a 3.

Part 4 - estimating your *Velocity*

The final part of the process deals with providing story point estimates with the dimension of time that has been avoided up to this point.

The concept of Velocity

Velocity in this context is defined as the number of story points of work the Solution Development Team can complete in a Timebox of a known duration. It works best where Timeboxes are all the same size and membership of the team is stable, although the occasional odd-sized Timebox and small variations in team make-up can be accommodated if necessary.

Where the velocity of the Solution Development Team is known, the membership of the team has not changed and the same baseline story has been used for estimating the most recent stories it is a simple exercise to work out how many Timeboxes will be needed to deliver them.

Given a team with a known velocity of 30 story points per 2 week Timebox and given a total of 120 story points of work, 4 Timeboxes should be planned to fulfil all the stories.

Where the velocity of the Solution Development Team is not known, the velocity itself will need to be estimated. Two techniques are commonly used to do this: *Commitment based planning* and *estimating by decomposition*. Often both techniques can be used in the order below.

Commitment-based planning

Estimating velocity by commitment-based planning requires the Solution Development Team to select a high priority story from the Prioritised Requirements List and ask themselves *"If this was the only thing we had to do as a team could we fulfil this story in a single Timebox?"* If the answer is "yes" then team select another high priority story and ask themselves *"If these two stories were all we had to do as a team could we fulfil both of them in a single Timebox?"* If the answer is "yes" then team select another high priority story and so on until the answer is "No - I don't think we could complete all of those stories". At that point that story would be put to one side. Where appropriate, some stories that appear smaller than the rejected story would be considered until the last one is put aside or accepted as the final story that could be included. The total of the story points for the accepted stories becomes the estimated velocity for the team.

Bearing in mind that the estimating described here is the estimating that will be carried out during the Foundations phase, the stories selected, one by one, for estimating should all be candidates for inclusion in the first Timebox in the Evolutionary Development phase. This technique can also be used to validate an existing assumption of velocity where that exists.

Estimating by decomposition

Estimating by decomposition can be used to validate the estimate from the commitment-based planning. At this point, the Solution Development Team will effectively pull forward the Investigation step from the first *structured* Timebox, understand the full detail of the requirement and work out exactly how they are going to fulfil the selected stories. The detailed estimates from the decomposition of each story into the development and testing tasks should be made in *ideal person hours* or *ideal person days* whatever is most sensible. (Ideal time assumes time when the team members can focus exclusively on the work of the Timebox. This is always less than the hours in a "working day", since, in reality, there are always other activities to be done). The validation comes from understanding whether the new estimate is close to the previous estimate. Having identified all the work needed to fulfil the stories, does the estimate for all the work match the capacity (the available person hours) the team has to compete it within the boundaries of the Timebox? When estimating velocity, working out the capacity should include reserving time for Daily Stand-ups, Timebox reviews, part-time working etc. but not extraordinary activities such as company-wide meetings, holidays, doctors appointments etc.

If the two estimates are close then the velocity estimated by commitment based planning can be considered accurate. If they are significantly different then the estimate should be adjusted to a level that the Solution Development Team are confident to commit to.

On-going validation of Velocity

During the Evolutionary Development phase, as Timeboxes are completed the actual story points completed should be captured. This data can then be used to validate the estimate of velocity made during Foundations and in turn, in line with the concept of planning and re-planning based on best available estimates, this can be used to predict what stories will be incorporated into the Solution Increment deployed at the end of the Project Increment. When predicting final outcome, it is common to use an average based on the last 3 Timeboxes, which smooths out any anomalies from a single Timebox.

In summary

Planning Poker is a sophisticated team-based estimating tool that has nothing to do with luck or gambling. It combines a number of respected estimating techniques into a simple effective estimating process and provides an opportunity to use multiple techniques to validate estimates. It also improves team communication and builds a shared understanding of the stories, the assumptions made and the differing impact of individual stories on the various technical roles. Planning Poker has proven to be accurate and effective if done properly and, in combination with velocity, provides a sound basis for planning and re-planning based on outcome-based measurement.

Appendix D
Index

AgilePM

This index is in alphabetical, word by word order. It does not cover the Contents list or Foreword. Location references are to chapter and section number, e.g.

bottom-up estimating, 20.3.2, 20.5.3

indicates that information on bottom-up estimating can be found in Chapter 20, sections 3.2 and 5.3.

Abbreviations: Fig = Figure

acceptance criteria
    see also quality
    confirming in Timebox, 17.8.2.1
    defining, 13.5; 19.4.3
    on reverse of User Story cards, 19.3.3

Agile Alliance, 2.2

Agile projects
    see also projects
    choosing DSDM as Agile approach, 2.5
    differences between Agile approaches and DSDM, 2.4
    relationship with DSDM, 2.2

application
    difference from other Agile approaches, 2.4
    difference from traditional approaches, 2.3
    reasons for choosing DSDM, 2.5

benefits
    of facilitated workshops, 12.2
    of using DSDM, 2.6

Benefits Assessments, 8.2.14; 16.15.1-15.2; 21.3.6
    see also milestone products

Big Visible Charts (BCVs), see Team Boards

bottom-up estimating, 20.3.2, 20.5.3
    see also estimating

Business Advisors
    change control, 9.4.3
    responsibilities, 14.2.1
    role, 7.2.2.3, 7.3.10; 14.2.2.3, 14.12
    testing perspective, 9.3.5; 12.3.4.3

Index

Business Ambassadors
    change control, 9.4.3
    responsibilities, 7.3.7; 12.3.4.3; 14.9.1
    role, 7.2.2.2, 7.3.7; 14.2.2.2, 14.9
    testing perspective, 9.3.5
    Timebox planning, 17.8.2.1-8.2.2

Business Analysts
    assessing project benefits, 21.3.6
    balancing priorities, 17.4
    relationship with Project Manager, 14.16.4
    responsibilities, 7.3.5; 13.5; 14.7.1; 19.4.1, 19.4.3
    role, 7.2.2.1-2.2.2, 7.3.5; 14.2.2.1-2.2.2, 14.7

Business Cases, 8.2.2; 15.3.2-3.3; 16.3.1-3.2; 20.5.2
    see also evolutionary products

business engagement in projects
    see also Instrumental Success Factors (ISFs)
    active involvement of business roles, 5.4.2; 13.4
    commitment of time, 5.4.1
    general, 5.4
    supportive commercial relationships, 5.4.3

business interests
    see also roles
    Business Advisors, 7.3.10
    Business Ambassadors, 7.3.7
    Business Sponsors, 7.3.1
    Business Visionaries, 7.3.2

business needs, focussing on, 4.2; 13.2-3

Business Sponsors
    provision of information to, 13.2
    relationship with Project Manager, 14.16.1
    responsibilities, 7.3.1; 14.4.1
    role, 7.2.2.1, 7.3.1; 9.2.1; 14.2.2.1, 14.4

Business Visionaries
    attendance at Daily Stand Up, 17.9
    change control, 9.4.3
    relationship with Project Manager, 14.16.2
    responsibilities, 14.5.1; 17.6; 21.3.6; 24.2.1
    role, 7.2.2.1, 7.3.2; 14.2.2.1, 14.5

change, responding to, 2.3; 13.7
change control, 9.4.3; 13.7
    see also project control
chat facilities, 18.2.3
    see also communication
collaboration
    see also teams; workshops
    barriers to, 18.3.2
    collaborative people, 18.3.3
    collaborative testing, 9.3.2
    collaborative workspaces, 18.2.3
    customer collaboration, 2.3
    definition, 18.3.1
    effective collaboration, 18.3.2
    general, 4.4; 18.1, 18.4
    leadership, 18.3.7
    Project Manager responsibilities, 13.4
    T-shaped skills, Fig 18d
    workplace culture, 18.3.6
commercial relationships, 5.4.3
    see also stakeholders
common sense, 3.1, 3.3, Fig 3a
communication
    see also workshops
    co-located teams, 18.2.6
    communication skills, 18.2.1
    day-to-day, 18.2.5

Index

        see also Team Boards; Daily Stand-ups

    distributed teams

        communication models, Figs 18a-b

        general, 18.2.7

    examples of poor communication, 18.1

    general, 4.8; 18.4

    planning effective communication, 18.2.2

    Project Manager responsibilities, 13.8

    types of communication, 18.2.3

    use of specialist terminology, 18.2.1

    within Solution Development Teams, 5.3.2-3.4

    within teams, 18.2.1

    words v. pictures, 18.2.4, Fig 18c

composition of DSDM, Fig 3a

conferencing methods, 18.2.3

  see also communication

configuration management, 12.3.3

Consolidation (DSDM structured timebox step 3), 17.8.2.1

control, see project control

cost

    as project variable, 3.2, Fig 3b

    delivery on budget, 22.3.3.2

Could Have priorities

    see also MoSCoW prioritisation

    agreeing priority levels, 17.4.1

    balancing priorities, 17.3.1, Fig 17a

    business expectations, 17.5

    definition, 10.2.3

    use, 17.2

creation of DSDM, 1.1

customer collaboration, 2.3

    see also collaboration

Daily Stand-ups
    general, 11.3; 18.2.5.2
    Project Manager role, 17.9
    transparency of process/progress, 5.6; 9.4.2
    updating of Timebox Plans, 8.2.11

deadlines, importance of, 13.2

decision-making, 5.3.1

defects, 9.6.5

definitions, 1.1-2

Delivery Approach Definitions, 8.2.5; 15.3.2-3.3; 16.6.1-6.2
    see also evolutionary products

delivery of solutions
    general, 4.1
    incremental, 4.6; 5.5
    timeliness, 4.3; 13.3

Delivery Plans
    see also evolutionary products; Project Increments
    definition, 8.2.6
    Deployment phase, 15.3.5; 21.3.5
    Feasibility phase, 15.3.2; 21.3.2
    format, 13.9
    Foundations phase, 15.3.3; 20.5.2; 21.3.3
    planning horizon, 9.2.2
    Project Manager responsibilities, 13.3

Deployed Solution, 8.2.10

Deployment phase
    see also process
    objective, 6.6
    planning, 21.3.5
    Project Manager input, 15.3.5

Development Approach Definitions, 8.2.5; 13.5; 15.3.2-3.3
    see also evolutionary products

Index

documents
- see also products
- as means of communication, 18.2.3
- value of, 8.3; 16.17

DSDM
- benefits, 2.6
- choice of as Agile approach, 2.5
- creation, 1.1; 2.1
- relationship with Agile projects, 2.2
- simplification, 1.2

DSDM Coaches
- responsibilities, 14.15.1
- role, 7.2.2.3, 7.3.13; 14.2.2.3, 14.15

DSDM Structured Timeboxes
- see also Timeboxes
- diagrams, Fig 11a; Fig 17b
- general, 11.2-2.1, 11.5; 17.8.2-8.2.1

email, 18.2.3
- see also communication

empowerment
- Solution Development Teams, 5.3.1; 9.4.4
- teams, 7.1

end-to-end testing, 9.6.6
- see also testing

Epics, 19.3.2-3.3, 19.4.1-4.2
- see also User Stories

estimating
- see also project planning
- common sources of uncertainty, 20.2
- coping with uncertainty, 20.2
- cycle, 20.4
- general, 9.2.3; 20.6
- key points, 20.1
- overview, 20.1

       review, 20.4

       styles

              bottom-up, 20.3.2

              choice, 20.3.3

              general, 20.3

              top-down, 20.3.1

       throughout the lifecycle

              Evolutionary Development phase, 20.5.3

              Feasibility phase, 20.5.1

              Foundations phase, 20.5.2

              general, 20.5, Fig 20a

              top tips for Agile Project Managers, 20.6

Evolutionary Development phase

       see also process

       objectives, 6.5

       Project Manager input, 15.3.4

       risk management, 23.1

evolutionary products

       see also products

       Business Cases, 8.2.2; 15.3.2-3.3; 16.3.1-3.2; 20.5.2

       Delivery Plans, see Delivery Plans

       Development Approach Definitions, 8.2.5; 15.3.2-3.3; 16.6.1-6.2

       estimating, 20.5.3

       Evolving Solutions, 8.2.10; 16.11.1-11.2

       general, 16.1

       Management Approach Definitions, 8.2.7; 15.3.2-3.3; 16.8.1-8.2

       planning, 21.3.4

       Prioritised Requirements Lists (PRL), see Prioritised Requirements Lists (PRL)

       quality, 22.2.5

Index

        requirements during, 19.4.3

        Solution Architecture Definitions, 8.2.4; 15.3.2-3.3; 16.5.1-5.2

        Timebox Plans, 8.2.11; 9.2.2; 13.9; 16.12.1-12.2

        Timebox Review Records, 8.2.12; 15.3.5; 16.13.1-13.2; 17.8.2.1

Evolving Solutions, 8.2.10

        see also iterative development

face-to-face communication, 18.2.3

        see also communication

facilitated workshops, see workshops

Feasibility Assessments, 8.2.8; 15.3.2; 16.9.1-9.2

        see also milestone products

Feasibility phase

        see also process

        completion of Project Approach Questionnaires, 5.7

        consideration of requirements, 8.2.3

        creation of Business Case, 8.2.2

        estimating, 20.5.1

        general, 15.2

        objectives, 6.3

        outlining Management Approach Definition, 8.2.7

        planning, 21.2, 21.3.2

        Project Manager input, 15.3.2

        quality, 22.2.5

        requirements activity, 19.4.1

        use of Terms of Reference in, 8.2.1

features, as project variable, 3.2, Fig 3b

Foundation Summaries, 8.2.9; 15.3.3; 16.10.1-10.2

        see also milestone products

Foundations phase

        agreeing lifecycle of project, 6.8

        baselining Management Approach Definition, 8.2.7

        Business Case, use in, 8.2.2

        estimating, 20.5.2

        Iterative development planning, 12.3.2

        objectives, 6.4; 15.2

        planning, 21.3, 21.3.3

        Project Manager input, 15.3.3

        quality issues, 22.5

        re-assessment of Project Approach Questionnaires, 5.7

        requirements activity, 19.4.2

        returning to during project, 6.4; 21.3.7

        Solution Development Team involvement, 15.3.3

        solution maintainability, 22.2.3

free format Timeboxes

        see also Timeboxes

        diagrams, Fig 11b, Fig 17c

        general, 11.2, 11.2.2, 11.5; 17.8.2, 17.8.2.2

functional requirements (FRs), 19.2.1.1

        see also requirements

governance processes, products used in

        Feasibility Assessments, 15.3.2

        Foundations Summaries, 15.3.3

        general, 8.1, Fig 8a

        Project Review Reports, 15.3.5

        Terms of Reference, 8.2.1

        Timebox Review Records, 8.2.12; 15.3.5

increment retrospectives, 15.3.5

incremental delivery of solutions

        general, 4.6; 5.5

        Project Manager responsibilities, 13.6

incremental planning, 21.3.7

        see also project planning

individuals/interaction, 2.3; 3.1

        see also collaboration

Information Radiators, see Team Boards

Instrumental Success Factors (ISFs)

    business engagement

        active involvement of business roles, 5.4.2; 13.4

        commitment of time, 5.4.1

        general, 5.4

        supportive commercial relationships, 5.4.3

    DSDM project approach, 5.2

    general, 5.1, 5.8

    incremental delivery, 5.5

    iterative development, 5.5

    Project Approach Questionnaires, see Project Approach Questionnaires (PAQ)

    Solution Development Teams, see Solution Development Teams (SDT)

    testing, 5.5

    transparency, 5.6

Investigation (DSDM structured timebox step 1), 17.8.2.1

ISFs, see Instrumental Success Factors (ISFs)

iterative development

    controlling, 12.3.3

    general, 4.7; 12.3.1, 12.4

    planning, 12.3.2

    Project Manager responsibilities, 13.7

    quality, 12.3.4-3.4.3

Kanban Boards, see Team Boards

leadership, 18.3.7

Management Approach Definitions, 8.2.7; 15.3.2-3.3; 16.8.1-8.2

    see also evolutionary products

management by exception, 9.4.4; 14.15.6

    see also project control

management by objective, 14.15.6

    see also project control

management interest

    Project Managers, 7.3.4

    Team Leaders, 7.3.6

Manifesto For Agile Software Development, 2.2

McConnell, Steve, quote, 20.2

milestone products
- see also products
- Benefits Assessments, 8.2.14; 16.15.1-15.2; 21.3.6
- Feasibility Assessments, 8.2.8; 15.3.2; 16.9.1-9.2
- Foundation Summaries, 8.2.9; 15.3.3; 16.10.1-10.2
- general, 16.1
- Project Review Reports, 8.2.13; 15.3.5; 16.14.1-14.2
- Terms of Reference, 8.2.1; 16.2.1-2.2; 19.4.1

Minimum Usable SubseT (MUST)
- see also MosCow prioritisation
- business expectations, 17.5
- general, 4.5; 10.2.1
- guaranteeing delivery, 3.2; 13.2; 17.2

modelling
- see also models
- general, 12.2.1, 12.4
- perspectives, 12.2.2, Fig 12a

models, definition, 12.2.1
- see also modelling

MoSCoW prioritisation
- Business Vision, 17.6
- combining with Timeboxing, 17.1
- Could Have items, 10.2.3
- decomposing high level requirements, 17.7
- effect on solution quality, 22.2.1
- general, 3.2; 10.1, 10.4
- managing business expectations, 17.5
- Must Have items, 10.2.1
- priorities
  - agreeing, 17.4.1, 17.7
  - assigning, 17.8.1
  - balancing, 17.3.1, 17.4, Fig 17a

discussing, 17.4.3

levels of priority for requirements, 10.3

Project Manager responsibilities, 13.2

relationship to Business Vision, 17.6

re-prioritising at end of Project Increment, 17.4.3

review during project, 17.4.2-4.3

Should Have items, 10.2.2

testing, 9.3.4

use in practice, 17.2, 17.11

Won't Have this time items, 10.2.4

MUST, see Minimum Usable SubseT (MUST)

Must Have priorities

see also MoSCoW prioritisation

balancing priorities, 17.3.1, Fig 17a

definition, 10.2.1

use, 17.2

non-functional requirements (NFRs), 19.2.1.2

see also requirements

outcome-based measurement, 9.4.1, Fig 9a

see also project control

outcome-based planning, 9.2.1

see also project planning

PAQs, see Project Approach Questionnaires (PAQ)

people, 3.1, Fig 3a

see also stakeholders

philosophy, 3.1, 3.3, Fig 3a

planning, see project planning

Post-project phase

see also process

objectives, 6.7

planning benefits assessment, 21.3.6

Project Manager input, 15.3.6

practices, 3.1, Fig 3a

pragmatism, 3.1, 3.5, Fig 3a

Pre-project phase

    see also process

    general, 15.2

    objectives, 6.2

    planning, 21.3.1

    Project Manager involvement, 15.3.1

principles

    Build Incrementally from Firm Foundations (Principle 5), 4.6; 13.6

    Collaborate (Principle 3), 4.4; 13.4

    Communicate Continuously and Clearly (Principle 7), 4.8; 13.8

    Deliver on Time (Principle 2), 4.3; 13.3

    Demonstrate Control (Principle 8), 4.9; 13.9

    Develop Iteratively (Principle 6), 4.7; 13.7

    Focus on the Business Need (Principle 1), 4.2; 13.2

    general, 3.1, 3.3, Fig 3a; 4.1, 4.10; 13.1

    Never Compromise Quality (Principle 4), 4.5; 13.5

    top tips for Agile Project Managers, 13.9

prioritisation of requirements, see MoSCoW prioritisation

Prioritised Requirements Lists (PRL)

    see also evolutionary products

    description, 16.4.1

    Feasibility phase, 15.3.2

    Foundations phase, 15.3.3

    general, 8.2.3

    roles/responsibilities, 16.4.2

    User Stories, 19.4.2

    Won't Have this time requirements, recording, 10.2.4

PRL, see Prioritised Requirements Lists (PRL)

process

    configuration of for projects, 6.9

    Deployment phase, 6.6; 15.3.5; 21.3.5

    diagrams, Fig 6a, Fig 15a

Index

Evolutionary Development phase, 6.5; 15.3.4; 23.1

Feasibility phase, see Feasibility phase

Foundations phase, see Foundations phase

general, 3.1, Fig 3a; 15.1, 15.4

lifecycle of project, 6.8; 15.2

overview, 6.1, 6.10

Post-project phase, 6.7; 15.3.6; 21.3.6

Pre-project phase, 6.2; 15.2, 15.3.1; 21.3.1

quality

    delivery on budget, 22.3.3.2

    delivery on time, 22.3.3.1

    DSDM approach, 22.3.2

    formality of process, 22.3.4

    general, 22.1, 22.4

    predictability, 22.3.3, 22.3.3.3

    requirement for, 22.3.1

process interests

    DSDM Coaches, 7.3.13

    Workshop Facilitators, 7.3.12

products of DSDM process

    diagram, Fig 8a

    evolutionary products

        Business Cases, 8.2.2; 15.3.2-3.3; 16.3.1-3.2; 20.5.2

        Delivery Plans, see Delivery Plans

        Development Approach Definitions, 8.2.5; 15.3.2-3.3; 16.6.1-6.2

        Evolving Solutions, 8.2.10; 16.11.1-11.2

        Management Approach Definitions, 8.2.7; 15.3.2-3.3; 16.8.1-8.2

        Prioritised Requirements Lists (PRL), see Prioritised Requirements Lists (PRL)

        Solution Architecture Definitions, 8.2.4; 15.3.2-3.3; 16.5.1-5.2

        Timebox Plans, 8.2.11; 9.2.2; 13.9; 16.12.1-12.2

        Timebox Review Records, 8.2.12; 15.3.5; 16.13.1-13.2; 17.8.2.1

    general, 3.1, Fig 3a; 8.1, 8.3; 16.1, Fig 16a, 16.17

    milestone products

        Benefits Assessments, 8.2.14; 16.15.1-15.2; 21.3.6

        Feasibility Assessments, 8.2.8; 15.3.2; 16.9.1-9.2

        Foundation Summaries, 8.2.9; 15.3.3; 16.10.1-10.2

        Project Review Reports, 8.2.13; 15.3.5; 16.14.1-14.2

        Terms of Reference, 8.2.1; 16.2.1-2.2; 19.4.1

    RACI summary table, 16.16

Project Approach Questionnaires (PAQ)

    Feasibility phase, 21.3.2

    general, 5.7

    risk management, 23.4

    use in tailoring DSDM

        general, 24.1-2, 24.3

        individual PAQ statements, 24.2.1

project control

    demonstrating, 4.9

    management by exception, 9.4.4; 14.15.6

    management by objective, 14.15.6

    outcome-based measurement, 9.4.1, Fig 9a

    Project Manager responsibilities, 13.9

    responding to change, 9.4.3

    transparency of process/progress, 9.4.2

Project Increments

    see also Timeboxes

    MoSCoW prioritisation, 10.3; 17.4.3

    reviews of Business Case, 8.2.2

    updating of Project Review Reports, 8.2.13

project-level roles

    see also roles

    Business Analysts, 7.3.5

    Business Sponsors, 7.3.1

    Business Visionaries, 7.3.2

    levels of engagement, 14.2.3

    general, 7.2.2.1; 14.2.2.1

    Project Managers, 7.3.4

    Technical Coordinators, 7.3.3

Project Managers
- see also projects
- assigning MoSCoW priorities, 17.8.1
- balancing priorities, 17.4, 17.7
- Daily Stand-ups, 17.9
- decision-making, 17.4.3
- leadership, 18.3.7
- relationships
  - Business Analyst, 14.16.4
  - Business Sponsor, 14.16.1
  - Business Visionary, 14.16.2
  - other stakeholders, 14.16.7
  - Solution Development Team, 14.16.6
  - Team Leader, 14.16.5
  - Technical Co-ordinator, 14.16.3
- responsibilities
  - for principles
    - collaboration, 13.4
    - communication, 13.8; 18.1, 18.2.2
    - control, 13.9
    - delivering on time, 13.3
    - focussing on business needs, 13.1-2
    - incremental delivery of solution, 13.6
    - iterative development, 13.7
    - quality, 13.5
  - for processes
    - Deployment phase, 15.3.5
    - Evolutional Development phase, 15.3.4
    - Feasibility phase, 15.3.2
    - Foundations phase, 15.3.3
    - Post-project phase, 15.3.6

        Pre-project phase, 15.3.1

        general, 7.3.4; 9.2.1; 14.3.1

        role, 7.2.2.1, 7.3.4; 14.2.2.1, 14.3; 15.1, 15.4

        top tips, see top tips for Agile Project Managers

project planning

        Deployment phase, 21.3.5

        diagrams, Fig 9b, Fig 21a

        estimates, 9.2.3

        Evolutionary Development phase, 21.3.4

        Feasibility phase, 21.3.2

        Foundations phase, 21.3.3, 21.3.7

        general, 9.1, 9.7; 21.1-2, 21.4

        incremental planning, 21.3.7

        outcome-based planning, 9.2.1

        planning horizons, 9.2.2

        Post-project phase, 21.3.6

        Pre-project phase, 21.3.1

        quality, see quality

        testing, see testing

        throughout the lifecycle, 9.5; 21.3

        top tips for Agile Project Managers, 21.4

        tracking and control, see project control

Project Review Reports, 8.2.13; 15.3.5; 16.14.1-14.2

        see also milestone products

project variables, 3.2, Fig 3b

projects

        see also Project Managers

        business engagement in, 5.4-4.3

        configuring DSDM to suit, 6.9

        control of, see project control

        difference between traditional approach and DSDM, 2.3

        historic failure of, 2.1

        lifecycle, 6.8; 15.2, Fig 15b

        management, see Management Approach Definition

        planning, see project planning

Index

        tailoring DSDM to project, 17.2-2.1

quality

        acceptance criteria, 9.6.3; 13.5

        across the lifecycle, 22.2.5

        as project variable, 3.2, Fig 3b

        assessments, 9.6.5

        assurance, 8.2.5

        compromising, 4.5

        general, 9.6, Fig 9c; 22.4

        high-level requirements, 9.6.2

        high-level risk analysis, 9.6.1

        iterative development, 12.3.4-3.4.3

        overview, 22.1

        process quality, see process quality

        Project Manager responsibilities, 13.5

        solution quality, see solution quality

        top tips for Agile Project Managers, 22.4

quality reviews, 12.3.4.1; 22.3.5

questionnaires, see Project Approach Questionnaires (PAQ)

quotes, McConnell, S., 20.2

RACI Summary Table, 16.16

        see also products

Rapid Application Development (RAD), 1.1; 2.1; 23.3

Refinement (DSDM structured timebox step 2), 17.8.2.1

requirements

        categories

            general, 19.2.1

            functional requirements (FRs), 19.2.1.1

            non-functional requirements (NFRs), 19.2.1.2

        definition, 19.2

        DSDM lifecycle phases

            Evolutionary Development phase, 19.4.3

            Feasibility phase, 19.4.1

>>>> Foundations phase, 19.4.2

>>>> general, 19.4

>>> general, 19.1, 19.5

>>> top tips for Agile Project Managers, 19.5

> resources, ensuring availability, 13.2

> responsibilities

>> see also roles

>> Business Advisors, 14.12.1

>> Business Ambassadors, 14.9.1

>> Business Analysts, 7.3.5; 14.7.1

>> Business Sponsors, 7.3.1; 14.4

>> Business Visionaries, 7.3.2; 14.5.1

>> DSDM Coaches, 14.15.1

>> Project Managers, see Project Managers, responsibilities

>> Solution Developers, 14.10.1

>> Solution Testers, 14.11.1

>> Team Leaders, 7.3.6; 14.8.1

>> Technical Advisors, 14.13.1

>> Technical Coordinators, 14.6.1

>> Workshop Facilitators, 14.14.1

> risk analysis, 9.6.1; 23.4

> risk management

>> general, 23.1, 23.5, Fig 23a

>> project risk

>>> major risk sources, 23.2

>>> mitigation using DSDM approach, 23.3

>>> risks to DSDM approach, 23.4

>> risk areas, 23.1

>> top tips for Agile Project Managers, 23.5

> roles

>> see also responsibilities

>> Business Advisors, 7.3.10; 14.12

>> Business Ambassadors, 7.3.7; 14.9

>> Business Analysts, 7.3.5; 14.7

Index

Business Sponsors, 7.3.1; 14.4

Business Visionaries, 7.3.2; 14.5

DSDM Coaches, 7.3.13; 14.15

DSDM Team Model, 7.2.1, Fig 7a; 14.2.1, Fig 14a

fulfilment, 7.2.3; 14.2.4

general, 7.1, 7.4; 14.1, 14.16

levels of engagement, 14.2.3

project-level, 7.2.2.1; 14.2.2.1

Project Managers, 7.3.4; 14.3

Solution Developers, 7.3.8; 14.10

Solution Development Teams, 7.2.2.2; 14.2.2.2

Solution Testers, 7.3.9; 14.11

supporting, 7.2.2.3; 14.2.2.3

Team Leaders, 7.3.6; 14.8

Technical Advisors, 7.3.11; 14.13

Technical Coordinators, 7.3.3; 14.6

Workshop Facilitators, 7.3.12; 14.14

Scrum, using DSDM alongside, 2.5

'servant leaders', 18.3.7

Should Have priorities

see also MoSCoW prioritisation

agreeing priority level, 17.4.1

balancing priorities, 17.3.1, Fig 17a

business expectations, 17.5

definition, 10.2.2

use, 17.2

soft skills, 18.2.1

Solution Architecture Definitions, 8.2.4; 13.5; 15.3.2-3.3; 16.5.1-5.2

see also evolutionary products

Solution Developers

responsibilities, 12.3.4.3; 14.10.1

role, 7.2.2.2, 7.3.8; 14.2.2.2, 14.10

Solution Development Teams (SDT)

empowerment, 5.3.1; 9.4.4; 17.10

  engagement, 14.2.3

  Evolutionary Development phase, 6.5

  Foundations phase, 15.3.3

  general, 5.3

  relationship with Project Manager, 14.16.6

  responsibilities, 9.2.1

  risk management, 23.1

  roles

    Business Ambassadors, 7.3.7

    Business Analysts, 7.3.5

    general, 7.2.2.2; 14.2.2.2

    Solution Developers, 7.3.8

    Solution Testers 7.3.9

    Team Leaders, 7.3.6

  size, 5.3.4

  skills, 5.3.3

  stability, 5.3.2

  Timebox plans

    creation, 8.2.11; 17.8.2.1

    updating, 13.9

  Timeboxes

    agreeing changes to, 17.10

    attendance at kick off, 17.8.2.1

Solution Increments

  creation, 6.5

  delivery, 13.9

  functionality, 22.2.3.1

  general, 4.6; 8.2.10

solution/technical interests

  Solution Developer, 7.3.8

  Solution Tester, 7.3.9

  Technical Advisor, 7.3.11

  Technical Co-ordinator, 7.3.3

Index

Solution Testers
- see also testing
- responsibilities, 12.3.4.3; 14.11.1; 19.4.3
- role, 7.2.2.2, 7.3.9; 14.2.2.2, 14.11

solutions
- delivery
  - general, 4.1
  - incremental delivery, 4.6; 5.5; 13.6
  - Project Manager responsibilities, 13.3
  - scope of features delivered, 22.2.1
  - technical quality, 22.2.2
  - timeliness, 4.3
- maintainability, 22.2.3-2.3.3
- quality
  - advantages of DSDM method, 22.2.4
  - general, 22.1-2, 22.4
  - maintainability of solution, 22.2.3-2.3.3
  - technical quality of solution, 22.2.2
  - scope of features delivered, 22.2.1

stakeholders
- collaboration, 18.3.4
- collaborative testing, 9.3.2
- communication with, 18.2.2
- definition, 3.1
- managing expectations, 13.8
- relationship with Project Manager, 14.16.7
- timely involvement in project, 13.4, 13.9

story point estimating, 20.3.1

Structured Timeboxes, see DSDM Structured Timeboxes

supporting roles
- see also roles
- Business Advisors, 7.3.10
- DSDM Coaches, 7.3.13
- general, 7.2.2.3; 14.2.2.3
- Technical Advisors, 7.3.11

Workshop Facilitators, 7.3.12

T-shirt estimating, 20.3.1
- see also estimating

tailoring DSDM to projects, 24.1-3

TDD, 9.3.6

Team Boards, 5.6; 8.2.11; 9.4.2; 13.8; 18.2.3, 18.2.5.1

Team Leaders
- see also teams
- relationship with Project Manager, 14.16.5
- responsibilities, 7.3.6; 14.8.1; 18.3.7; 21.3.4
- role, 7.2.2.2, 7.3.6; 14.2.2.2, 14.8

Team Models, 7.2.1, Fig 7a; 14.2.1, Fig 14a
- see also responsibilities; roles

teams
- coaching by Project Manager, 13.4
- co-located, 18.2.6
- communication, 18.2.1
- confidence-building, 13.3
- culture, 13.4
- distributed, 18.2.7, Figs 18a-b
- DSDM concept, 18.3.4
- empowerment, 7.1; 13.4
- leaders, see Team Leaders
- selection of members, 18.2.1
- team goals, 18.3.5
- teamwork, 4.4; 5.3.3; 14.1

Technical Advisors
- responsibilities, 14.13.1
- role, 7.2.2.3, 7.3.11; 14.2.2.3

Technical Coordinators
- attendance at Daily Stand-ups, 17.9
- relationship with Project Manager, 14.16.3
- responsibilities, 12.3.4.3; 13.5; 14.6.1
- role, 7.2.2.1, 7.3.3; 14.2.2.1, 14.6

Index

teleconference Stand-ups, 17.9; 18.2.3

    see also Daily Stand-ups

Terms of Reference, 8.2.1; 16.2.1-2.2; 19.4.1

    see also milestone products

Test-driven Development (TDD), 9.3.6

    see also testing

testing

    see also Solution Testers

    collaboration, 9.3.2

    end-to-end, 9.6.6

    independence, 9.3.5

    Instrumental Success Factors, 5.5

    integration into project, 9.3.1

    prioritisation, 9.3.4

    repeat testing, 9.3.3

    responsibilities, 12.3.4.3; 13.5

    running tests, 9.6.4

    test-driven development, 9.3.6

    test preparation, 9.6.4

    Timebox step 2: Refinement, 17.8.2.1

    types of, 12.3.4.2

Themes, 19.4.1-4.2
    see also User Stories

time
    as project variable, 3.2, Fig 3b
    delivering on time, 4.3; 22.3.3.1

Timebox Plans, 8.2.11; 9.2.2; 13.9; 16.12.1-12.2
    see also evolutionary products

Timebox Review Records, 8.2.12; 15.3.5; 16.13.1-13.2; 17.8.2.1
    see also evolutionary products

Timeboxes
    see also Timeboxing
    close-out, 15.3.4; 17.8.2.1-8.2.2
    daily stand-ups, see Daily Stand-ups
    dealing with changes to, 17.10
    definition, 11.1
    DSDM structured timeboxes
    diagrams, Fig 11a; Fig 17b
    general, 11.2-2.1, 11.5; 17.8.2.1
    estimating sessions, 20.5.3
    free format
        diagrams, Fig 11b; Fig 17c
        general, 11.2, 11.2.2, 11.5; 17.8.2.2
    general, 11.1, 11.4-5, Fig 11c; 17.8.2
    incremental delivery of solution, 5.5
    kick off, 15.3.4; 17.8.2.1-8.2.2
    length, 17.8.1
    MoSCoW prioritisation, 10.3
    planning in Evolutionary Development phase, 21.3.4
    project control, 9.4.1, Fig 9a
    Project Manager responsibilities, 13.2-3
    User Stories, 19.4.3

Timeboxing

Index

    see also Timeboxes

    balancing priorities, 17.4

    combining with MoSCoW prioritisation, 17.1

    general, 3.2; 11.1, 11.5

    use, 17.8, 17.11

top-down estimating, 20.3.1

    see also estimating

top tips for Agile Project Managers

    Benefits Assessments, 16.15.2

    Business Cases, 16.3.2

    Delivery Plans, 16.7.2

    Development Approach Definition, 16.6.2

    DSDM principles, 13.9

    DSDM products, 16.17

    estimating, 20.6

    Evolving Solutions, 16.11.2

    Feasibility Assessments, 16.9.2

    Foundation Summaries, 16.10.2

    Management Approach Definition, 16.8.2

    MoSCoW prioritisation, 17.8.1

    people/teams/interactions, 18.4

    Prioritised Requirements Lists, 16.4.2

    project planning, 21.4

    Project Review Reports, 16.14.2

    quality planning, 22.4

    requirements, 19.5

    risk management, 23.5

    roles/responsibilities, 14.17

    Solution Architecture Definition, 16.5.2

    tailoring DSDM to project, 24.3

    Terms of Reference, 16.2.2

    Timebox Plans, 16.12.2

    Timebox Review Records, 16.13.2

    Timeboxing, 17.11

tracking and control, see project control

transparency, 5.6; 9.4.2

uncertainty in projects, 20.2
    see also estimating

User Stories
- cards, 19.3.3
- definition, 19.3.1
- Evolutionary Development phase, 19.4.3
- example, 19.3.3
- Feasibility phase, 19.4.1
- format, 19.3.2
- Foundations phase, 19.4.2
- guidance on creating, 19.3.4
- prioritisation, 10.1

'Waterfall' approach to projects, 2.1; 20.1; 23.3

wide-band Delphi, see story-point estimating

Won't Have this time priorities, 10.2.1; 17.2, Fig 17a
    see also MoSCoW prioritisation

working hours, 13.3

working software, 2.3

Workshop Facilitators
- responsibilities, 14.14.1
- role, 7.2.2.3, 7.3.12; 12.1, 12.4; 14.2.2.3, 14.14

workshops
- benefits, 12.2
- general, 12.1, 12.4
- records, 21.3.2
- retrospectives, 17.8.2.1
- success factors, 12.3

Printed in Dunstable, United Kingdom